pg 1 2   KT-367-987

Contents

Preface   v
Acknowledgements   x

 1 Sport, the Media and Popular Culture   1
 2 All Our Yesterdays: A History of Media Sport   19
 3 A Sporting Triangle: Television, Sport and Sponsorship   43
 4 Power Game: Why Sport Matters to Television   66
 5 Who Wants to Be a Millionaire? Media Sport and Stardom   86
 6 The Race Game: Media Sport, Race and Ethnicity   107
 7 Playing the Game: Media Sport and Gender   122
 8 Games Across Frontiers: Mediated Sport and   144
    National Identity
 9 The Sports Pages: Journalism and Sport   164
10 Consuming Sport: Fans, Fandom and the Audience   184
11 Conclusion: Sport in the Digital Age   204

Bibliography   223
Index   240

Sport, is of course one of the very best things about television; I would keep my set for it alone. (Raymond Williams, *The Listener*, 1 August 1968)

GOLFONOMICS: The Ball Game that became the richest Sport on Earth. (*The Independent*, 19 September 2008)

Sport needs, attracts, and must deal with money and power and the backers will always be looking to buy or take their share of the glory. How are we to police the line between the realms of power and play, economic space and social space? The production and consumption of modern sport clearly is political, albeit with a small 'p'. (David Goldblatt, 'Taking sport seriously', *Prospect*, No. 141, December 2007)

Power Play

Sport, the Media and Popular Culture
Second edition

Raymond Boyle and Richard Haynes

Edinburgh University Press

For Noelle, Lauren and Liam (RB)
For Susan, Alice and Adam (RH)

Edinburgh University Press Ltd
22 George Square, Edinburgh

Reprinted 2010

www.euppublishing.com

Typeset in 11/13 pt Stempel Garamond by
Servis Filmsetting Ltd, Stockport, Cheshire, and
printed and bound in Great Britain by
CPI Antony Rowe, Chippenham and Eastbourne

A CIP record for this book is available from the British Library

ISBN 978 0 7486 3592 4 (hardback)
ISBN 978 0 7486 3593 1 (paperback)

Preface

THE MEANING BEHIND THE SPECTACLE:

Giant scrolls? Human kites? An army of drummers? Clifford Coonan decodes the symbols of the ceremony China used to tell its story to the world. (*The Independent*, commenting on the opening ceremony of the Beijing Olympic Games, 9 August 2008)

A decade of change: media sport 2000–8

The increasingly central role that sport plays in public life was clearly evident in the UK during August 2008. In the light of Team GB's Olympic success, sporting media stories were everywhere, and significantly often in mainstream broadcast, print and online news coverage. At these moments the already increasingly porous boundaries between sports news and news news disappear completely.

Sports such as cycling, not normally given an extensive media profile, found itself and its stars, such as triple gold medal winner Chris Hoy, being centre stage in the media spotlight ('Golden Hoy: the Scot who made Olympic History', the front page splash in *The Herald*, 20 August 2008). There were numerous news stories that focused on the politics of sport. These included the debate about whether Team GB should have an all British football team at the 2012 London Olympics. The Prime Minister at Westminster Gordon Brown, a Scot, having given much political thought to defining 'Britishness', advocated such a move. He clashed with Alex Salmond, First Minister and leader of the Scottish National Party government in Edinburgh, who argued against such an arrangement, going further to suggest that Scotland should have its own distinct team at the Olympics. Two other Scots, Sir Alex Ferguson, manager of Manchester United, and Sir Sean Connery, promoting his autobiography at the Edinburgh book festival, were pulled into the wider media and public debate. Other political stories around in August 2008 included the impact that the success of the Beijing Games might have on China's growing position within the world economy. While stories relating to the likely impact that the London Games in 2012 may have on the arts and cultural heritage industries that will see National Lottery money diverted to the Olympics began to reappear again following what appeared like an cessation of hostilities during the 24/7 media coverage of the Beijing Games.

The summer of 2008 had also seen those perennial footballing under-achievers Spain triumph at the European Football Championships held in Switzerland and Austria. This was accompanied by much discussion of the so-called 'new Spaniards' who were, if we were to believe media coverage, setting aside traditional nationalist rivalries to unite behind the Spanish national team ('Spain revels in new spirit of unity as football team heals division', *Observer*, 29 June 2008), while on the tennis courts of London and Beijing, Spain's Rafael Nadal's success at both Wimbledon and the Olympics helped showcase the growing global sporting image of that country. In the UK, by way of contrast, tennis player Andy Murray's Wimbledon tournament saw the British media increasingly fixated about the need to label the tennis star as Scottish and/or British (or more accurately a Brit), all of which led one media commentator, Alan Ruddock, to note:

> It confirms that the British media is, in reality, a London media, or at the very least an English media. The label [Brit] represents annexation, not appreciation, and confirms the prejudices of those who believe that London's editors have no knowledge of, or interest in, affairs outside the centre. (*Observer*, 6 July 2008)

Elsewhere in the global sporting landscape, the trajectory of sporting development and success increasingly reflected the wider shifts in international economic and political power relations. While India and China, both enjoyed staging successful high-profile sporting events in cricket and the Olympics, the sport of golf was being hit hard in the US by the credit crunch, but found itself thriving in the emerging economic powerhouse countries of Russia, India and China.

What all of the above serve to illustrate is that since the publication of the first edition of *Power Play* in 2000, sport has become even more a central component of mainstream popular culture as well as economic, political and public discourse. We would argue that a more commercially focused, demand-led, 24/7 media system has helped to facilitate the seemingly insatiable appetite for particular sporting discourses. These trends are not without paradox. While sports – and football in particular – have entered the mainstream media lexicon, more and more live sport is only available on pay-TV platforms. Despite this, events such as the free-to-air Olympics break through this barrier and are widely amplified if they carry what the media define as 'good news stories'. More and more mainstream news coverage is devoted to carrying sporting stories and the stars that the media sport industries work so hard to create, and the media management and PR industries work so hard to sustain and extract a commercial value from.

And yet despite this change, taking sport seriously remains something of a challenge. David Goldblatt (2007) has argued that a healthier sporting culture would be achieved if sports were accorded the same seriousness given to the performing arts, and subject to the same levels of 'transparency, sustainability and democracy that we expect in public life' (Goldblatt, 2007: 37). While this may be true, there is also evidence, almost ten years on from the publication of the first edition, that talking seriously about sports' cultural position and the role the media play in this process happens in a much more sustained and discursive manner than has ever been the case, certainly within a UK context.

When cultural critic Germaine Greer in a column on the arts can argue the case for why sports matter, things have clearly evolved. She notes how:

> Sport is perhaps the best way to demonstrate how culture works to enliven and leaven daily experience. We know that the Aztecs played ball games, and the annual ceremonial games were of crucial importance in the cultural life of the Mesoamerican peoples. Our reasons for risking bankruptcy in staging the Olympics Games are cultural. But sport does not simply bring people together; it also divides them, sometimes with murderous effect. What is more important is that, when well-managed, the battle on the pitch is a stereotyped outlet for aggression and conflict; this symbolic warfare inspires acres of newsprint, much of it better written than anything on the comment pages. (*Guardian*, 24 March 2008)

Such examples of a critical intervention in the discourses that surround media sport, while still rare, are more common than they were a decade ago, from Beckham to Rooney, from Andy Murray to Lewis Hamilton, discussions about the relationship between sport and national identity, sexism in sport, sports corruption and the economics of media sport and digital sports rights are all topics that seep into mainstream areas of journalism.

It also demonstrates the extent that sport, more than at any other time in its history, has been explicitly pulled into the orbit of commerce and business. Sport, and the media themselves, are now integral components of what are often called the entertainment or cultural industries, despite sport's strange exclusion from the UK government's official definition of the increasingly ubiquitous 'creative industries'. This section of the economy has become increasingly important over the last decade as the revenue streams and the employment opportunities offered across the creative industries of sport, music and media have mushroomed.

Sport has become important to those working within Media Studies and beyond, even if they have little actual interest in sports per se. The business of sport and its linkage with the media industries mean that today sport matters to those whose primary interest may lie in the economics of the media industries and the political issues which relate to regulation and media policy.

Another key driver in the upsurge of interest in media sport has been the extent to which issues of identity – ethnic, racial, regional, national and international – have moved centre stage in both academic and political public debate. The extent to which globalization is eroding distinctive national traditions and identities has seen sport, with its universal appeal, being examined for evidence of this economic and political process.

Cultural critic Martin Jacques crystallized some of the issues around race, sport, representation, politics and the process of globalization when he argued with regard to British motor racing driver Lewis Hamilton that:

> Hamilton defies the British white stereotype of young black men, perpetrated with a new vengeance by much of the media. He is highly articulate, extremely intelligent, very successful, blessed with great charm and likeability, and is close to his father, who has been a huge influence on him. Hamilton marks the arrival of a new black British role model – and a new kind of image for Britain in the world. (*Guardian*, 22 October 2007)

The last decade has seen a rise in the idea that sporting success can confer some sort of 'soft' power on a country as it competes on the global stage of media representation.

We have been fortunate in that as sports fans and media academics our twin interests neatly collide with each other and we hope that this background is reflected throughout this updated and revised edition of the book.

There is little doubt that the advent of digital broadcasting has signalled a new phase in the evolution of the relationship between sport and the media. What we wish to do in this book is to re-examine how the sport–media nexus has evolved to its present state and investigate what have been the implications of this for sporting and media organisations and their supporters and consumers.

For some, sport will appear to be a massive triviality and in essence when the games of sport are looked at in isolation this may well be true. However, for the millions of fans around the world who invest financially and emotionally in these games, sport has always mattered. Unquestionably sport matters to big business and to those who drive the increasingly commercial and global media and entertainment industries. The power play involving the control and meaning of sport is one in which the media are absolutely centrally implicated. Let the games begin . . .

Acknowledgements

Thanks to all those who helped us put together the first version of the book in 1999. Since then Alina Bernstein and her work with the International Association of Mass Communications Research (IAMCR) Media and Sport Section has acted as a great facilitator for international discussion around media and sports issues. We would like to acknowledge her hard work as these section meetings have always informed and educated us. Along the way the work and thoughts of many have shaped our work (to them, thanks). The following have particularly sustained our interest in the field: Neil Blain, Alan Tomlinson, David Rowe, Garry Whannel, Philip Schlesinger, Simon Frith, John Sugden and Hugh O'Donnell. In addition we would like to thanks all the students at Glasgow Caledonian University, Stirling University and Glasgow University who have passed through various media sports courses and lectures since we began teaching about this topic, way back when . . .

Chapter 1

Sport, the Media and Popular Culture

Sport is at once both trivial and serious, inconsequential yet of symbolic significance . . . Sport in many cases informs and refuels the popular memory of communities, and offers a source of collective identification and community expression for those who follow teams and individuals. (Sugden and Tomlinson, 1994: 3)

. . . where *Il Sole* was available most of the prisoners, including politicals, read *La Gazzetta dello Sport*. (Observations made while in prison in Milan by Antonio Gramsci, in Forgacs, 1988: 376)

Introduction

Without question one of the great passions of the twentieth century has been sport. The opening decade of the twenty-first century suggests that this passion remains unabated. Sport continues to matter to thousands of players and fans across the globe, with differing sports playing a particularly important role in the cultural life of countries and people. While football is the global game, other sports such as baseball occupy a central position in American popular culture, cricket and Aussie Rules in Australian life, Gaelic games in Ireland, cricket and basketball in Caribbean culture, while rugby union is important in constructions of Welsh and New Zealand national identities.

However, the history of sport has also been to a large extent both dominated and documented by the mass media. Newspapers, film, radio and television broadcasting have all had a profound effect on shaping the popular and political culture of this century. While sport has always mattered beyond the confines of the pitch or the stadia, it has become increasingly intertwined with various media and television in particular.

Something, however, has begun to happen to this relationship in more recent times which has resulted in sport becoming increasingly important within the worlds of business and politics. This is illustrated by taking a snapshot of sports media stories moving in Britain in late 2008.

The Beijing Olympics have dominated media coverage during the summer of 2008, with coverage ranging from the human rights record of China, issues of media censorship, the faking of parts of the opening ceremony, the role of the Olympics in projecting China as a new superpower to the rest of the world, the economic importance of the Games to China, the unparalled success of Team GB at the Games and the role played by Lottery money in this achievement. In addition, the Beijing Games has focused attention on the politics that surround the staging of the 2012 Games in London.

In other sections of the media there are stories of the importance of football to the future success of ITV, the main commercial television channel in the UK, and the possibility of financial difficulties for Setanta Sports as the pay-TV channel challenges the dominant player BSkyB in the UK market. We also have the outcry from the Scottish Nationalist government about live Scottish international matches disappearing from free-to-air television, and criticism for the BBC and its failure to bid for live test match cricket. These stories sit beside calls for Scotland's triple Olympic gold medalist, Chris Hoy to be made a knight of the realm, and the double gold medal winning swimmer Rebecca Adlington to be made a dame.

All of these stories were covered in the sports, business and news pages of the print media, and given an extensive airing online and on both mainstream radio and television news. It appeared, certainly in Britain in 2008, that sporting issues, inevitably bound up with the media, had never mattered more and appeared to extend into areas of society previously immune to engaging in such a high-profile manner with the business of sport.

How and why has this has come about is something which this book seeks to explore. As will be evident from Chapters 2 and 3, there has always been a relationship between sport and the media, but we would argue that the ties between two of the great forces of twentieth-century popular culture have never been closer and this tell us much about wider cultural and social shifts in society. This chapter seeks to trace briefly the previous academic work that engages with aspects of the relationship between sport, media and identity and to provide the reader with a context within which to place the book. We examine the treatment of sport in sociological and historical encounters and then focus specifically on academic writing directly concerned with what we call 'media sport'.

Finally we outline the specific areas the book covers, identifying both the key themes addressed in the chapters which follow and how they interact with each other. In so doing we discuss our own broad theoretical approach to studying the complex relationship between media and sport and argue for an interdisciplinary awareness which locates this relationship within the specific wider economic, political and cultural contours of society. In so doing we hope that it invites the reader to engage and think about sport and the media in a more critical manner than they may have previously done. As will be clear from the discussion of previous academic approaches to sport and society, sport – and its media context – have increasingly mattered to academics.

Sport in sociology and history

An excellent overview of the position of sport within social theory is provided by Jarvie (2006). In his book Jarvie traces the influence that major sociological traditions have had on the sociology of sport and leisure. In the context of this work, while sociological encounters with sport are discussed, specific attention here is paid to the position of sport within the particular field of media/cultural studies.

Over the years, sociology had been largely indifferent to suggestions that the position of sport, and indeed leisure, in modern society was worthy of serious and sustained investigation. Leisure was viewed as unimportant, or at its most simplistic as the antithesis of work. Sport was perhaps one of the last major areas of human activity to be subjected to rigorous examination by sociologists.

The last decade or so has seen a seachange in attitudes towards the sociological study of sport and leisure and a substantial growth in the research and literature that focuses on the relationship between sport and society (Cashmore, 2005; Coakley, 2003; Houlihan, 2007; Tomlinson, 2006) Accompanying the movement of sport from the periphery of sociological enquiry has been a debate between sociologists and those working within media/cultural studies regarding the most suitable theoretical paradigms within which this work should be located. There is little doubt that the rise in popularity of Media Studies courses and the media's increased interest in sport have also focused the minds of scholars. As Bernstein and Blain suggest in their overview of the field:

> The study of the ways in which media and sport interact crosses boundaries and can be found in literature concerned with the sociology of sport, history of sport, gender studies, cultural studies, journalism, leisure studies and beyond. (Bernstein and Blain, 2002: 1)

To that list of subject areas you could also add Sports Studies, the rise of which has been significant in the last ten years in generating research around the sociology of sport. At the centre of much of this debate is the relationship between sport and power in society.

Sport and power

Those working from within the structure paradigm draw upon a Marxist analysis which posits sport and leisure activities as being determined by the economic and political contours of society. In addition, they cite the centrality of class and capital in shaping the choices open to individuals, and present the arena of sport and leisure as a terrain on which dominant and subordinate groups produce and reproduce power relations that exist elsewhere in a capitalist society. In short, sport and leisure became vehicles of social control which both exploited workers and expanded the hold of capital on all areas of human activity.

It is a far from monolithic theory, however, and feminists such as Hargreaves (1994) and Creedon (1994) have highlighted the importance of gender relations in shaping leisure patterns, while Cashmore (2005) has long been emphasizing the important role that race plays in determining the patterns of sporting behaviour among ethnic groups in Britain. The work of Hargreaves and Cashmore is closer to a process approach adopted by neo-marxists (also referred to as the 'cultural studies' approach). Horne et al. (1987) sum up the strengths of this neo-marxist approach as being threefold:

> It takes seriously the idea that sport and leisure practice must be understood as relations of power; it emphasises the role of the state and the economy in structuring sport and leisure activity in contemporary society; and it applies an open-ended approach to sport and leisure studies so that new developments can be examined in a non-dogmatic fashion. (Horne et al., 1987: 188)

Recent work by Horne (2005) has developed this approach to engage with the increasingly important role played by the media in shaping patterns of consumption and 'normalizing' the consumer society. While Rojek (1992: 8) recognizes that this 'cultural studies' approach is useful because of its recognition of leisure and sport as 'deeply rooted social processes', he also attacks this approach as being too deterministic and overtly concerned with class and capital. In addition, he quite rightly points out that all the case studies and fieldwork, despite their location within British cultural studies, have been centred on England and English society, failing to recognize the cultural differences that exist elsewhere, for example between Scotland and England.

Rojek places himself within another process paradigm, that of the 'figurational sociology' approach to the study of sport and leisure (Dunning and Rojek, 1992). Drawing heavily on the work of Norbert Elias, the 'figurational' sociologists view society as a series of interlocking and dependent groups whose interplay is in a constant state of development and change. In other words, they place the individual at the centre of a series of configurations which, as they move outwards, become more complex, with no one factor overtly determining the relationships between the individual and society, but a multiplicity of factors and social groups such as the family, schooling, housing and such like all influencing the individual.

Rojek argues that much of the difference between the cultural studies approach and the figurational sociologists has been overemphasized. He acknowledges that a fundamental difference between the two approaches centres on the figurational sociologists' assertion that all social science research should aspire to 'the conditions of detachment, a methodology of self-consciously distancing oneself from the object of study' (Rojek, 1992: 28), rather than what Rojek views as the politically motivated drive of cultural studies. However, he concludes that:

> The common respect for history, the common emphasis on the historical and social dimensions of the 'natural' and the 'obvious', the common application of cultural diversity and richness – these are not insignificant common denominators. (Rojek, 1992: 28)

There is much of value in this assertion. However, the fundamental difference between the approaches as to the location of power in society remains. Cultural studies researchers are accused of overemphasizing class as a determining factor in social relations, while figurational sociologists are accused of underplaying its centrality.

In addition, the subjectivity of the researcher in any research process and his/her ability to 'detach' themselves from that work remains a point of disagreement. Perhaps the most significant agreement between the scholars is that the various patterns of sport and leisure development should be viewed as a continual process, although they may disagree on the determining influences that shape this development. This debate has moved the study of sport and leisure from the margins of sociology and sociological enquiry. It has also seen debates around issues such as globalization, power and the role of politics in society mobilize sport as one of the domains through which these processes are played out (Andrews and Grainger, 2007; Andrews and Ritzer, 2007; Giulianotti, 1999; Miller et al., 2001; Rowe, 2003a).

Sport and historians

In addition to the body of work concerned with the sociology of sport, another area, that of social history, has also engaged with the study of sport. The need to place sport within a broader economic and political perspective has been recognized by social historians who have contributed much to the elevation of the study of sport within the academy, viewing it as a legitimate and fruitful scholarly activity which highlights the cultural, economic and political significance of sport to society. As Jones argues:

> Sport in industrial societies is an important economic, social and political activity in its own right, able to provide the specialist with vital evidence about labour markets, capital investments, class, gender and even international relations. (Jones, 1992: 2)

The interchange between historians and sociologists working within the field of sport has been dogged by debates surrounding the role of theory in any investigation. Put at its simplest, historians claim that sociological encounters with sport suffer from the weight of ideological baggage that scholars carry to the subject. They argue that sociologists use sport to legitimize particular theoretical positions. In addition, they suggest that these positions are in fact untenable due to a neglect in adequately historicizing the sporting and cultural context.

Despite this, most contemporary research into the media–sport relationship recognizes the importance of a historical perspective. Helland (2007) adds depth to his analysis of the commercialization of modern media sport by positioning it against a historical backdrop that adds context to his contemporary analysis of television sports rights, while Davies (2006) argues that the role and position of sport as a cultural form is central in understanding the making of modern American society. In the UK, the work of Polley (1998, 2006) has situated sports culture as a central element of the social and cultural history of British society. Within this narrative, the growing role of the media in shaping sporting discourse is also acknowledged.

The important role that sports have played in international politics has also been increasingly recognised through work such as Riordan and Kruger's (1999) significant study of the politics of sport in the twentieth century, while more recent work by Edelman et al. (2006) has examined the key symbolic role played by sport in the ideological battles that characterized the Cold War and Guoqi (2008) provides a timely reminder of the ongoing role that sport has played in both China's self-image and the one it projects onto an international stage. Indeed the merging of politics and national identity formation and sport is a theme also explored in key edited collections by Smith and Porter (2004) and Tomlinson and Young (2005).

Media Studies sport

A good deal of the sociological theorizing on sport has focused on the particular dynamics and ideologies embedded in sporting culture and the societies in which they are played. However, the media, television and the press in particular are playing a central role in producing, reproducing and amplifying many of the discourses associated with sport in the modern world. It is this process and its ideological fallout that has been of particular interest to media/cultural scholars. John B. Thompson argues that:

> Pop music, sports and other activities are largely sustained by the media industries, which are not merely involved in the transmission and financial support of pre-existing cultural forms, but also in the active transformation of these forms. (Thompson, 1990: 163)

Understanding this process of transformation and its implications is what has interested many key writers who focus on media sport (Goldlust, 1987; Whannel, 1992, 2001, 2008; Rowe, 1995, 2004, 2005; Wenner, 1998; Brookes, 2002) There has been an increasing recognition of the importance of examining both the political and economic structures of the media–sport relationship as well as its mediated representations – for example, the way in which television increasingly dictates when sporting events take place (moving Saturday football matches to a Sunday evening and such like). Barnett (1990) remains a good example of an empirical strand of the former; however, Whannel (1992) was not only concerned with the political economy of media sport but also has an equal interest in text and ideology. In other words, he was interested in looking at how media sport helped to promote particular ways of thinking about sport and society, for example the notion that politics has nothing to do with sport, and that black athletes are 'naturally' more gifted than white athletes.

Whannel is an central figure in media sports scholarship. During the 1980s he was one of the first in the UK to write in a sustained and critical manner about the relationship between sport and the media and has always retained an equal concern with both the political economy and ideological dimension of media sport. His account of the influences that shaped his work at this time offers a fascinating insight into the position of sport and the academy during this period and the key role that the development of media studies played in shaping research into sport (Whannel, 2008). Thus not only does his work examine the increasingly complex relationship that exists between capital, television and sport (through sponsorship, advertising and international marketing), but is also concerned with the ideological implications that such a process has on the sporting representations. One of Whannel's original objectives was to examine:

> What are the cultural and economic relations between television and sport, and how, if at all, has television transformed sport? What relationship is there between the cultural and economic level in this particular instance? (Whannel, 1992: 4)

More recently in his overview of the state of the field since the publication of his 1983 book *Blowing the Whistle*, Whannel argues that:

> We should never regard popular culture as epiphenomenal or marginal – it remains a central element in the political process. It constitutes a meeting ground between popular common sense and organized political discourse, and for that reason alone, it is vital that we continue subjecting it to analysis and critique. (Whannel, 2008: 237)

This seems a research agenda that remains particularly relevant in the digital age of the twenty-first century as we seek to track the continually evolving relationship between these two institutions.

Television and sport

As an academic field of enquiry and cumulative knowledge, the study and research into the relationships between television and sport is relatively new. Apart from the sporadic appearance of media or cultural studies of televised sport during the 1970s, the literature on the subject did not gain momentum until the 1980s and find a more systematic approach until the 1990s. Considering the amount of literature given over to other television genres (in particular news, current affairs and popular drama) or to other aspects of sporting configurations (specifically football hooliganism) it is surprising that academic research has taken so long to recognize one of the most pervasive aspects of our popular culture. Televised sport not only provides our main connection to sport itself, but also our ideas about nationality, class, race, gender, age and disability. It therefore presents a rich seam of material from which to investigate and understand our social, cultural, economic and political lives.

As Whannel (1992, 2008) has highlighted, the relative dearth of material on televised sport in the growing field of media studies was largely due to a schematic split in the academic analysis of television: first, textual or semiotic critiques that drew upon film theory; and second, socio-economic analysis that focused on production practices and the political organization of the media. The former approach is most recognizable in the British Film Institute (BFI) publication *Football on Television* edited by Buscombe (1975) that incorporated a series of textual readings on the televising of the 1974 World Cup. This exploratory work has proved very influential within subsequent research on televised sport, specifically related to the ideological components of sports broadcasts.

Analysis of the structural aspects of the sport–television nexus provides the alternate trajectory in the media study of sport which can be identified in the work of Rader (1984), Goldlust (1987) and Barnett (1990). These studies investigate the transformation of sport by television, in particular how such changes relate to the economic imperatives of television and sponsorship or the cultural policies of nation states in pursuit of public service criteria.

Other major studies, most notably Wenner (1989), Whannel (1992, 2008), Blain et al. (1993) and Rowe (1995, 2003b, 2004), have variously attempted to bridge this analytical gap through a mixture of political economy, textual readings and aesthetic concerns. These studies have a clear connection to the interdisciplinary agenda of British Cultural

Studies which had its roots in the Centre for Contemporary Cultural Studies at Birmingham University.

There has also been a growing research interest in the relationship between television and sports that originates from the areas of management studies and economics. Work focused on the political economy of the sports industries by the likes of Westerbeek and Smith (2003) and Nicholson (2007) emphasizes the managerial and marketing challenges posed by the global industry. The expansion in the marketing industries surrounding the sporting and creative industries in the last decade has meant that academic discourses about sport appear across the academy. Desbordes (2006) offers an international perspective on marketing and football – with television a key player – while Beech (2006) offers one of the key texts on the more general marketing of sport. Jeanrenaud and Kesenne (2006) and Gratton and Solberg (2006) offer an economic analysis of the changing relationship between the sporting and media industries.

The rise in the importance of football on television and the extent to which that television financially underwrites the sport has also generated work from sports economists such as Dobson and Goddard (2007) and Groot (2008).

Mediated sport and identity

There is now an established tradition of examining the relationship between representations of mediated sport and the society that produces and consumes them (Blain et al., 1993; Brookes, 2002; Rowe, 2003b; Hand and Crolley, 2006). These studies are often focused on particular media or specific sporting events and are concerned with the role played by mediated versions of sport in the process of identity formation around issues of class, gender, ethnicity and cultural and national identity.

Most are alert to taking a too media-centric view of social change. We would argue that the media can become one part of a complex relationship that helps link an individual to a larger collective grouping. At certain moments the media are important in legitimizing and giving a profile to groups of supporters, such as in the coverage of a successful Cup Final victory or the aftermath of a tragedy such as Hillsborough. At other times and in specific social circumstances their importance may be less. We suggest that even in a book about media sport we must be alert to the wider pressures, often political, economic and cultural, which frequently set the parameters in which media sport and its relationship with collective identities are being shaped. We will return to this below as we outline the structure of the book.

It is also worth noting some other key research areas around the media sport nexus that have become increasingly prominent in the decade since *Power Play* was first published. These include the importance of technology in shaping sporting culture, in particular the extent to which that digital technology has both strengthened traditional aspects of the media–sport relationship – big brands such as the BBC and BSkyB still dominate UK media sports – and also disrupted traditional relationships – the rise of the Internet has impacted on print media specifically. Allied with this there has been a growing interest in the profession, practice and impact of sports journalism across the digital media landscape (Boyle, 2006; Steen, 2008), while debates around sport and governance, the importance of sports rights in a digital economy and the impact of globalization on both the media and sporting industries have all been key areas of interest in the last decade as the economy of the sports industries have become more prominent. These developments are we hope reflected in this new version of the book.

Mapping the field and the structure of the book

Any study of the increasingly symbiotic links between sport and the media should offer an entry point into wider debates and concerns which we feel are central in media studies. The study of media sport provides an arena in which students can investigate some of the wider issues concerned with media, power and ideology. In this book we are particularly interested in:

1. the political economy of media sport;
2. the relationship between sport, media and identity formations of gender, race and nation;
3. the consumption of sport and the role of audiences in the communication process.

To understand any of these political, economic and cultural processes involves placing both sporting and media institutions within a larger frame of reference – a field of play which recognizes that sporting forms and mediated versions of these forms are continually being shaped by and in turn shaping culture as a whole. While the media are becoming increasingly powerful in driving the form and content of modern sport and its relationship with its supporters they are not doing this in isolation from wider economic or cultural shifts in society. In other words, we argue that to examine the sport–media relationship we need to encompass a broader range of vision beyond simply focusing on the mediated discourses of sport circulated by the media.

Despite the usefulness of some aspects of postmodern theory in examining mediated textual representations of sport, we suggest that a more rooted concern with the economic, political and social structures which remain central in determining our lives is also more likely to increase our understanding of the role of media sport in contemporary society.

Historical perspective

The early part of the book identifies the key role of a historical perspective on the relationship between various media and sport when attempting to understand the contemporary situation. Historian Martin Polley (1998: 9) has argued that not only does a historical approach allow us to understand the broader political and economic factors shaping sports events in the past, but 'it can offer a sense of long- and short-term trends that are not always visible to present-centred disciplinary approaches'. Broadly speaking we argue that, while sporting and media institutions have evolved and developed individually with their own distinctive traditions, practices and ideologies, there has always been some interface between these cultural forms. Initially the press, then newsreel and radio and more recently television have not only used sport as media content, but often helped to change and reconstruct the position of sport within society. For example, we see newspapers helping to facilitate the commercial development of sports such as football in Britain through sponsorship and media exposure, or radio amplifying sporting contests such as gaelic games in Ireland during the 1920s into truly national sporting events.

Thus Chapter 2 examines the origins of modern sport and mass communications, focusing on the early sporting press and how the relationships established between radio broadcasters and sporting authorities in Britain during the early part of the century helped mark out the relationship which would evolve between sport and television later in the century. It also highlights the extent to which tensions in the relationship between sport and various media are not new and are characteristic of each new stage of technological development.

Political economy

In Chapter 3 we turn our attention to what we call the sporting triangle of media sport: the relationship between television, sponsorship and sport. For much of the later part of the twentieth century this inter-relationship has constituted the key drivers which have shaped and continually reshaped sport as a cultural and ideological form and as a commercial/business entity. The media in their various forms have increasingly become the economic underwriter of modern sport, and we want to examine how in the digital twenty-first century this relationship has become more explicit.

We argue it is impossible to understand fully the relationship between mediated sport and forms of representations which are discussed later in the book without a grasp of the underlying economic structures which have increasingly intertwined sporting and media forms and institutions both nationally and internationally.

One of the aspects that a historical analysis of media sport highlights is the extent to which the relationship between sporting and media forms is continually being driven by wider economic and cultural shifts in technology and broadcasting regulation. Thus, while Chapters 2 and 3 highlight the historical and economic developments in media sport, the final chapter focuses on sport in the digital age. Here we argue that we are in another stage of development in a relationship which seeks to reconcile the tensions between continuity (one of the media appeals of sport is its 'traditional' character and history) and change (both in media regulation and in new technological innovations). Indeed the themes of continuity and change are ones that run throughout the book, as does a central concern with the impact of both marketization and digitization on the media–sport relationship.

Sport and media sport

In Chapter 4 we turn our attention to the key role that television in particular plays in transforming sporting forms into media events. There is an equal concern here with examining both why television needs sport, as well as how it constructs the mediated version of sporting contests. In other words, there is a recognition that, at times, sports coverage can provide both ideological and economic benefit to particular media systems.

Thus the ability of the BBC to call itself a national broadcaster is reinforced, or undermined, by its ability to deliver national sporting events to the country. This becomes increasingly problematic not simply because of commercial competition, but because broadcasting has to reflect the new political realities of a devolving UK state. Too often broadcasters – and indeed some academics studying media sport – have not been aware that, for people in Glasgow or Edinburgh, the Football Association is actually the English football association and 'national' sporting events may be understood or viewed differently by the Scottish, English, Welsh or Irish. On the other hand, a commercial broadcaster such as BSkyB or Setanta may view sport simply as a key 'media product' to be used to attract and sustain a subscription base among viewers. As we argue in Chapter 4, this does not of course mean that it will necessarily be ideologically neutral. In other words a broadcaster may mobilize established ideological discourses of Scottishness (passion, grit, determination) for commercial reasons in order to sell Scottish football to a predominately English audience (Haynes and Boyle, 2008).

Chapter 4 also focuses on the ways in which production codes and practices of television sport have become established, including areas such as modes of address – commentary, highlights and action replays. Central here is the way in which sport gets constructed by various media into narrative forms which not only make sense of particular sporting stories, but often reinforce and reconstruct wider values and attitudes in society.

This chapter also examines whether stylistic differences in the treatment of sport on television exist between terrestrial and satellite broadcasters. Both this and the following chapter build on the historical and economic analysis outlined in the earlier part of the book. Chapter 5 demonstrates the close ideological and business links between sport and the media in the promotion of sports stardom. We examine how transformations in the media–sport relationship have highlighted tensions between amateurism and professionalism.

Building on Chapter 3 we explore the key role that the sports agent plays in creating the sports star with both commercial and ideological spin-offs for the structure of sport and our understanding of its position in society. This chapter also reminds us of the important role that media sports stars play in sustaining aspects of the mythical dimension of sport in society and creating both heroes and villains whose appeal extends beyond the confines of the sports field.

Media sport and representations of race, gender and nationality

As we noted above, we do not take a media-centred view of social development. However, it remains true that mediated discourses of sport play an important part – at times more crucial than others – in reproducing, naturalizing and even constructing values, attitudes and sometimes prejudices which circulate in wider society. It is also important to recognize that often particular ideological formations of identity exist in and around sporting subcultures, for example the often masculine culture which surrounds sports such as football. Mediated versions of sport may choose to ignore or amplify certain aspects of this culture for a range of reasons. Thus any sectarian overtones surrounding a Celtic v. Rangers football match may be played down by television coverage, keen to highlight 'the atmosphere' at a match, but less happy to examine some of the more unsavoury elements which exist in and around such matches.

This part of the book examines the ideological role that mediated coverage of sport plays in constructing and reproducing various discourses centred around race, gender and nationality. Chapter 6 looks at sport and social inequality, stereotypes and discourses of race in media sport, black and Asian athletes and media sport, and sectarianism and sport. The following chapter asks is media sport a male preserve? It examines stereotypes and discourses of gender in media sport and the extent to which female sports journalists and presenters are challenging professional ideologies of gender.

We would argue that often the intersection of media–sport representations and issues of identity are not clearly demarcated, so issues of gender, race and nationality often collide. However, for the purposes of the book we examine them separately while aware of the complexity and interplay between them.

Chapter 8 focuses on media sport and the civic nation, looking at how international sports coverage often carries with it a broader political agenda. This can also operate at the national level, where sport and its attendant coverage often become a focal point for an expression of a range of collective identities. This process can call into question the complex relationship that exists between discourses which circulate in the media about sport and its collective power. This is not to suggest that, at certain moments in the political and cultural life of communities, sport does not offer an important forum for collective expression and identity. Rather, that caution is required in simply reading media representations (and interpretations) of events as accurate indicators of

political and cultural realities. Put simply, we would argue that sometimes they are, and sometimes – often depending on who is telling or
retelling the story – they are not.

The burden of expectation placed on sport (often by the media) and
the treatment of events given by media institutions is closely related
to deeply rooted historical, political and economic factors (Blain and
O'Donnell, 1998; Puijk, 1997). This approach remains alert to the
range of influences (social, economic and political) which continually
construct aspects of personal identities and in turn connect these to
wider patterns of collective experience.

Media consumption: fans and audiences

We are not suggesting that the media simply deposit various ideas on
an audience which in turn unproblematically absorbs them. Nor do
we think that the various media institutions are simply constructing or
creating various discourses. As we argue in the latter part of the book,
these discourses are of course themselves influenced by wider social,
economic and political pressures. For example, different versions of a
country's national character may be used for differing political, economic or cultural reasons.

A UK national newspaper can mobilize the importance of football
in Italian life in its travel section to sell to its readers the glamour,
designer style and excitement of combining football and shopping on
a weekend visit to Milan, while a political story about the growth of
right-wing extremism in Italy may note how football has become a
recruitment ground for some of these groups. In other words, particular configurations of discourses drawing on sport and national character can often be used for differing reasons in differing media. This is
not, however, a 'media-centred' view of society, where the media are
the origins of all discourses that circulate within society at any given
time. Rather we argue that they are part of a complex interrelationship
between groups in a society who come to understand themselves in
part through internal group dynamics, and in part by defining themselves against 'others'.

Chapter 9 examines the key production role that journalism and
sports writing plays in both imposing narratives on sporting contests
and developing the mythic aspects of sports' wider appeal. In Britain
the recent explosion in sports writing appears concerned with documenting the private world of the British male, while in America, sports
writing with a longer literary pedigree often appears more concerned

with using sport as a way of defining and understanding aspects of American myth and identity. The consumption of media sport through broadcasting and print media is discussed in the following chapter, particularly against the backdrop of changes in the ecology of media sports outlined earlier in the book.

Conclusion

Since the publication of the first edition of the book there have been a number of significant changes in both the academic study of media and sport and within the sports and media industries themselves. Within the academy the rise of sports studies and the area within that subject that focuses on sport and society has grown. The sporting terrain is now routinely mobilized by the academy as an area of study across subjects as diverse as management studies, cultural economics, public relations, public policy, media and cultural studies, journalism studies and sports studies. Much of this work has been around the business of sports, and the opportunities that the fledgling sports economy offers graduates across sponsorship, event management, media rights and marketing.

At the same time tremendous change in the media industries, driven by commercialization, digital technology and regulatory change, has helped enhance the position of some sports as central aspects of media culture in twenty-first century Britain (Boyle and Haynes, 2004). In an increasingly demand-led media system, sports content has seen its value enhanced and its presence leak out into mainstream areas of popular culture as well as wider public and political discourse. From mainstream news bulletins to growing print and online coverage, the explosion of journalism about sports and sports journalism has been striking in the last decade (Boyle, 2006; Steen, 2008).

One impact of this process has been the public realization that sports do not exist in a political vacumm and that the central role of money in shaping sports culture has become increasingly explicit. It has never been harder to argue (although that does not stop sections of the media doing so) that we need to keep politics out of sport. Sports have always been mired in politics both with a small 'p' (sport as part of power relations) as well as having at times a more overt political dimension. From Britain's record gold medal success in Beijing 2008 being attributed to significant financial investment from the National Lottery in key sports to the acknowledgement that only a few clubs can win the English football Premiership given the gulf in wealth that exists between the top clubs and the rest, money matters in elite sport like never before. Partly as a result of this, the issue of public trust in both sports culture and the media more generally has become an important part of the agenda that surrounds the narratives of media sport in the opening decade of this century.

Our final chapter on sport in the new media age both pulls together some of the issues raised while also setting out some of the structural changes and implications of the latest stage in the evolution of the sports–media relationship. We would argue for a multidisciplinary approach to the subject, one which recognizes the importance of the political economy of media sport as well as the ideological and political dimension to media coverage of sporting forms. By political in this context we mean the ways in which power is organized in society, and the ways in which formulations of power are both maintained and often challenged by groups and individuals.

To shed some light and understanding on how the media function within the wider political, economic and cultural contours of the digital society appears to us to be one of the tasks required of media studies. Drawing freely from the social sciences we hope this examination of the complex relationship between the media and sport will go some way to increasing our understanding of how two of the great forces of the twentieth century – sport and the media – have become intertwined in a twenty-first century global business relationship which brings both pain and pleasure to many and increasingly generates profit for a select few.

Chapter 2

All Our Yesterdays:
A History of Media Sport

Sport . . . is probably the biggest thing in the land. It occupies the thoughts, and empties the pockets, of countless millions. (Trevor Wignall, sports journalist, *Daily Express,* 1936)

A glance at the world showed that when the common people were not at work, one thing they wanted was organised sports and games. (James, 1963/83: 153)

Introduction

Mediated versions of sport are one of the key areas of culture which give us a sense of a lived history. One of the particular appeals of sport, for both the media and supporters, is the extent to which the narratives or stories which surround sport act as a bridge between the present and the past. Sporting events need to have a history and a longevity to feel important. In Australia, international cricket is dominated by the Ashes series with England, a competition given extra impetus by the long rivalry between these two countries. As we argue in Chapter 4, television increasingly helps to create – and at times even invent – this historical dimension for more recent sporting events. However, it is important that we have some historical perspective on the institutional relationship that has evolved between the media and sport, particularly as it is the former that has told the history of sport for much of the twentieth century.

This chapter aims to highlight some of the major transformations in the historical relationship between sport and the media: from the emergence of a popular press to the beginnings of an international sports–media nexus. We shall explore this relationship by investigating various media in turn: the press, cinema and newsreels, radio, and finally television. However, it is important to stress that each new mode of communication did not develop in isolation from the others.

It is unquestionable that mass communications have transformed sport from what Holt (1989: 12) refers to as an 'orally transmitted popular culture' to a mass culture with mass spectatorship. However, oral traditions continue to pervade sport and the interplay between sport as popular culture and various media forms is historically complex. There is no simple linear transformation of sport by modern communication systems and technologies. Neither, of course, is this a one-way street – sport has also played its part in the transformation of media industries. Therefore there is much to be learnt from the historical relationship between sport and the media.

Down the years how the media have affected the way in which sport is played, spectated and organized, and the importance of sport in the social and economic history of media industries, offers an insight into the current transformations and tensions that arise in the sport–media nexus which are examined later in the book.

Origins of sport and the media: the sporting press

Media sport is a product of modernity, that phase of western civilization which transformed European societies, 'resulting from the explosive interaction between capitalism, technology and human linguistic diversity' (Anderson, 1991: 45). It is no coincidence that the institutions through which 'print-capitalism' was diffused in the late seventeenth and early eighteenth centuries, namely the church, the armed forces, the public schools and the universities (Mann, 1992), are the very same media through which modern sporting practices emerged in the late eighteenth to mid-nineteenth centuries (Holt, 1989).

It is during this latter period that folk games, played under the patronage of the aristocracy, started to be transformed and codified, swept up by the spread of industrial capitalism and urbanization in an era of unprecedented change (Hargreaves, 1986). In Britain these processes set in motion the morphology of the modern nation and gradually led to the ascendancy of a powerful middle class which appropriated many aspects of popular sporting custom. Previously, sport had developed as an integral part of localized ritual amusements quite often associated with religious festivals.

Early industrial society, motivated by the tenets of modernism, led to the rational belief that sport represented 'progress' and 'moral improvement' (Real, 1998: 17). However, as Holt has argued, the

Victorian transformation of sport, particularly in the public schools, does not suggest that modern sport's antecedents were either crude or met with a rapid decline (Holt, 1989: 12–14). Commonly known rules and the dissemination of results or victories were well established in some areas by the late eighteenth century and, as we shall see, a fledgling sporting press had begun to emerge during this period.

Sports print media

Contrary to popular belief, sport has a rich literature which stretches back into the eighteenth century. One of the earliest chroniclers of traditional sporting pastimes was J. Strutt, whose publication *The Sports and Pastimes of the People of England* was published in 1801. From bear-baiting to knur-and-spell Strutt recorded for posterity a vivid picture of the English at play. Where Strutt documented some of the more esoteric and brutal aspects of pre-industrial popular recreations, other writers turned their attention to emerging codified sports.

As early as the 1720s and 1730s the first accounts of village cricket were captured in heroic verse. These romantic visions of pastoral England were written in Latin and provide a pre-Georgian impression of one of the oldest team games. Later, in the early 1800s, reports of village cricket were serialized in *The Lady's Magazine* by the sketch artist Mary Russell Mitford. Her prose was critical of a growing professionalism in the sport which she viewed as the antithesis of the gentlemanly art. In one issue she is noted as saying: 'Everything is spoilt when money puts its ugly nose in' (cited in Martineau, 1957: 98) – a romantic sentiment that is wholly recognizable and an early indicator of the ideology of amateurism.

Sport was very marginal to the news agenda of the respectable press of the late eighteenth early nineteenth centuries. The cost of producing daily or weekly newsprint due to restrictive pressures of censorship and stamp duty ('taxes on knowledge') meant that sport could not compete for space in a copy-scarce environment. Even the cheap journalism of the radical press, which by the 1830s challenged the hegemonic control of ownership and licence enjoyed by the respectable press, as well as appealing to a predominantly working-class audience, could not find room for urban recreations. Instead, a wholly separate sporting press emerged to cater for genteel interests in horse racing, prizefighting and blood sports.

One aspect of the sporting press was to communicate and help legislate the organization of sport. For example, horse racing had long enjoyed the patronage of the aristocracy, and in 1751 a group of socially elite owners joined to form the Jockey Club which remains the administrator of the sport. The Jockey Club's rules of racing were published in its own official organ, the *Racing Calendar* (Vamplew, 1988: 47). The publication allowed both the policing and capitalization of the racing programme. Any races not advertised in the *Racing Calendar* were not recognized by the ruling body, enabling a strict control of the sport's administration. It can be seen, from this example, that the dispersion of rules was crucial to the reform of traditional sporting forms from pre-industrial popular culture and reflected the broader shifts in the economic and the political spheres of early industrial capitalism.

Gambling and advertising

The growth of popular gambling was a second and more economic focus for the growth of a sporting press. Vamplew (2008) has argued that many of the rule changes published and distributed by the early sporting press were motivated by the needs of gambling. Sports-minded gentry required a forum from which to wager their bets, and the press became 'full of little calls to combat' (Clapson, 1992: 16). Daily newspapers like *Bell's Life* in London (orig. 1822) were stakeholders for the aristocratic 'fancy' on prizefighting and were full of news and gossip about 'the ring'. By the mid-nineteenth century *Bell's Life* enjoyed a circulation of more than 30,000 (Mason, 1988: 46), although censure and regulation of illicit betting began to gain ground, spurred on by the liberal press and evangelical campaigns of the National Anti-Gambling League.

However, the use of the telegraph from the 1860s reinvigorated off-course betting on horse racing, enabling sporting newspapers to develop a national average from the transmission of racing odds and results from the 'Tattersall's Rings' (exclusive betting enclosures at racecourses) and deliver it to an expectant working-class betting market. As Clapson (1992: 28) has illustrated, from the 1870s the sporting press expanded in its range and tenor. In Britain, Manchester became the provincial capital of the sporting press, dominated by the publisher Edward Hulton. During this period Hulton published two major daily sports newspapers, *Sporting Life* (orig. 1859, replacing *Bell's Life*) and the *Sporting Chronicle* (orig. 1871). For those opposed to gambling such papers represented the 'cheap and the sensational' and, by popularizing gambling and the commercial dimension of sport, had irreparably damaged the spirit of sport.

If gambling had opened up the commercial potential for a sporting press from the early 1800s to the 1870s, it was the sporting evangelists who forged another wave of sporting publications designed for the burgeoning recreations of the English middle class. Lowerson (1993) has traced the rise of some of these specialist sporting publications during a wave of middle-class enthusiasm for sport from 1870 to 1914. The view of sport as 'improving', providing spiritual as well as bodily virtue, was central to this movement. The growing popular press provided an essential vehicle for disseminating the evangelical zeal of a section of the middle class who promoted the therapeutic value of sport.

Through the patronage of the sporting press both traditional and modern sport enjoyed an unprecedented promotional boom. Economically driven by advertisements the sporting press developed a more graphic layout afforded by cheaper block printing. Hunting, which had long received the patronage of the socially grand *Field* magazine, was joined by the more commercial *Shooting Times* (orig. 1882) and *Horse and Hound* (orig. 1884), which were heavily laden with advertising for manufacturers of tack and firearms among other essential hunting and shooting equipment. *The Field* had also transformed itself to incorporate ball games, specifically the summer pastimes of lawn tennis and croquet. Here was an instance where the sporting press moved directly into the business and administration of sport – the proprietors of *The Field* offered a silver trophy to inaugurate the Wimbledon Championships held by the All England Croquet Club in 1868 (Lowerson, 1993: 253).

For those in positions of power in sports administration the rapidly expanding sporting press was a means to communicate the social and cultural parameters of sport. For example, the weekly *Athletic News* (orig. 1875), another of Hulton's publications from Manchester, disseminated the unofficial, but authoritative, 'voice of football'. The paper was closely allied to the northern-based Football League and enjoyed an impressive circulation in excess of 180,000 at its prime (Mason, 1988: 48). Edited by J. J. Bentley from 1892 to 1900, who would go on to be President of the Football League, the *Athletic News* took a strong view on any moral transgression of football's codes and etiquette. This was particularly true where gambling by players and officials was concerned and the paper eschewed any 'tipsters' or horse-racing results from its pages.

The Edwardian era saw pressure on daily newspapers to increase their sporting coverage. The newspaper industry had seen a rapid acceleration of newspaper chains, with press barons such as Northcliffe and Beaverbrook shaping the content and layout of their papers. Economic pressures to boost circulation to satisfy the demands of advertisers led to a more universal outlook on content, and sport fitted into a broader magazine miscellany.

The sporting press had proved very successful in tapping into the nation's captivation with sport. The establishment of regular fixture lists and seasonal events within many spectator sports provided a steady flow of stories and results for the sporting press to report. Tipping sheets and football coupon papers had emerged in the 1880s, albeit on an ephemeral basis. However, by 1900 local newspapers were beginning to employ their own specialist 'tipsters' and conduct variants of what became the football pools, whose lead was soon to be followed by the national press, including the *Daily Mail,* the *Daily Mirror* and the *Daily Express,* as well as the Sunday editions.

As we have already mentioned, newspapers began to sponsor sporting occasions for the promotional effect association with new professional sporting heroes might bring. For example, the *News of the World* sponsored the first Professional Golfers Association (PGA) matchplay championships with £200 in prize money after professional golfers had threatened a strike over inadequate payments (Lowerson, 1989: 203–4). As the PGA tournament grew in the 1920s and 1930s the championship began a long association with the *Daily Mail* in 1936. The growth of sports coverage in the national popular press spelt the death-knell for many of the independent daily and weekly sporting papers that by the 1930s had dwindled to just a handful of publications predominantly catering for horse racing.

Europe's sporting press

The demise of a specific sporting press in Britain contrasted with the growing strength of daily sport newspapers in continental Europe. The *Gazzetta dello Sport* in Italy was launched on the eve of the first Olympic Games held in Athens in 1896. The paper was born of a merger between two newspapers *La Tripletta* and *Il Ciclista* that had supported an early Italian passion for cycling.

As with its British counterparts, the *Gazzetta* began to sponsor sporting events, the inauguration of the cycling race, Giro Ciclistico, fostering closer ties between sport and the press. Today the *Gazzetta* enjoys an unprecedented position in the Italian press having embedded itself in the daily culture of Italian newspaper readers and it has gained in recognition abroad with the spread of interest in Italian football which has been facilitated by increased television coverage.

Cycling and motorsport also played a key role in the establishment of a French daily sports paper *L'Auto-Velo*, later to become *L'Équipe*. Established in 1900 by Henri Desgrange, founder of the Tour de France in 1903 (Wheatcroft, 2005), *L'Auto* changed its name to *L'Équipe* on the Liberation of occupied France and was integral to the re-establishment of the Tour in 1946 as well as instigating new European competitions in football, basketball and athletics. *Gazzetta*, *L'Équipe* and the Spanish sports newspaper *El Mundo Deportivo* (founded in 1906) have been the guardians of the meaning of sport in their respective national cultures, developing distinctive forms of sports journalism from that developed in Britain (see Chapter 9).

The sports journalist

Sports writers themselves were emerging as a specialist breed of journalist. Cricket had long enjoyed a level of serious writing about the game. The Cricket Reporting Agency had been established in the mid-nineteenth century as had several statistical compendiums on cricket, the most famous being John Wisden's *Cricketers' Almanac*, first published in 1864. Wisden, characterized by its 'yellow half-brick' appearance, became an essential read for cricket enthusiasts and was the most visible example of a growing interest in sporting minutiae.

More elaborate prose on cricket emerged in the 1920s and 1930s through the writing of Neville Cardus of the *Manchester Guardian*. Formerly a music critic, Cardus had turned to cricket after suffering a breakdown and recuperating at Old Trafford, the home of the Lancashire County Cricket Club. Cardus used his self-taught musicology to express the rhythms of the game and the performance of the men who played it. A more detailed examination of the sports journalist's craft is made in Chapter 9; however, in this historical context, it is important to note the break from the rather cursory and formulaic tradition of sports writing that emerged during this period.

The 1921 Ashes tour by Australia caused an outpouring of new journalism on cricket and prompted several national newspapers, including *The Observer*, to take its coverage of the sport more seriously. However, this brand of journalism did not have a wide appeal. Less highbrow newspapers, such as the *Daily Mirror*, turned to a brasher mode of address in the coverage of sport in a clear attempt to attract a young working-class readership. Sport was entertainment that was kept separate from 'hard news'. As Trevor Wignall – quoted at the top of the chapter – a sports journalist from the *Daily Express*, reflected in 1936:

> Football had a place of its own in newspapers, and even Test cricket was regarded as something that should not be mixed with politics or a read-able murder. Sport, as this is composed, is probably the biggest thing in the land. It occupies the thoughts, and empties the pockets, of countless millions. (Wignall, 1936: 6)

As with today, the coverage of sport from the turn of the twentieth century was highly selective. Heavily dominated by men's sporting achievements, often associating the manliness or courageousness of a performance with a fervent patriotism, sports coverage was schemati-cally divided into 'naturalized' seasons of sport: football, rugby and steeplechase horse racing in winter, and cricket, tennis, golf, athletics and flat horse racing in summer. In this way, the press socialized their readers into the place of sport in society, setting parameters for the communication and significance of sport.

The press rarely questioned the politics of sport, and only where scandal and corruption arose did it remind its readers of the sanctity of sport founded on the amateurist values of its administrative leaders (Inglis, 1987). Until the press was faced with the competition and immediacy of broadcasting, newspapers could rely on a voracious appetite for sports news and results from a largely male audience.

Sport on newsreel

It is interesting and significant that the period in which sport gained mass popularity as a form of entertainment coincides with the inven-tion, innovation and commercial exploitation of the moving image. Although sport can engage all the senses it is perhaps the sight of the elite sports performance that most catches the imagination and stirs the emotions. It is debatable whether film contributed to the mass popularity of spectator sport. Rather, sport has been used by film as a device for exploring human emotion and form, with all its sense of achievement, failure, courage, athleticism, ritual and occasion. However, in return, film has captured and reproduced the often mes-meric and heroic moments of sport, as well as the corporeal aspects of people at play.

Film and sport

In the 1890s the Lumière brothers, Thomas Edison, Robert Paul and others had begun to show actualities or 'topicals' as a way of exhibiting their versions of a mechanical eye that would capture a moving image. Exhibiting short sequences in travelling fairs and music halls the pioneers of film engineering were more interested in the intellectual challenge of manufacturing equipment than the images they created. However, some films did focus on specific subjects and sporting events featured prominently in the productions of this band of inventors and scientists.

An early illustration of this practice was Robert Paul's film of the 1896 Derby from Epsom Downs where his camera, located twenty yards behind the finishing post, captured the winning horse owned by Edward, Prince of Wales, named Persimmon, later to be screened at the Alhambra Theatre, London (Fielding, 1972: 18). Other sporting events were staged deliberately for the camera, for example Thomas Edison captured a boxing match featuring Billy Edwards in his New York studio in 1895, later to be exhibited in peep shows. Boxing, moreover, became a staple of these early films.

On one occasion in 1899 both the Edison and Biograph companies produced films on a prizefight between Jeffries and Sharkey that was later recreated in a more successful 'fake' film produced by Sigmund Lubin for the Vitagraph company that used two impersonators instead of the actual pugilists (Fielding, 1972: 16). The exercise of 'faking' actual events for film indicated the intense rivalry that grew among the competing companies as each sought to promote their own technological achievements. The subject matter appeared to take second place behind the technology, 'intended simply as short-lived novelties, designed to demonstrate the convincing qualities of their projectors and cameras' (Puttnam, 1997: 27).

The discovery and restoration of the Edwardian 'actuality films' of Mitchell & Kenyon discovered in the early 1990s provide valuable evidence of early interest in sport on film (Toulmin, 2006). The films, developed into major television series for the BBC, show a range of sports events mainly shot in the North of England revealing a burgeoning period of spectator sport in Britain. Although principally made of short highlights Toulmin (2006: 144) suggests they 'show how the growth of particular different sporting activities became tied to this new technology and was a major factor in developing an audience for the institution of cinema'.

Newsreel began in earnest in Paris when Charles Pathé started the Pathé Journal in 1908. Newsreel gave order to the 'topicals' that had previously entertained the patrons of travelling fairs and sideshows. Pathé had understood that the renting of film was the most economical method of reaching wider audiences than hitherto possible. The rise of newsreel coincided with the process of industrialization of film production. The expansionist building programme to house film exhibition led to the construction of cinemas across Europe.

Newsreels helped to fill cinema programmes, and were commercially circulated. The French companies Pathé and Gaumont dominated the market and built up economies of scale through extensive distribution networks. With locally fixed audiences the demand for film content rapidly increased. The same film could be screened in several countries at once, with amendments to captions to suit the localized needs of different language communities. The system of weekly releases went a long way to satisfy the hunger for film entertainment from mushrooming cinema audiences.

Sporting entertainment and 'exclusives'

Although the First World War had produced a fillip to the craft of newsreel production in terms of camera operation, direction and editing, the market demand for entertainment drove its expansion during the 1920s. Traditional values of objective journalism were forgone for the principles of storyline and dramatic effect. Sport matched the industrial need for entertainment, providing ready-made spectacles for the newsreel companies to capture and release to mass audiences.

During the 1920s, photojournalism of sporting events was underdeveloped and technically poor. Moving images of sport filled this niche with an array of popular sporting events. Boxing, football, cricket and horse racing were staple favourites, and reels on large sporting occasions, like the Henley Regatta or yachting from Cowes, provided the mass audience with a window on culturally exclusive worlds of sport that were demarcated by class and social distinction.

As power in the film industry shifted to Hollywood during the interwar period, American companies expanded their operations in Europe with the introduction of sound in 1929. British Movietone News, owned by Twentieth Century Fox, headed this audio-visual revolution in newsreel, famously interviewing the Prime Minister, Ramsay MacDonald (Aldgate, 1979: 22). The entry of American corporations promoted vociferous competition among newsreel producers and distributors. Sport was at the centre of these rivalries that reached their height during the 1930s.

The intense rivalry between newsreel companies led to an escalation of 'exclusives', where film of individual events was secured through payment to the various governing bodies of sport. Gaumont paid up to £2,000 for the rights to the Grand National alone (Aldgate, 1979: 24) and other events such as the Cup Final, by the 1930s well established at Wembley Stadium, warranted similar fees.

Reflecting on the 'golden age' of newsreel, cameraman Ronnie Noble recalled the practice of 'pinching' in the highly competitive environment for film footage from sport. The war for coverage led to all manner of pirate activities in order to 'get one over' the opposition. Scaffolds were erected around perimeter fencing, cameras were smuggled into stadiums by a variety of cunning strategies and aeroplanes were deployed to capture remote footage with long-focus lenses. 'Pinching' was an essential quality for the newsreel cameraman and was deliberately used to spoil the value of rival newsreel companies:

> A really first-class pinch is one that remains undetected until the story hits the screen. The satisfaction is not only in getting pictures of the event, but in putting the story on the screen simultaneously with the 'rightful' company's claim of exclusive pictures. (Noble, 1955: 100)

Pirating certainly enlivened the working day of those cameramen who travelled the length and breadth of the country to deliver the best pictures for cinema audiences.

However, because sports rights cost newsreel companies dear for film they could not guarantee was exclusive, there was a pressure to pool resources and access to events. The main reason for this tendency was the sense that sporting authorities were overtly capitalizing on the newsreel war, causing much grievance and resentment.

The filming of Test Match cricket, for instance, proved notoriously difficult to police. Test grounds were not only large, with many possibilities for smuggling cameras through the gates, but also were surrounded by buildings that overlooked the arena offering numerous vantage points for clear, uninterrupted and legally secure coverage. Attempts to prevent such 'pinching' led to extreme measures of balloon barriers and spotlights to blind cameramen. Unfortunately, the projectionist's moves also interfered with the crowd's enjoyment of the game and even distracted the players themselves.

Newsreels, according to Huggins (2007: 97) helped broaden the appeal of sport and in the case of football changed the perception of the sport from an exclusively working-class pastime to 'a widely accepted part of popular culture'. They continued to cover sport into the 1960s; however, with the decline and fragmentation of the cinema-going audience, due, in the main, to the rising popularity and ubiquity of television, the newsreel lost its resonance and ability to tell truly the whole story of events. Radio commentaries had given instantaneous reception from sport, and television then added the moving image in people's homes with the comfort and ease of turning the switch. Nevertheless, newsreels stand as a significant historical document on sport from the turn of the twentieth century to the immediate postwar years. They capture the wider feel of the event itself, with as many shots of the crowd as the play on the field and, for this alone, are valuable anthropological texts.

Sport on radio

Britain was still frayed and shaken by a war it had won, and ration books still mattered more than any written by Shakespeare, but sport helped provide the promise of a better tomorrow in one heady and irresistible package. (Radio sports commentator, Bryon Butler, 1997: 18)

The immediacy of radio

The introduction of radio in 1922 posed an immediate threat to the dissemination of news by the local and national press. Radio enjoyed the power of immediacy and the ability to go out and about to deliver on-site accounts from sport. Even the most efficient of the Saturday specials run by many local newspapers were pushed to turn the day's news around and distribute their publications to their agents before 7 p.m. in the evening. Radio news, therefore, posed a real threat to the livelihood of many journalists, printers and salesmen and women who relayed the afternoon events to the hundreds of thousands of eager readers waiting to gain information on the day's results, whether it be in football, rugby union, rugby league, cricket or horse racing. One of the most vociferous opponents of radio was Lord Riddell, who represented the Newspaper Proprietors' Association (NPA) before the Sykes Committee of 1923 that had looked at the regulation of radio in the UK. It was believed that a results service and running commentaries from sport would seriously damage the sale of newspapers and between 1922 and 1926, before the BBC became a Corporation by Royal Charter, the results service from sport was restricted to bulletins after seven o'clock (Briggs, 1961: 172; Whannel, 1992: 13–14).

BBC radio sport

On becoming a Corporation in 1926, the BBC was given the freedom by the Postmaster-General to provide outside broadcasts (OBs) from sport. The BBC soon developed a sequence of firsts from sport in a portfolio of programming that included a results service, eyewitness accounts, running commentaries and talks. The results service fed the appetite not only of the sports enthusiast but also the rapidly growing number of households that completed a pools coupon in the hope of getting rich quick.

This posed some ethical problems for the BBC whose conservative moral tone was compromised by indirectly supporting the rapid rise of mass gambling through the pools during the interwar period. Eyewitness accounts and running commentaries offered the sports fan a new engagement with sport. The immediacy of radio outside broadcasts provided the sports fan with an unparalleled access to sport. Central to the ideology of programming from sport was the rhetoric of public-service broadcasting championed by the BBC's first Director General, Lord Reith. Enshrined in this concept was a belief in the power of broadcasting to enlighten its audience culturally, informing them of important political events, as well as providing entertainment during the 'lighter' moments of programming.

Sports programming clearly fitted into the latter definition of the BBC's cultural mission under Reith's direction. Sport provided a way of broadening the BBC's appeal to a wider audience, reminiscent of the way in which it has been used to introduce new communicative platforms like pay and digital television at the dawn of the twenty-first century. In response to criticism of the place of sport in the serious agenda of broadcasting the growing constituency of BBC listeners soon began to make their voice heard, as this reply to a letter of criticism to the Radio Times from 1930 makes clear:

> Sport is not a plague to be avoided, and one must be very bigoted to switch off whenever it is mentioned. Even an 'Indiscriminate Listener' should understand that the average healthy-minded man be as keenly interested in the latest cricket score as in (say) a revolution in Mexico. Something must come first, and whether news or sport matters little

to the ordinary listener – I enjoy both. Your correspondent should learn to be tolerant; after all, narrow-mindedness has done more harm to the old country than sport. (J. W. Coxon, letter to the *Radio Times*, 20 June 1930)

BBC radio and sports rights

By the early 1930s the BBC soon had a portfolio of sporting events placed in a broadcasting calendar that resonated with the winter and summer seasons of sport. (Scannell and Cardiff, 1991)

Now well-established events – the Scottish and English Cup Finals, Test cricket, the Boat Race, the Grand National, the Derby, the Five Nations rugby union internationals, Wimbledon and the Open Golf Championship – were the portals to a shared national culture, and radio gave them a wider audience and significance. However, the arrangement to broadcast some events was reliant on the goodwill of the various governing bodies of sport concerned.

The BBC had taken the Corinthian principle that business and sport did not mix and that, because it was promoting such events to a national audience, it had a right to broadcast without payment. The BBC's principled defiance hid a wider agenda to gain dominance in the coverage of sport, feeling that, because the press did not have to pay for access into sports arenas, neither should they (Haynes, 1999). The sports' authorities were not of the same opinion, and believed the BBC's attempt to gain universality of reception and access to sport was proving a threat to their own status as providers of entertainment. In particular, the authorities and the NPA were afraid of the possible effects public broadcast of running commentaries would have on attendance at sporting events and the circulation of newspapers.

The intransigence of some sporting bodies to adhere to the public-service rhetoric of the BBC included the English Football Association which prohibited access to the 1929 Cup Final between Bolton Wanderers and Portsmouth. Here, the BBC resorted to a series of eye-witness accounts by a number of reporters who had paid for entry into Wembley and then rushed to a flat in Chelsea where they delivered a summary of events (Haynes, 1999).

A further ban by the FA in 1930 brought matters to a head and the BBC conceded to pay a facility fee of £1,000 for entry into the stadium. However, the director of OBs Gerald Cock was far from satisfied with the FA's conflation of sport and business:

> [It] is a dismal prospect when the governing body of a sport originated, built up, and entirely supported by amateurs, should be captured by professionals whose whole interest apparently is commercial. (*Radio Times*, 28 March 1930)

Cock's view hints at the socio–cultural background of BBC personnel, many of whom held Oxford or Cambridge 'blues' and carried the sporting ethics founded in the amateurist origins of organized sport during the nineteenth century.

The sporting rivalries of the two universities figured highly in the early OBs from sport, not only the annual 'Boat Race' but also the Varsity rugby union match from Twickenham, athletic events with American universities Princeton and Cornell in 1931, and football from Highbury.

Producing sport on radio

When radio outside broadcasts from Britain's sporting arenas began in 1927 the technical and logistical problems greatly outweighed any concern with the structure and quality of the programmes. The early years of the BBC's promotional arm, the *Radio Times*, and its annual review of the year, the BBC Handbook, are full of references to the technical difficulties in the broadcasting of sport. Experiments with OBs brought some humorous results as the following recollection of a pioneering broadcast from the Derby suggests:

> In the now distant days of 1926, while a contract with the newspapers precluded the broadcasting of one word of descriptive matter of events as they were taking place, attempts were made to broadcast some Derby 'atmosphere' from Tattenham Corner . . . Listeners will remember that terrible Derby. From early in the morning to late afternoon the rain came down in torrents, and during the Race, not only were there no sounds from the hoofs in the soft going, but even the bookies, tipsters and onlookers were more occupied in taking shelter under their umbrellas than in speeding home the winner. (BBC Handbook, 1928: 143–4)

Similar experiments were made at speedway tracks, where all that could be heard was the roar of the bikes as they neared the microphone. It became clear that in order to convey the sporting scene a new form of narrative speech needed to be introduced.

Radio sports commentary

Running commentaries from sport became the mainstay of BBC Radio's sports production. Before the innovation of the li p-microphone that isolated and shielded the commentator's voice from the surrounding roar of the crowd, running commentaries were conducted from small huts erected near the pitch, racecourse or track. The commentators themselves invariably came from an 'Oxbridge' background, were ex-sportsmen themselves, and were employed through a network of friends and acquaintances, largely developed at university or in the Armed Forces. Commentary was a craft that had to be learned (Booth, 2008).

A mellifluous delivery of words was a central feature of good commentary, the guidelines for which were set by the BBC's second director of OBs Seymour Joly de Lotbiniere. De Lotbiniere set the parameters of good practice, and devised a way of sound-testing potential commentators, as well as keeping a rigorous check on the quality of broadcasts with a regular meeting of his staff following the weekend's sport where his critiques began with the ominous phrase: 'Programmes since we last met'. Running commentaries from sport produced some of the most popular household names on British radio. From the interwar years names such as George Allison (football), Captain Teddy Wakelam (rugby union and cricket), Graham Walker (motorsport – and father of Murray Walker), Wynford Vaughan-Thomas (rugby union) and Howard Marshall ('The Voice' of cricket) educated and entertained a rapidly growing audience. In the late 1940s, John Arlott (cricket), Rex Alston (cricket, rugby union and athletics), Max Robertson (athletics and tennis), Raymond Glendenning (football, horse racing and boxing), Stewart Macpherson (boxing and ice hockey) and G. V. Wynne-Jones (rugby union), fresh from their experience of war, provided a new vigour and artistry to sports commentary, more professional in the rudiments of broadcasting than the previous generation of practitioners.

The BBC also introduced new sports programming in the postwar era, most notably *Sports Report* in 1948. Produced by the Scot, Angus Mackay, *Sports Report* was the flagship results service of the BBC's Light Programme, which 'brought in reports from no fewer than 15 towns up and down the country within the space of 30 minutes' (Mackay, 1997: 13).

With television not yet established, the programme introduced new stars of broadcasting and sport, in particular the Irish presenter and commentator Eamonn Andrews, and attracted more than 12 million listeners in the 1940s and 1950s (Butler, 1997: 18). The programme flitted across the country, and in some cases across the world, to on-the-spot reporters who had been given chapter and verse by Mackay to keep their summaries concise and articulate. The demands of producing a programme so quickly after the event are captured in the following words from Mackay himself:

> Sports Report goes out so soon after the end of the day's sport that, far from having a complete rehearsal, we are usually working from hand to mouth while it is being broadcast. (MacKay, 1997: 13)

The other outstanding element of the BBC's sports programming became *Test Match Special*. In the formative years of sports commentaries, cricket was not considered to be a viable option for extensive coverage, not only because it took up a lot of airtime, but because it was thought the listener would get bored with a ball-by-ball account. Therefore cricket was largely restricted to eyewitness accounts from Tests until regular commentaries began on *Test Match Special* in 1957 with England's series against the West Indies (see Johnston, 1968, and Martin-Jenkins, 1990, for comprehensive historical accounts of cricket on radio and television).

The key to cricket commentaries was the wider picture magically and majestically captured by the likes of John Arlott, Rex Alston and, latterly, Brian Johnston during a lull in play. As producer Robert Hudson argued in 1968:

> It is in the filling of these pauses in play that the commentator really reveals his quality; his timing must be as precise as the batsman's in the middle – so that he rounds off the point he is making just as the bowler wheels round to bowl the next ball. (Hudson, 1968: 35)

By the time television sports programming began in earnest during the 1950s radio had already set the codes and practices of OBs from sport and, most importantly, the standards the audience had come to expect from the BBC's sports service.

Origins of televising sport

Of all the media discussed in this chapter – and indeed this book – television has shaped our contemporary view of sport more than any other. The history of sport that television often presents to us is, in fact, a history of televising sport. All the 'golden moments' of sport are worked and reworked by television to re-present the 'world of sport' in new ways and combinations.

However, as we have already reviewed, modern sport had existed long before television entered our homes and communities. To understand this state of affairs fully we need to analyse critically the origins of this relationship, to ask how and why this relationship began, and to decipher what this history means in an omnipresent world of televised sport.

Continuities of radio and televised sport

The history of televising sport in the UK is intimately related to the history of radio outside broadcasts from sport. Technically, many of the people involved in BBC radio were also the pioneers in television sport. The first Director of Television at the BBC was Gerald Cock, previously head of outside broadcasts in radio. Such ties meant that sport became a key instrument in the promotion of television as a new form of entertainment.

Institutionally, the connections between BBC producers and the administrators of sport were also of value. The new-found engagement between broadcaster and sports administrator allowed a honeymoon period for television sport to develop on an experimental basis. As with radio, a major fear had been the possible effect television broadcasts would have on actual attendance at sports events. This remained an issue that would never go away, and would ultimately cost television dear.

As this suggests, the relationship between sport and television has not always been sanguine and throughout their historical association the struggles over the representation of sport through the lens of the camera and the microphone, who this mediation is for, and when or how it is delivered, have often proved volatile. The main causes of these disruptions and altercations have been a set of conflicting agendas that reflect the historical infrastructures of sport and the unique political economy of British broadcasting formed by an uneasy marriage between public-service broadcasting and publicly regulated commercial (otherwise labelled 'independent') television.

Any history of televised sport should, therefore, consider the political economy of this 'match made in heaven' (Goldlust, 1987: 78) as well as those technical innovations that have helped to transform the way in which sport is delivered to our homes.

BBC television sport

When the BBC Television service began broadcasting in November 1936 there was a great scepticism about what the medium could achieve. Certainly, with regard to sport, there was no sense that sport would be dominated by this new form of entertainment. BBC radio was still consolidating its position in the British living room and television was nothing short of a frivolous gimmick. For Gerald Cock, sport and outside broadcasts in general offered the most effective way of attracting an audience for what was a considerably unknown entity.

In order to promote the new medium the *Radio Times* introduced a new column under the pseudonym 'The Scanner' that showed a preoccupation with promoting the technological dimension of outside broadcasts from sport. For example, preceding the first televising of a rugby union international between England and Scotland from Twickenham in London during March 1938, there appeared an early indication of the logistical difficulties facing the BBC technicians in their attempts to provide the clearest possible 'depictive form' of the play. Twickenham was to become the first sports stadium to be permanently equipped for television, and the *Radio Times* informed its readers that three cameras were to be positioned within specially constructed wooden huts in the West Stand, thirty feet from the ground placed level with the half-way line and the two 22-yard lines.

The *Radio Times* gave an expectant impression of what viewers might see:

> With skilful use of the telephoto lens the ball or the forwards on top of it should be seen the whole time. A 'sticky' pitch slowing up the game will probably make a better picture. (*Radio Times*, 11 March 1938)

The fragility of the image can be sensed from this account, and the positioning of the cameras was clearly viewed as the optimum use of the telephoto lenses to capture the play in each third of the field. The sheer bulkiness of the technology required to transmit from sport, specifically the mass of cable involved, severely restricted the mobility of the equipment. The problems of economically marshalling the technology needed on location took many years to resolve.

This, inevitably, enforced certain time constraints. For example, in 1938 the coverage of England against Scotland from Wembley on Saturday, 9 April, was preceded by a light-heavyweight title fight between the boxers Len Harvey and Jock McAvoy on Thursday,

7 April, which left twenty-nine hours between the broadcasts. As The Scanner suggested, 'come behind the scenes, and you will see that, far from being ample, the twenty-nine hours' interval is giving something in the nature of a rush job' (*Radio Times*, 22 April 1938).

This relative immobility is symbolic of the transitional period in media technology. It was a time-consuming (and labour-intensive) process and virtually pre-Fordist in comparison to other forms of communication at this time (radio reached over ninety per cent of the population by 1938). Processes and techniques had yet to be fully standardized and programmes had yet to be formalized in any coherent, recognizable way. The mass consumption of television was still some way off.

Sports rights and competition

For the duration of the Second World War BBC Television was put on hold. On resumption, the first major sports broadcast came from the London Olympic Games in 1948. This event kick-started a whole series of innovations during the immediate postwar period. New, more sensitive, CPS Emitron cameras were introduced, providing a higher degree of depth of field and focus (Whannel, 1992: 64).

Allied to this innovation was the introduction of 'zoom lenses' mounted on turrets giving OB directors the ability to focus on individual players instead of actual play. First used in the coverage of horse racing from Ascot in 1951, the new lenses brought a five-to-one ratio, which was a vast improvement on the previous two-to-one system, allowing a process of personalization, to give the viewer a 'privileged insight' into the sport (Clarke and Clarke, 1982: 72).

Transformations in sports programming were also emerging in the early 1950s after a series of decisions on broadcasting policy. Firstly, issues of copyright had led governing bodies to restrict access to sport. In 1944, led by the Greyhound Racing Association, many of Britain's leading sports organizations formed the Association for the Protection of Copyright in Sport (APCS). The APCS was fearful of the 'rediffusion' of televised sport in public places and attempted to enforce their own copyright on the performance of sports women and men, much akin to the legal rights of an author, composer or playright (Haynes, 1998: 215–18).

These cool relations thawed after the Labour government's Committee on Copyright announced in 1952 that the rights to television sports performance should be vested in the broadcaster on agreement of remuneration to sports promoters for any loss of revenue incurred. This opened the way to a series of deals between the BBC and sport, including the rights to the 'Matthews Final' of 1953 for £1,000.

The second major shift in broadcasting policy was the introduction of commercial television in 1955. The Independent Television Authority reflected broader shifts in British popular culture after the austerity of the immediate postwar years. It also broke the broadcast monopoly of the BBC and introduced more lively, populist forms of programming.

As Whannel (1991) has highlighted, the BBC was initially slow to respond to its new competitor in most areas of programming except, that is, for sport. From 1954 to 1958 the BBC introduced three new sports programmes that came to be the staple diet of sports broadcasting in Britain. These were the mid-week sports omnibus *Sportsview* (1954), the Saturday evening highlights package *Sports Special* (1956), and the star in the BBC's portfolio of sports programming, the Saturday afternoon sports magazine *Grandstand* (1958), which ran for forty-eight years until January 2007.

All three programmes placed great value on winning the 'family audience', appealing to both the sports lover and the uninitiated. *Sportsview*, introduced by Peter Dimmock, was designed to combine filmed material with studio comment and interviews, with much emphasis placed on sporting personalities. *Sports Special*, the forerunner of *Match of the Day* later to be launched on BBC 2 in 1964 after the introduction of videotape, was introduced by Kenneth Wolstenholme and was built on the back of the BBC's exclusive deal with the Football League for edited filmed highlights. Finally, *Grandstand*, introduced by David Coleman, brought together previously disparate live outside broadcasts from sport under one umbrella programme, and was invariably structured around horse racing. Together, the BBC's portfolio of sport made it very difficult for the disparate ITV franchises to gain a foothold in the televising of sport market.

ITV sport

The first ITV companies to introduce sport into their schedules faced an upward struggle to gain the confidence of suspicious governing bodies and restricted funds for sports rights. ITV managed to poach some talent from the BBC, like producers Bill Ward and John Graydon, and also recruited from within sport itself, including Wolves and England skipper Billy Wright who joined the Midlands-based Associated Television as chief sports advisor in 1956.

ITV sought new avenues of televised sport including a mobile unit to film the Monte Carlo Rally for the Associated Rediffusion (AR) programme *Calvalcade of Sport*, 'behind the scenes' interviews with sport personalities in *Sportstour*, and the Wednesday evening programme *Sports Formbook* that discussed the following week-end's sport with racing journalist John Rickman giving the latest tips from the racecourses and stables. ITV also famously introduced wrestling to its sports programming, screened twice a month by AR in 1956.

Transformations in sport were also delivering new experiences for the viewer. Until the 1950s the Football Association and the Football League had resisted the introduction of floodlighting. However, many games had been played under floodlight outside the auspices of the FA Cup and League programme. Specifically, clubs such as Wolves began to pit their skills against international competition, invariably under floodlight in front of the TV cameras (Haynes, 1998: 218–21). Both the BBC and ITV companies revelled in the opportunity to show international stars like Ferenc Puskas on British screens, introducing viewers to a new era of mid-week European football that would blossom in the late 1960s with the triumphs in the European Cup of first Celtic and then Manchester United.

Global TV sport

Other international sporting occasions like the Olympic Games and the World Cup were also gaining wider recognition during this period. Television helped bring such events into the living rooms of the nation. The introduction of a cross-continental association of broadcasters in 1954 called 'Eurovision' allowed viewers the first live pictures from the World Cup in Switzerland (1954) and Sweden (1958), followed by the Rome Olympics in 1960. Through the amalgamation of public-service broadcasters under the auspices of the European Broadcasting Union (EBU) the internationalism of sport was disseminated to a wider public, the philosophy of which resonated with the desire of broadcasters to bring new exotic experiences into people's homes on a transcontinental basis.

These exchanges relied upon some four thousand miles of connecting land lines, with forty-four transmitters. The ideological motivation for the exchange, from the British perspective, is identifiable within the following quote published in the *Radio Times* from the BBC's Chief Technician, M. J. Pilling:

> We have tried to advantage the universality of the picture as a way of overcoming the language barrier. This has led us to develop much more along the lines of shared programmes. (*Radio Times*, 21 May 1954)

The World Cup of 1962 from Chile and the Olympic Games of 1964 from Tokyo were beyond the reach of land lines and denied British viewers any live action from these events. However, the BBC and ITV companies went to extreme lengths to provide pictures as soon as they could from the other side of the world.

For the Tokyo Games this meant the first use of satellite technology, although only to restrict the delay of recorded material. Using the Syncom III satellite of the US Navy which covered the Pacific region, the EBU recorded three hours of action in the United States then flew video tape to Europe for transmission on the same day. The true immediacy of satellite broadcasts of sporting events from around the world did not arrive until the Olympic Games from Mexico in 1968. Both ITV and BBC sent out their own camera crews and presenters to provide on-site 'unilateral' broadcasts, to complement the universal EBU broadcasts. This allowed far more focus on British athletes, and has since become the standard way of covering such global sporting events.

The 1970 World Cup from Mexico added colour to the immediacy of live satellite transmission. With England looking to retain their World Championship and the brilliance of the Brazilian team that included Pele, this tournament inaugurated a new era of global television, capturing the imagination of millions of viewers worldwide. As the 1970s progressed, other sports entered the global playing field, most notably boxing. The 1974 fight between George Forman and Muhammad Ali, known as the 'Rumble in the Jungle', raised heavyweight boxing to unprecedented heights, both as global spectacle and the efficacy of sports superstardom. The fight, thanks to television, is legendary in twentieth-century popular culture and was recently revisited in the film documentary *When We Were Kings*.

In many respects, the 1970s and early 1980s were the 'golden years' of British sports broadcasting. Operating as a duopoly, the BBC and ITV companies enjoyed the fruits of a highly limited spectrum for television in the UK. The introduction of Channel 4 in 1982 opened up some new vistas for sports broadcasting, providing an outlet for previously marginalized sports such as American Football from the NFL in the United States, and previously unseen sports like sumo wrestling from Japan. However, the dominance of the BBC as the national broadcaster of sport would be sustained until the late 1980s and early 1990s when, under challenge from new cable and satellite broadcasters, the Corporation began to be outpriced in the battle for inflationary sports rights and the relatively settled landscape of television sport would be dramatically altered for broadcasters, sporting bodies, viewers and supporters.

Conclusion

What we have suggested in this chapter is that there has always been a relationship between various media and sport. At an institutional level this is a relationship that has evolved and developed, often accompanied by a substantial degree of tension. Sport and the media were two cultural forms which simply proved to be irresistible to each other as the century progressed.

The remainder of the book looks at how this history has informed the shape of modern media sport. Chapter 4 examines in detail what exactly television wants from sport in the first decade of the twenty-first century, while the sporting stars and heroes which the media help to create are scrutinized in Chapter 5.

In this brief historical context we have examined two sides of the triangle which constitutes modern sport, television and sport itself. The third, sponsorship, and its interplay with the other two is an absolutely vital component in the story of the evolution of the contemporary media–sport experience and it is to this area which we now turn our attention.

Chapter 3

A Sporting Triangle:
Television, Sport and Sponsorship

Sponsorship remains one of the world's most important forms of marketing communications expenditure, and sport is still the major recipient for the money that corporations commit to sponsorship spending each year. (Chadwick, 2007: 287)

A squad to win the Rugby World Cup (and plenty of new business). (2007 advert for Benchmark Sport Holdings, a company that controls a network of brands and businesses involved in developing revenue streams from sports entertainment events)

Introduction

Since 2000 the European market in sports sponsorship has risen by 40 per cent to be valued in 2008 as worth in the region of £5 billion (*SportBusiness International*, January 2008). This growth is all the more remarkable given that a European Union Directive in 2005 signalled an end to tobacco advertising and sponsorship of sport and, as we note below, the tobacco industry had been one of the key sectors driving sports sponsorship since the 1960s. However, the escalation in value of sports-related sponsorship is indicative of other trends that have been shaping media sport in the new century. One has been the expansion in sports content on television across primarily pay-TV platforms, fuelled by a more commercially orientated broadcasting industry; the other has been the continuing commercialization and commodification of sports content that has occurred in the last decade as the sports industry has consolidated its position by entrenching elite sport within the entertainment and corporate sectors of the economy.

At the end of the decade it is almost impossible to have a discussion of elite sports without someone mentioning the importance of 'branding', how football clubs can 'add value' to their brand and 'develop and reposition' it in 'emerging global markets'. When the Abu Dhabi United Group, the overseas investment arm of the Abu Dhabi Royal Family, took over Premier League football club Manchester City in September 2008, the strategic aim of Sulaiman al-Fahim was not to make money out of the club, but rather to use the club's media profile as a space to promote Abu Dhabi as a tourist destination. The lexicon of sports language has been transformed by the discourse of advertising and marketing.

In this chapter we attempt to make sense of the complex relationship which has evolved at the very centre of national and international sport – a triangular relationship between sport, sponsors and television which now increasingly drives the shape and development of sporting contests. Building on the previous chapter we focus on the historical link there has always been between sport, the media (television in particular) and sponsorship. As we point out, this relationship is not new and, as Cashmore (1996: 163) has noted, its roots date back to the initial growth of professional sport:

> The development of the sports goods industry dates from the last quarter of the nineteenth century, paralleling the growth of organised sport.

However, what also becomes clear is that the last forty years or so have witnessed a tightening of the stranglehold that sponsors in conjunction with television exert on major sporting events.

Later, we examine the centrality of this sporting triangle in shaping the contemporary national and international sporting experience. Here we look at recent events such as the 2007 Rugby World Cup finals to examine the extent to which funding from sponsors and television underpin their economic structure. Finally, we ask what are the tensions and contradictions inherent in such a relationship for all the parties involved. In particular, how will what Garry Whannel (1992: 151) has called the increasingly powerful 'interlocking forces of television and sponsorship' shape sport and its audiences in the future?

The good old days? Sport and sponsorship

A triangular relationship has developed in recent years that has come to dominate the economic structure of modern sport. Sports governing bodies, sponsors and television have become intertwined in an alliance that has transformed sport in Britain and throughout the world. Professional sport in Britain today relies on commercial sponsorship and money from the sale of television rights for its financial survival. Sponsors are keen to secure media exposure, the most desirable being television, thus sports are desperate to achieve a television space for their sport and their sponsor(s). As this pattern develops it seems that sport is increasingly becoming an adjunct of the advertising industry. Why has this come about?

Martin Polley (1998: 63–84) convincingly argues that sporting activity has always had a contact of sorts with commercial sponsors. Initially this took the form of aristocratic patronage. By the nineteenth century it involved members of the landowning classes becoming involved in popular recreation through forms of patronage. This was perceived as a means of promoting the social order, as well as providing an opportunity to increase the standing of the landowner among the lower classes.

In Britain, the later part of that century saw a fundamental reorganization of sporting activity along both professional and commercial lines, with mass spectator sport as we understand it today evolving during this period (Holt, 1989). Many of the governing bodies of sport that exist today were founded around this time. As the commercialization of popular activities increased, reflecting the commercial opportunities that the new industrial urban environment offered to some, so the business opportunities offered by sport increased also.

As patronage declined due to the economic and social dislocation caused by the development of industrial capitalism, so commercial sponsorship increased. Two of the most popular spectator sports in Britain, football and cricket, enjoyed varying degrees of contact with commercial sponsors. As early as 1896, for example, Nottingham Forest were sponsored by Bovril when they appeared in that year's FA Cup Final, while elsewhere in Europe the origins of the modern Tour de France cycle race date from a commercial sponsorship deal which used the race to promote the newspaper *L'Équipe*. However, this level of sponsorship involvement would seem minuscule when compared with the expansion in this area that was to occur during the 1960s.

1960s: the sponsorship game

A number of currents and cross-currents were responsible for the sudden growth in the level of sports sponsorship that was to occur from this period onwards. One major factor was the financial crisis that professional sport found itself in as a result of the falling revenue that accompanied the decline in attendances. During the early 1950s over 40 million people regularly watched professional football in Britain. By the 1960s this had declined to under 30 million and, despite a brief resurgence after the English World Cup victory in 1966, attendances continued to drop. This pattern was repeated in all the major spectator sports in Britain. Gate receipts provided the main source of revenue for these sports.

The shift away from spectator sport was part of a wider shift in the leisure pattern of postwar Britain. As the suburbs grew, leisure activities were becoming increasingly domestically orientated, a trend accentuated by the growth in the popularity of television. In addition, as the British economy enjoyed a period of relative buoyancy, the increase in discretionary income resulted in the development of a more aggressively commercial pattern of leisure activity. Sport suddenly found itself competing for the public's attention in an increasingly competitive marketplace.

Allied with this was the internal structure of the sports governing bodies themselves. Most of the organizations were still run along amateurish and paternalist lines and were incapable of dealing with the problems that the changing nature of leisure activity posed to their sports. Against the backdrop of these changes, it was the banning by television of cigarette advertising in 1965 that provided the incentive needed for major corporate involvement in sports sponsorship.

Many of the initial corporate sponsors of televised sport were those companies who viewed sponsorship as a way of securing television exposure, not only on commercial television, but also on the 'advertising-free' public-service BBC TV. During this period sport was particularly vulnerable to the overtures of the commercial sponsor. A sport's ability to secure television coverage thus became a key factor if it wished to attract potential sponsors.

As we argue in the next chapter, television has always viewed sport as an important part of its schedules. Historically, sports programming proved to be cheap, popular and easily scheduled. The fees that sport receives from television, although initially disproportionally small, have in recent years mushroomed with increased competition in the television marketplace with the result that governing bodies of sport are keen to go to any lengths to accommodate television.

In 1966, sports sponsorship accounted for less than £1 million of the revenue received by sport in Britain. By the mid-1970s this figure had risen to £16 million (1976) with a further growth to £46 million by 1980. By the early 1990s the amount of money generated by commercial sponsorship had jumped to over £250 million and by 2006 the UK market was worth over £450 million (IposMori, Sportscan, March 2007). Globally it has been estimated that expenditure on sports sponsorship grew between 1989 and 1996 from $3 to $11 billion (*The Economist*, 6 June 1998); by 2008 the North American market alone was worth $11.6 billion (*SportBusiness International*, January 2008) and the European sports sponsorship market was worth £5.26 million in 2007 (Rines, 2007).

Initially, cigarette sponsors such as Benson & Hedges (cricket and snooker) and John Player (cricket and motor racing) used sponsorship of televised sport as a means of evading the television ban on cigarette advertising and obtaining 'piggy-back' exposure on the advertising-free BBC television. Such was the success of these arrangements for the sponsors involved that the range of corporations involved in televised sport began to grow. In addition, there were sports suppliers, the most famous being the sportswear firm Adidas, who began to use the television age of sport to establish a global marketing platform (Smit, 2007).

Why sponsor sport?

The reasons why companies choose to sponsor sport vary. They can be looking to achieve an increase in the public profile of the company, as well as increasing public awareness of the product/services that the company offers. The association of the company/product in the minds of the consumer with a particular sporting image is also a factor in determining which sport companies may choose to sponsor.

During the 1970s the condom manufacturer Durex became involved in the sponsorship of motor racing as part of the company's strategy to 'normalize' their product. Sports sponsorship has also proved a very cost-effective means of achieving these aims. Major corporations also use sport as a place at which clients can be entertained. The growth of corporate entertainment through the 'tented villages' that now accompany most major sporting events is another manifestation of the increasing links between business and sport.

By the early 1980s it became increasingly clear that sport was becoming firmly positioned within the broader communication strategies of corporations. Whitson (1998), focusing on North America, clearly demonstrates how the linkages between professional sport and the media industries had evolved in the 1980s and 1990s to such a degree that he identifies 'a new kind of corporate integration in the media and entertainment industries' (p. 59).

In 2007 the Spanish sponsorship market was worth €550 million with the Santander bank the largest domestic sponsor. In that year they got involved with Formula 1 motor racing and calculated that the promotional value of their €21 million investment was worth at least four times that (*SportBusiness International*, March 2008). With the bank's international market profile they viewed the international television coverage of the sport in Europe and South America as offering a perfect fit with their communications and corporate strategy to increase brand awareness in a competitive market.

Not only does high-profile televised sport offer a range of marketing, public relations and advertising opportunities which extend the range of public awareness for particular companies, but increasingly in North America this also involves media corporations not simply providing the television channels which deliver this 'sports product', but also owning the sports clubs involved. Thus through vertical integration media corporations can control both distribution and content. The extent to which this pattern has emerged in the UK is examined in more detail later in the chapter.

While for corporations involved in the sports/leisure industry the benefits for brands of a close association with a sporting elite are clear (note how both Nike and Reebok during the 1980s overtook rivals such as Adidas in market share by aggressively pursuing such a policy – see Chapter 5 for more details). At a national and international level non sports-related companies can benefit hugely from close involvement with sporting teams and individuals. For example, Visa's close involvement with the 2007 Rugby World Cup (Official Worldwide Partner and Official Payment Service) was part of a long-term relationship they have nurtured with the sport and has been driven by the aim of building brand awareness across global markets while increasing point-of-sale use of their cards (Glendinning, 2007).

The sports broker

As we have seen, corporations have clearly defined aims in sponsoring sport. As capital penetration of sport has increased, there has been a corresponding growth in the consultancy agencies which link the sponsor with the sport. These agencies have become the new power brokers in the alliance between sport and commerce, helping to provide the linkage points in the television/sport/sponsorship axis.

Worldwide one of the largest of these agencies is International Management Group (IMG). Originally formed by Mark McCormack In 1960 his initial interest in sports management evolved around golf. Gary Player, Arnold Palmer and Jack Nicklaus were three of his first clients (see Chapter 5). Soon his organization began to diversify into other sports such as tennis, while he used his sporting and business contacts to help facilitate the development of the television arm of his empire, Trans World International (TWI).

By the time of his death in 2003 IMG was the largest independent producer of sports programming in the world. Today IMG is a global sports, entertainment and media operation. Not only does it manage top sports people, but through its subsidaries such as TWI and Tiger Aspect Productions, it produces around 11,000 hours of content a year distributed across all media platforms. However, they were by no means the only players in the game.

In the UK one of the main trailblazers in the development of sports brokers was Patrick Nally, whose WestNally pioneered the model of sports marketing which would be put to good effect in the world of both the Olympics and the FIFA World Cup by ISL (International Sport and Leisure) which exclusively marketed both events globally.

There is now a range of agencies; some, such as Ketchum Sport and Sponsorship, have diversified out of PR and other areas of communications services to form agencies working across marketing, PR, event promotion and sponsorship. Indeed one of the defining changes over the last forty years has been the integration of a range of communication services through agencies, a process quickened by the need to have a range of knowledge and skills to work across the digital media landscape and its multi-platforms.

As we examine below, governing bodies of sport employ such agencies to find exclusive sponsors for their sporting events, and to sell both the television and arena advertising rights to potential clients. Television exposure becomes of central importance both in generating substantial rights revenue and providing global exposure for sponsors who in turn pay handsomely to have their company linked with a premier sporting event. Given the massive sums of money now involved in elite sport this has also lead to potential unhealthy relationships between such organizations and some governing bodies of sport. ISL, which worked closely with FIFA, collapsed in 2001 with debts in the region of £150 million. A Swiss court case in 2008 into accusations of fraud and embezzlement revealed that ISL had paid about £66 million in 'bribes' to secure various marketing and television rights contracts (*Daily Telegraph*, 13 March 2008), while, as we note in Chapter 9 when we focus on the area of sports journalism, the powerful brokers of elite sport, including key sponsors such as Adidas or Nike, have also become more adept at managing their assets or brands and the media coverage that plays such an important part in this circuit of communication between sport, commerce, image and the fans (Boyle, 2006). In contemporary sports marketing, managing the 24/7 media is a key function in the battle to maximize your investment.

Global sports sponsorship: branding cricket

As a result of television becoming the driver of elite professional sport, it has come to dictate when, where and in what form sport can take place. The list of such examples of the economic stranglehold that television has over some sports would prove exhaustive if reproduced here. However, one example is the World Heavyweight Boxing title fights which take place in London that are often staged at midnight in order to suit the American networks which are showing the fight live. In the global fight to secure the television rights for sport the American networks dominate. The East Coast of the USA is the most densely populated part of the country, thus offering the audience that advertisers are anxious to reach and television can deliver.

Major sporting events such as the Olympic Games are staged to suit American television networks (NBC specifically) who are anxious to secure a return, through advertising revenue, on their capital outlay used in buying the television rights. In the case of the FIFA World Cup, it has been European television that has dictated, even when the finals have been played in America. Both the 1986 finals in Mexico and the 1994 finals in the USA saw some of the matches being played during the hottest time of the day in order to provide European television with prime-time live football.

At a national level, sports such as cricket have changed due to television's insatiable appetite for more 'entertaining' forms of sports programming. This has resulted in the development of the one-day game, to the detriment some would say of the longer, more traditional Test matches, while in Australia television was instrumental in the initiation of the floodlit day/night matches. The sport now has one-day internationals, a one-day World Series and a limited-overs Sunday League competition, all initiated by television and supported by sponsors keen to secure exposure.

The creation in 2008 of the Indian Premier League (IPL) marked a new stage in the development between television, cricket and sponsorship. The creation of the IPL in cricket-obsessed India marked two trends in global sport. The first demonstrated the ongoing battle for the control of sport between competing media organizations desperate to secure lucrative content and both sponsorship and advertising revenue. When the owner of Zee-TV, a major broadcaster in India, set up the Indian Cricket League, the reaction of the Indian Cricket Board was to sanction a rival IPL and sell the ten-year rights to the country's Sony Television and the Singapore-based World Sports Group for £800 million (in the UK, pay-TV company Setanta secured the rights). The IPL creates eight franchises supported by both corporate India and wealthy individuals who bid for seventy-eight top international players in an auction (with the winning bid for each player becoming their annual salary). DLF Universal, an Indian company, paid around £30 million for a five-year sponsorship deal, with Pepsi becoming the official drink of the tournament in a £6 million deal.

The second is around the governance of the game and the increasing difficulty of harmonizing what has become a global sporting calendar.

The IPL is fundamentally a domestic Indian competition that allows each team to have eight overseas players, but its short season clashes with the English cricket season and potentially with international test matches. However, in a country that generates up to 70 per cent of cricket's global income, money and powerful media and business interests exert massive influence on the sport and raise the more general question regarding elite sport in the twenty-first century: who is sport actually for? With its showbusiness style auction, wealthy franchise owners and media and sponsorship financial underwriters, the IPL demonstrates how a sport such as Indian cricket has become deeply embedded – and indeed dependent on – a complex relationship between commerce and the media.

Of course this is not an entirely new development and the importance that sports place on their ability to secure television exposure means that rules have always been changed or altered to suit the needs of television. Barnett (1990) notes how American football was overtly tailored to fit neatly into the pattern of advertising breaks on American television. Indeed, such is American television's desire to guarantee a resolution of the sporting contest that a number of rule changes in various sports ensure that the matches cannot end in a draw.

In snooker, a sport largely reinvented by BBC television in the 1970s, matches were shortened to suit television. Domestic football matches in both England and Scotland which traditionally took place on a Saturday afternoon, now, thanks to exclusive television deals, are played on any day of the week at any time, much to the inconvenience of the actual travelling supporter.

Europe's premier football club tournament the European Champions Cup which was a home and away knock-out competition has metamorphosed into the Champions League format to maximize the financial benefits for the top clubs and to provide more content for television companies. Central in this process has been the intention of the governing body of European football (UEFA) to secure the greatest monetary gain through the marketing of television rights and sponsorship opportunities of this new tournament through The Event Agency and Marketing AG (TEAM) formed in 1991 (Sugden and Tomlinson, 1998: 93–7). The success of the UEFA Champions League (in marketing terms) has been the result of UEFA and TEAM controlling the event, its television branding, and the position of the elite sponsors (integrating them into the television coverage) in a precise and consistent manner, allowing UEFA to 'optimise the potential of the golden triangle of soccer, TV and sponsorship' (Holt, 2007: 61). To this end UEFA will revamp the tournament in 2009–10, with the showpiece final being moved from a Wednesday to a more lucrative Saturday night prime-time television slot for the first time in the history of Europe's premier football tournament.

The model of international sports sponsorship and marketing which dominates in twenty-first century owes much to perhaps the most important Olympics of recent times. These were not necessarily the most important in athletic and sporting terms, but signified a new era had arrived in the commercialization of global sport. The games in Los Angeles in 1984 set new benchmarks in the marketing and sponsorship relationships which have now become an integral part of international sport.

The Olympics 1984–2008: from LA to Beijing

The growth of televised international sport is inexorably bound up with the developments in satellite and video technology, and how the medium has used these developments to enhance the spectacle of sport on television. With the launching, in 1962, of the first communication satellite Telstar, a new era of international sport was about to begin. The 1964 Tokyo Olympics were received, via satellite, in thirty-nine countries. Developments in colour television during the 1960s, and video technology also, enhanced the quality of picture that television could offer the viewer thousands of miles from the event.

The battle between the American television networks to secure the rights to screen these major events has resulted in an upward spiral in the amounts of money each network is willing to bid for the event. Such are the massive costs incurred by the host city in staging the games (Montreal is still paying off the debt it incurred during the hosting of the 1976 Games) that with the realization that the spiral in television fees was levelling out, the organizers targeted alternative sources of revenue.

Select corporate sponsors would become official Olympic sponsors marketing their products/services under the Olympic logo. In LA there were thirty official sponsors paying between $4 and $15 million for the privilege. Among the largest of this elite group were Coca-Cola (official Olympic drink), McDonald's (official caterers), Kodak (official film), Levi-Strauss (official clothing), Visa (official credit facilities), Anheuser Busch (Budweiser, official alcoholic drink) and so on.

Allied with this, the sponsors involved also bought much of the advertising space available throughout ABC's television coverage of the games. For instance, Coca-Cola and Levi-Strauss between them bought $70 million worth of air time in addition to their sponsorship deals. The Olympic stadiums remain among the few international sporting arenas that do not carry perimeter advertising. While the International Olympic Committee (IOC) feels that this helps to preserve the 'pure' athletic atmosphere within the stadiums, one wonders how long the IOC can resist the pressure from sponsors to relinquish this policy.

This contradiction between overt commercialism and the mythical aura of sporting activity presents an interesting dilemma for television, sports governing bodies and potential sponsors. The apolitical 'world of sport' full of mythical unsullied heroes that television likes to portray becomes increasingly difficult to substantiate as capital penetration of sport becomes more overt. For many the 1984 LA Games were a celebration of corporate capitalism, an arena where human activity was transformed into an economic process that fuelled the consumption of corporate goods and services. It was a process that television both mediated and played a crucial role in sustaining. Sport has become synonymous with corporate image, television entertainment and consumer capitalism and, for sponsors and marketers, global sporting events would never be the same again.

Much of what LA achieved through its private selling of the Games has been adopted by other organizations around the world. The 1996 European Football Championships played in England had eleven official corporate sponsors arranged by ISL who were working on behalf of UEFA. Sponsors paid £3.5 million for the exclusive rights to advertise in the stadia and up to £10 million on related advertising and marketing. In addition, official suppliers such as Microsoft provide free of charge goods and services worth at or around £10 million (Abel and Long, 1996: 19). As an evaluation report of the sponsorship opportunities offered by 1996 concluded:

> An event such as the European Football Championship is a major media occurrence and can provide a superb marketing platform for brand and image communication worldwide. In particular, if sponsor companies are willing and able to underpin and support their headline sponsorship with other marketing activity, these opportunities are further enhanced. (Easton and Mackie, 1998: 113)

The global marketing strategies of these multinationals have become an integral part in the staging of an international sporting event. Such is the size of the financial undertaking involved in staging these events, and the inability of the organizers to find alternative sources of funding, that this concentration of a cluster of corporate sponsors involved in sport will continue.

Expenditure on such events may or may not be viewed as a legitimate area for state involvement. China, for example, viewed the staging of the Beijing Games of 2008 as part of its wider strategy of opening up the country economically to global business, while the UK government has diverted Lottery money away from the Arts in an attempt to support funding of London 2012. Sports organizers have firmly set out their stall (and are being encouraged by governments to do so) to woo the private sector. The sponsorship and marketing template developed and refined since the 1984 Olympics with various tiers of corporate sponsorship has allowed global brands to view investing in major international sporting events as a key aspect of broader communications strategies.

The 2008 Beijing Olympics was simply the latest example of the process kick-started in LA in 1984. In China the opportunity for companies to break into this vast and emerging market resulted in the Games attracting record deals and even outstripping the FIFA World Cup in terms of corporate sponsorship. The twelve top-tier elite sponsors such as Kodak, Samsung, Visa and Coca-Cola all paid more than £100 million in deals over two or three Olympics, but all viewed Beijing as commercially the most important. These twelve sponsors can use the Olympic logo globally in their marketing, while the next tier sponsors are international firms such as Adidas and VW who want greater exposure in China and local national companies such as CNC and Air China who can only use the logo within China, but through media coverage will get global exposure.

The next level sees Olympic suppliers in a range of sectors such as Snickers supplying Olympic snacks! Beijing 2008 developed the template further by allowing three drink sponsors, rather than one given the scale of the domestic Chinese market – both Tsingtao and Yanjing sat beside Budweiser on the platform of supply sponsors. The London 2012 Olympic Games had by 2008 secured second-tier sponsorship deals totalling £230 million. The London Games needs to raise around £650 million in sponsorship in order to successfully meet its costing targets as with every Olympics the scale and scope of the financial dealings around the event get larger and more complex.

The media and marketing the rugby world cup 2007

Increasingly sport is strategically managed and marketed to produce maximum commercial yields for sports federations, media corporations, sponsors and advertising concerns. The depth of this commercial activity was witnessed in the media marketing of the 2007 Rugby World Cup which was held in France (with, for reasons of purely sports politics, some matches in both Cardiff and Edinburgh). The world cup, organized by the International Rugby Board (IRB), the sport's governing body, has grown in commercial and media profile since its launch in 1987 in Australia and New Zealand.

The 2007 tournament made a profit of almost £80 million for the IRB, who uniquely in world sport retain the profits of such tournaments rather than the national organizing boards. The key revenue streams were broadcast rights (55 per cent); sponsorship and official licensing (25 per cent) with travel and hospitality making up the remainder. In the UK, it was ITV who had payed £40 million for the combined rights to the 2007 and the previous 2003 tournaments. However, due to the time difference of the 2003 tournament in Australia, the majority of that fee, £30 million, was paid for the French finals which allowed ITV to show games in peak time. In a difficult advertising and ratings year for ITV this proved to be a lucrative proposition for the struggling commercial broadcaster.

When England beat Australia in the quarter-final of October 2007 to reach a surprise semi-final with France, ITV added £6 million to their advertising revenue as slots for the semi-final doubled in price to £100,000. As we discuss in more detail in the following chapter, in a digital multi-channel age which has seen television viewing actually increase but the audience share decline for individual channels such as ITV1 and BBC1, live international sport has become a key feature of what has been called 'event television'. In an era of growing on-demand television it remains one of the few television genres that needs to be watched live in the schedule to enjoy fully.

When England reached the final of the 2007 tournament it provided ITV with its largest grossing advertising revenue weekend of the year. When allied with its coverage of the Formula 1 motor racing championship live from Brazil (with British interest in the sport revived by the emergence of Lewis Hamilton – see Chapter 5 – as a genuine world champion contender), the advertising and associated sponsorship around television coverage of these events generated £16 million for ITV. The largest audience of the year of 14.9 million tuned in to watch England fall at the final hurdle to South Africa. However, for the national and global sponsors who associated themselves with this media sports event, the exposure on prime-time television represented nothing but success in the raising of brand awareness.

From England shirt sponsors Nike through to top-tier French tournament sponsors such as Visa and official supply sponsors such as Toshiba, the various advertising tie-in campaigns and the extensive media coverage of the tournament resulted in it being the most commercially successful rugby tournament ever.

Global sport: changing the rules

Continual upheavals in the broadcasting environment are having a significant impact on the relationship between sport and sponsors outlined above. Within a UK context the rise in the 1990s of satellite and cable delivery systems and the Rupert Murdoch-controlled BSkyB in particular altered not only the media landscape in this country, but marked another stage in the ever closer corporate synergy between the media and sporting industries The extensive marketization of British broadcasting over the last decade when allied with the impact of digital technology has resulted in rights for elite sports events increasing in value as the ability to secure a 'live' audience in a multi-channel age of time shifting and downloadable content becomes more difficult (see

Chapters 4 and 11). The role of sponsorship has also become more important within the broader marketing and communications mix, as traditional models of advertising have come under pressure in the always-on age of the Internet.

The regulatory framework within which broadcasting in the UK has historically operated was also loosened considerably following the 1990 Broadcasting Act. One notable change was the rise of sponsored programming, particularly within the commercial television sector. Sponsors no longer simply sponsored sporting events broadcast by television, they also sponsored the programmes themselves. This has become a particular feature of entertainment, drama and sporting output on both terrestrial commercial television and satellite themed sports channels. What is striking is how relatively quickly this model is now part of the wider iconography of sport on television. Football and rugby managers and players are rarely interviewed unless against the backdrop of corporate and media sponsors, with a range of logos filling the screen of the viewer.

In the UK, money for sports rights from BSkyB has become a major revenue stream for professional sport; in return, that company dominates the television coverage of a number of major sports, in particular English Premiership football (Boyle and Haynes, 2004).

As television becomes the major sponsor of sport in the UK, commercial sponsors increasingly are having to make arrangements not solely with the sports with which they wish to associate, but also with the television companies which control the exposure of that sport on either a free-to-air or subscription basis.

For example, 2008 saw Sony pay £3 million to replace Honda as the sponsor of the ITV coverage of Formula 1 racing for that year's championship. By embedding itself in the opening credits and ad break intros and exits, Sony achieves a distinctive position in the television coverage of a sport cluttered with a host of brands and sponsors. Having a core sponsor also lowers the production cost for ITV in covering the sport. What has changed in this sponsorship relationship in the last decade is that in the digital multi-platform age Sony sponsors not just the race and qualifying coverage on ITV1 but the highlights on ITV4, and crucially is integrated into the interactive coverage delivered through the UK's most popular F1 website run by ITV.com. The web-based element of any deal is now crucial in allowing a particular kind of access for the sponsor to quite often the most dedicated of fans who use the related website for additional information and as a platform to watch video material.

Although with ITV allowing the BBC to gain exclusive coverage of Formula 1 from 2009, how the Corporation will integrate the sponsors and commercial liveries that dominate the sports visual image will be indicitive of how far the sponsors have 'naturalized' their place in television's (whether PSB, commercial or pay-TV) coverage of the sport and the extent to which regulators are happy for this to happen.

Formula 1, a trailblazer of tobacco-sponsored sport, has successfully reinvented itself in the light of the 2005 European Union Directive that prohibited tobacco advertising and sponsorship on television. Mobile telephony, media and technology companies, drinks and online gaming organizations dominate the sports sponsorship landscape in 2008. Yet the latter sectors are coming under European pressure to go the way of tobacco sponsorship. For while the gaming industry in 2008, through online gambling companies, are the largest investors in shirt sponsorship in the English Premier League, the anti-gambling and alcohol lobby has become stronger over the years. As Jamie Singer (2008: 19) argues:

> Despite lobbying from the industries themselves, the parallels between the current pressures and voluntary undertakings given by the drinks and gaming industries and the efforts made by the tobacco industry are striking. It is now possible that the £110 million the drinks industry invested in sport in 2006 and the many millions the gaming industry currently invests may only be with us for a finite period of time. If this is the case, sport must look to other sources of revenue.

In the fast-moving commercial world of television sport, sponsors' logos are not simply confined to the field of play or sports stadium but are increasingly central in the actual coverage of the event itself.

In a competitive deregulated media market where channels are busy branding themselves in order to stand out in a crowded marketplace, exclusive sports coverage has become increasingly important as a revenue generator for television.

The last decade has also seen another development in the sponsorship of sport that is directly related to the money that television has poured into certain elite sports such as football. In the UK this has seen a North American sports franchise business model become an increasingly central part of the landscape of the British game. There was outrage in 1998 at the failed attempt to take over at a cost of £625 million one of the biggest clubs in Britain, Manchester United, by Rupert Murdoch's BSkyB television operation. While globally relationships between television companies and sports clubs have existed for some time, most notably in North America, but also in European countries such as Italy through entrepreneurial figures such as Silvio Berlusconi, what the Manchester United deal appeared to signify was the beginning of a new phase in the continually evolving sport–media–sponsorship axis in the UK. Ten years on and eight English Premiership football clubs are under foreign ownership and control.

The majority of these owners want to introduce a more sports franchise model to clubs such as Manchester United (US-based Glazer family paying £831 million), Aston Villa (US-based Randy Lerner paying £62.6 million) and Liverpool (US-based Hicks and Gillett paying £298 million). Sponsorship relationships with global and local companies are at the core of this business as are close links with media organizations as the 'brand' is promoted and developed in key markets in Asia and North America. Even Chelsea's cash-rich Roman Abramovich (who bought the club paying £140 million in cash) has set in place a marketing infrastructure at the club geared to developing revenue streams through sponsorship partnerships, particularly in the Asian market. While the Abu Dhabi Royal Family view taking over Manchester City as part of their strategy to promote that country as it competes with Dubai as one of the key tourist locations in that part of the Gulf.

What is clear is that the last ten years has seen increased competition in the television market (from pay-TV platforms in particular) for content and as a result the continual escalation in the money television pays into sports like football. When this is combined with the intrinsic value of live sports content in the digital age in capturing particular audiences (young and male) for sponsors and media organizations, this combination has tightened and intensified the relationship between sponsors, television and sport in the last ten years.

Where only the sponsored survive (and related issues)

Commercial sponsorship wants to be associated with success. Sponsorship of this type is not patronage and companies expect a commercial return on their involvement in sport. Despite the claims made by many 'socially responsible' companies that they sponsor non-televised community events, this aspect of commercial sponsorship remains minimal when compared with the total revenue allocated to sponsoring televised sport. In Britain it has been estimated that sponsorship of youth sporting events accounts for 0.5 per cent of the total sponsorship budget.

What the sponsor gives, the sponsor can take away. Money tends to follow the successful high-profile sports. Image becomes all important to the sport, with its financial survival becoming dependent on its ability to attract favourable media coverage. As the sponsor becomes more important, the need to sanitize the televised image of the sport increases as does the desire to distance sports from anything which may be deemed political or controversial. Horne (2006: 93) has also argued that 'patronage and sponsorship should not be confused, and sponsors enter into an agreement motivated by some commercial interest.'

The sport of cycling has been subject to a number of high-profile doping incidents in the last number of years that have significantly dented both the public image of the sport and its appeal to corporate sponsors. In 2007 one of the largest sponsors in the sport Deutsche Telekom, who sponsored the T-Mobile team, dramatically ended its involvement with the sport. As Hamid Akhavan, chief executive of the German company, explained:

> We arrived at this decision to separate our brand from further exposure to doping in sport and cycling specifically. (*The Times*, 28 November 2007)

It is not always the most obvious issues, such as drugs in sport, that cause issues or present risk in an era of increased concern about the importance of brand management.

The journey of the Olympic flame from Athens to Beijing in the run-up to the 2008 Olympic Games was in effect one long media commentary focused not on the Olympic spirit, but rather the poor human rights record of China in Tibet. For some Olympic sponsors such as Samsung the demonstrations that dogged the journey of the torch also impacted on their promotional activity built into their sponsorship package. In London, for example, they had arranged for competition winners to be present during the visit of the torch to that city. Instead they found their guests caught up in egg-throwing protests which left some of the competition winners upset and distraught by the whole event. Significantly, no mention of the protests in London, Paris and San Francisco which both disrupted the journey of the torch and dominated the television news coverage in April of that year appeared on the official Beijing 2008 Olympic website, despite this site carrying heavily edited video footage from London and Paris.

Conflicts of interest

As the relationship between commerce and elite sport deepens so too does the importance for financial and corporate reasons of protecting that investment through image management. Often this brings sports and sports stars into conflict with journalists and journalism who are covering events and stories – or at least it should. In reality the rise of public relations and media management techniques once associated with Hollywood and the entertainment business are now common-place in the increasingly commercial and image-conscious world of sport and sports journalism and journalists often either implicitly or explicitly play along (Boyle, 2006).

We examine some of this in more detail in Chapter 9 when we focus on sports journalism. However, it is worth noting at this stage that as the money that flows into elite sport from television and the related commercial sponsorship has continued to grow in the last decade, so too has the influence of corporate sponsors on controlling access to their individual or collective clients.

Interviews with top stars become a promotional opportunity for stars to name-check sponsors, products or events they are associated with. In an age of visual idents and logos it is often hard to tell if some sports interviews are editorial or advertising content.

Thus, as the links between sport, sponsors and the media become ever closer, it also becomes more difficult for media which are party to particular relationships to be clear sighted in their reporting of events involving key sponsors, clubs and such like. It is perhaps ironic that any decline in the levels of critical scrutiny of sport by either the print or electronic media is occurring at a time when, given the massive amounts of television-generated money now circulating in the higher echelons of sport, the temptations to cheat or to get involved in corrupt dealings has never been greater.

The winner takes it all

While winning has always been an aspect of sporting activity, the increasing commercialization of sport has amplified the importance that has become attached to success. Sporting success has become equated with financial solvency. Television's thirst for 'entertainment' has also led to an infatuation with elite and successful sporting indi-viduals and teams. Sponsors target their resources towards the top of the sporting tree. The concern over the use of drugs in sport has tended not to connect this alarming growth industry with the increasing commercial incentives on offer to the top sportspeople who succeed.

The increasing linkages between sport, television and commerce have also coincided with a converging in the values that are supposedly held to be dominant in sport. The close relationship between sport and television inhibits the space available for critical debate about the effects on sport and sporting subcultures of television's commodification of this aspect of popular culture into another area of light entertainment.

Television's treatment of sport as an activity that occurs in some apolitical vacuum is increasingly being challenged by the very process it has helped facilitate. As links between the 'world' of business and the 'world' of sport become more overt, so the separation of these worlds becomes more difficult to sustain. Rather than being an arena free from the economic structures that dictate our working environment, sport is also seen as being subject to these self-same influences.

While sport has always operated within the economic parameters of the social system that it finds itself in, television has denied this in its representation of sport. As capital penetration of sport, both amateur and professional, increases, this facade becomes more apparent.

Sports organizations have never seen themselves as purely profit-maximizing businesses; however, this is changing. As the importance of television money and commercial sponsorship increases so does the ability of the TV/sponsor to, if not push, then certainly nudge the sport in particular directions.

Significantly, while the rallying cry of many of the key players involved in reshaping the television–sponsorship–sport axis has been the need to loosen regulation or open up the market to competition, either in the media or commercial marketplace, what is actually emerging are new patterns of control which restrict open competition.

Who's in control?

In Formula 1 motor racing, a sport built on money from sponsors and television, the governing body is the Fédération Internationale de l'Automobile (FIA). Bernie Ecclestone is its vice president for marketing; in 1996 the FIA signed over the rights to market the sport and sell it around the world until the year 2010 to companies owned by Ecclestone.

As Williams (1998: 9) notes, he is also chairman of the Formula One Constructors' Association that represents the competitors and also chairman of something called Formula One Administration – a company which collects, divides and distributes the revenues from the circuit owners, race sponsors, television companies and trackside advertisers . . . he is in an unique position: poacher, gamekeeper and lord of the manor too.

In addition, according to *The Economist* (6 June 1998), he can offer one-third discounts to broadcasters around the world who 'agree not to show other "open wheeler racing" – which is doubtless why America's IndyCar series gets relatively little exposure outside the United States'.

Such are the powerful links between corporate business and political culture that politicians are often reluctant to get involved in disputes which may harm important political/media relations. Occasionally politicians do step in, such as in the United States in 1992 when, due to political pressure, the Supreme Court exempted the sport of Baseball from its antitrust laws. However, unquestionably, television and sports sponsorship have helped pull elite performance sport into the mainstream of consumer capitalism.

There are other drivers of change in the relationship that have emerged over the last few years and central among these has been the rise of the Internet and digital media more generally.

The new age of sponsorship?

Tony Webb is clear that sports sponsorship in the European marketplace has significantly changed in recent years. He argues that:

> From a simple, uncomplicated, media exposure opportunity, the industry can now present a multimedia platform designed to communicate effectively with the ever-changing needs of consumers. Communications channels have increased in number and in type and can provide an enormous choice, depending on need. (Webb, 2008)

We have already noted above how the interactive aspect of the Internet and the intregal role played by websites in what is now called the 360 degree commissioning of sports content (producing content that can be delivered across platforms such as television, the web and mobile devices) means that for sponsors the online world is becoming as important as the traditional offline environment.

With a younger demographic of digital natives now regularly engaging with sports-related content online, sponsorship deals and

partnerships are reflecting the growing complexity of media consumption patterns. Becoming embedded in online content is a crucial
element of contemporary sponsorship arrangements, but in addition
adding something to the online experience, rather than simply selling
your message is viewed as one of the key changes in the contemporary
industry (Phelops, 2008).

For sports rights holders this also means rethinking how they
enter partnerships with sponsors, many of whom will be technology
partners who may bring particular expertise to the online market for
sports content. Phelops (2008) has outlined the increasing complexity
involved for both sponsors and rights holders as the offline and online
worlds merge as part of a wider mediascape of sports content. From
the structuring of these relationships to their evaluation (for example,
simply looking at audience figures for television forms only part of
the picture regarding the potential success of any sponsorship involvement which now must include web traffic), new and emerging models
are being road tested.

Conclusion

Sporting cultures, while always linked with commercial forces, have
never been more intertwined given the growth of the sports media in
the multi-platform era. In more recent years, British sport has undergone a series of rapid and dramatic transformations.

One has been the introduction of more sophisticated marketing
and promotional strategies both by sporting bodies keen to attract
the interest of television and mobilize the growing influence of the
Internet and by the television companies themselves who want to
maximize the return on their investment in the rights to deliver sports
content across their organization.

The cultural critic Reuel Denney (1989) recognized this media-led
process during the 1950s in what he termed 'the decline of lyric sport'
and the rise of 'spectorial forms' which function like 'rationalized
industries' where the codes of spectatorship for sport and the media
are virtually one and the same. Such an argument leads us to ask if there
is a difference, and if so how can we any longer discern this?

While the sports sponsorship industry continues to develop models
of partnership in the digital age, at its core television remains important as the medium that views sport as another part of its entertainment programming that delivers potential audiences to advertisers
and attracts subscribers to new delivery platforms. In an era that sees

UK advertisers in 2009 spending more on the Internet (around £3.6 billion) than on television (£3.4 billion) for the first time, key sports content remains crucial for the mainstream television industry. There are few areas of content that allows, say, ITV to increase the cost of its 30-second advertising slots by 50 per cent to £200,000 other than 'event television' such as the 2008 UEFA Champions League final between Manchester United and Chelsea.

The economic and regulatory environment in which television finds itself helps to shape the nature and character of the programmes it broadcasts. It also dictates what sports should be shown and how they should be presented. It is this particular aspect of the sport–media relationship to which we turn our attention in the next chapters.

Chapter 4

Power Game:
Why Sport Matters to Television

In a world were you can download anything, you can't download live sport. Anything live becomes more important. The price paid by broadcasters [for live elite sport] will continue to go up. (Greg Dyke, former Director-General of the BBC, *The Observer*, 28 October 2007)

It is always difficult to explain the point of sport to those who do not like it. Non-aficionados will never be persuaded to take pleasure from ball skill or pace. But the level at which sport can be understood by anyone is as a story: as a narrative which must build to a decisive climax and in which character is revealed through actions. (Mark Lawson, Forever England, *Guardian*, 2 July 1988)

Introduction

Television to all intents and purpose controls large sections of contemporary sport. What we want to do in this chapter is examine some issues centred around the reasons why television is so interested in sport (in some sports more than others) and how this relationship alters what appears on our screens from that which we may witness in sporting stadiums. Part of this involves what Garry Whannel (1992) calls the transformation of sport by television, and we highlight some of these key practices below. However, as was evident from the previous chapter, a central element in the sport–television relationship revolves around the economics of the broadcasting industry, and its use of sport as 'television product' in the drive to secure audiences and subscribers. The first part of the chapter examines what television demands from its sports and the economic benefits which this strand of programming can offer television. Then we briefly examine the case of snooker, a sport largely reinvented for television in the late 1960s and early 1970s. How did television transform this sport to such an extent that it became the most exposed sport on television during the 1980s, and what does its decline as a television sport a decade later tell us about the television–sport relationship?

Next we draw on the pioneering work of Whannel (1992) and look briefly at some of the visual transformations that turn a sporting event into television sport. Given the fast-changing nature of televisual technology, we examine the extent to which the treatment of sport has changed over the years, looking at cricket. Finally we focus on the key – and often underestimated – role that commentators play in this process of transformation. In so doing we broaden out our argument to suggest that sports commentary has played a key role in shaping how we come to think and talk about sport and its position in contemporary society.

What television needs from sport

Audiences and advertisers

Economically sport matters to television, be it public-service broadcasters or commercially driven terrestrial and satellite companies. At certain times, such as during major international football tournaments, it delivers large audiences outside peak-time viewing, something which is becoming rarer as the audiences fragment in a multi-channel environment. During the 2006 World Cup, for example, it was estimated that 81 per cent of the UK population (45 million people) watched some part of the tournament. Both the BBC and ITV had average audiences near 6 million with significantly larger viewing figures for the games involving England where peak audiences of up to 20 million viewers are not uncommon.

As Mark Lawson noted above, the commercial value of these television events is their ability to appeal both to the committed sports fan, and also the peripheral sporting viewer who becomes interested partly due to the narratives which television, in conjunction with the press, construct around the event. People also get interested for reasons of an ideological nature connected with national pride and an identification with a wider collective experience (see Chapter 8). This can make for some exceptional viewing patterns, including 2 million viewers staying up in the early hours of the morning to watch Paula Radcliffe in the Women's 2008 Olympic Marathon (Mosey, 2008). The fillip that sport can produce for mixed programming channels is a global phenomenon. NBC, the American channel tied more closely to the

Olympic movement than any other, has influenced the scheduling of Olympic events to ensure advertisers are reaching US peak-time audiences. Shortly after the record eight gold medal haul of US swimmer Michael Phelps, NBC claimed over 200 million viewers had watched the Games (83 per cent of the US TV audience), with an average audience of 29.8 million (Holmwood, 2008) – for once, a nation was distracted away from its dominant professional sports.

Revenue from advertising reached more than $1 billion for the period of the Games, enabling the network to recoup some of the $2.2 billion television rights fee it had paid for the 2008 and 2012 Games. The demands of advertisers can sometimes reach the absurd. In 2008 NBC delayed the televising of the Men's 100m final from Beijing for twelve hours in order to reach a lucrative peak-time audience. The delay undermined the spectacle of Usain Bolt's world record run, many viewers having already known the result through news networks or the Internet. The public relations blunder with the US audience led to the rumour that the 'blue chip' event would be run after midnight in London 2012 in order to reach a peak-time audience in the States (Scott, 2008).

In the UK, similar demands are placed on channels that owe their survival to advertising revenue. As discussed in Chapter 3, for ITV1, The Rugby World Cup, Formula 1 and the Oxford and Cambridge Boat Race proved lucrative attractions for advertisers. In 2007 a peak audience of 15.8 million viewers watched England's defeat by South Africa in the Rugby World Cup Final (Dowell, 2007). A 30-second slot on ITV1 cost £300,000 (*SportBusiness International*, 2007) and the channel brought in £11 million in advertising revenue for that game alone (*SportBusiness International*, 2007). Formula 1 has one of the largest cumulative global audiences for any single sport. In the UK, with the rise to prominence of British driver Lewis Hamilton, average ratings for ITV1 steadily grew between 3 to 4 million, with the 2007 climactic Brazilian Grand Prix drawing more than 7 million viewers. In spite of the relative success of these sports, football remains the dominant television sport throughout Europe and ITV's flagship sports coverage retains its contract to screen live UEFA Champions League football.

Football is also the key driver in attempts to maintain pay-TV both in the UK and elsewhere in Europe. As Robert McChesney (1998: 36) points out:

> Sport is arguably the single most lucrative content area for the global media industry, a point understood best of all by Rupert Murdoch, CEO of News Corporation. Sport was crucial in making his British

Sky Broadcasting (BSkyB) the most successful satellite TV service in the world and in making the US Fox TV network a fully-fledged competitor to ABC, NBC and CBS.

Due to the emergence of dedicated subscription sports channels, these broadcasters are interested, where possible, in offering the popular sports exclusive and live to the consumer. As we noted in the previous chapter, this has resulted in increased competition for sports rights and as a result sports programming involving the most popular sports, such as football, cricket and rugby, is no longer the cheap form of programming it once was. While the economics of making money out of television increasingly views sports 'product' as vital, it is not the only reason why sports matter to television.

Prestige and profile

As we argued in Chapter 2, the BBC's historical image of itself as the national broadcaster owes much to the centrality of its sporting coverage. National sporting events such as the Scottish and English FA Cup finals have been projected by the BBC as part of the national fabric of British life down through the years. However, as we examine in more detail in Chapter 11, the BBC and public-service broadcasting (PSB) in general struggled to redefine itself as the ecology of broadcasting in Britain rapidly altered, first because of multi-channel pay-TV (Goodwin, 1998), and more latterly the rolling out of digital television platforms, high definition television (HDTV) and Internet protocol television (IPTV). Broadcasting rights to key sporting events and competitions have been stripped from the BBC's grasp by old and new competitors. From the mid-1990s, in a period of unprecedented change in the television coverage of sport, the BBC saw rights to the Ryder Cup, Formula 1, England Test Cricket, the Boat Race, the FA Cup, English and Scottish international football and other assortments of live and recorded highlights from sport lost, at some point, to rival broadcasters. Some of these sports returned to the BBC but at extreme financial cost. The BBC paid an undisclosed sum (read an exorbitant rights fee) to regain the television rights for Formula 1 from 2009. But the point to be made is that television sport is a highly competitive business driven by rights holders who auction rights to the highest bidder in a highly competitive market. Despite BBC protestations, part of these losses have stemmed from a reluctance to divert licence money away from other areas.

Sport should matter to the BBC because the Corporation's ability to deliver to a national audience key sporting events is one of the cornerstones of its PSB remit. It has also always lauded the claim that its coverage helps promote sport to a wider audience, a role it was keen to rekindle once the 2012 Olympic Games were awarded to London. In other ways BBC sport has pushed the frontiers of technology and the coverage of sport. All these elements were apparent in a speech by the BBC's Director of Sport Roger Mosey in 2007 when he proclaimed sport had a threefold function in the BBC. In a slightly defensive but upbeat speech he suggested BBC Sport is 'at the very heart of a public service proposition for the future', it 'can be in the vanguard of the next phase of the digital revolution' and 'has a unique role to play in our national sporting life' (Mosey, 2007a).

The BBC's bold development of their 360 degree coverage of the major events, with interactive television, broadband and mobile phone coverage of the Olympic Games and the World Cup, belies the massive growth in the coverage of sport across other free-to-air channels as well as the rise of new pay-TV competitors. Channel 4 and Channel 5 in the UK have used sport to give them credibility and profile in the marketplace as well as delivering lucrative audiences to advertisers. Channel 5 have successfully targeted bidding for one-off international football matches and European games involving English clubs and in so doing not only achieved some of the channel's largest audiences, they also considerably raised the profile of the station. The extent to which sports historically anchored to one channel are shifting from their moorings was perfectly illustrated in 1998 by the England and Wales Cricket Board's decision to award the rights to screen home test matches at a cost of £104 million (1999–2002) to Channel 4 (in association with the ubiquitous BSKyB), thus leaving the BBC after an association of almost half a century.

In 2006, the year after England regained the Ashes, Test cricket moved exclusively to Sky Sports denying British audiences of any live coverage of cricket on free-to-air television for the first time. A subsequent deal with the England and Wales Cricket Board in August 2008 worth £300 million meant all forms of live cricket would be exclusive to Sky Sports from 2010 to 2013. The deal, which also encompassed the launch of a new potentially lucrative Twenty20 competition in 2010 to challenge the success of the IPL in India (see Chapter 3) meant that British audiences not willing or unable to pay for Sky Sports coverage would be consigned to watching cricket highlights on Channel 5. The decision of governing bodies of sport to sell rights exclusively to pay-TV channels is contentious, not least because it deprives some young viewers from a particular televisual experience of sport. The ECB Chairman, Giles Clarke, criticized the BBC for not showing any interest in the rights, suggesting they had deprived millions of cricket-loving licence payers access to live Test cricket through a lack of prioritizing cricket in their coverage. The BBC countered that as long as Test cricket remained off the A Listed Events the rights would commercially be beyond their reach.

The dispute over Test cricket reveals there are wider ideological and political reasons for national broadcasters to carry national sporting events. Ironically, at a moment in the history of sport on television when there has never been more of it on our screens (particularly if we are willing to pay extra for it), it remains the case that there are in reality a small core number of mainstream sports which television is particularly interested in, with football and its fan base number one in the eyes of the television executives. There are economists (Hoskins et al., 1997: 91–2) who argue that in a multi-channel environment the main rationale for public-service broadcasters should be to offer programmes which carry an 'external benefit' to the citizen. While they include news and current affairs in these programme categories, they see no reason to include sport, arguing that this should be left to the private sector.

We would disagree with this analysis and indeed suggest it appears illogical given that part of the argument they advance for including drama within a PSB remit is that this programme category 'may provide external benefits in the form of an increased sense of identity and awareness of national/regional themes and values' (p. 91). We would strongly argue that this is exactly one of the functions which certain sporting events provide for a broad audience. One can imagine a lively debate if viewers in Scotland were asked to choose between having access to a television drama or a major international football and rugby match involving the national team. These issues and the extent to which governments should intervene in the operating of the sports–television marketplace are developed in more detail in Chapters 8, 10 and 11. It is also worth noting at this juncture the extent to which sport has come into contact with other areas of television output, in particular game shows (such as the BBC's long-running *A Question of Sport*). Programmes such as this are often a vehicle for sports stars (see next chapter) and, as we suggest below, firmly locate sport within the light entertainment sphere of television output.

Screening sport: old and new versions

> This is cricket for the Ritalin generation. Nine hundred and eighty-two
> runs scored, 34 wickets, the third-fastest 50 ever in Britain – 21 balls,
> cheer leaders galore and little boys dancing in the aisles doing pass-
> able impressions of the Kent captain, Robert Key. For those who still
> couldn't focus, there was an optional course of ECT in the lunch break.
> (Simon Hattenstone, 'Sportblog', Guardian.co.uk, 30 July 2008)

Between them Goldlust (1987), Whannel (1992) and Blain et al. (1993)
offer comprehensive overviews of the techniques used by television to
transform sporting events into television programmes. What we want
to do here is to examine briefly the extent to which changes in the
sports broadcasting environment looked at in the previous chapter and
the growth in satellite coverage of sport in the UK in particular have
altered the principles outlined in these books. We start with an analysis
of a phenomenon that has dramatically transformed the fortunes of
cricket, the ultra-short form of the sport called Twenty20 introduced
into English cricket in 2003.

   As the quote from *Guardian* sports journalist Simon Hattenstone
above suggests, the contrast of Twenty20 cricket to the drowsy nar-
colepsy induced by the traditional format of county cricket is startling.
Although the underlying laws of the game remain largely intact, in
many ways the two versions of the sport have little in common. One is
driven by the needs of television, commerce and entertainment values,
the other enjoys limited television coverage, is financially unstable
and is burdened by the weight of tradition. As journalist Paul Weaver
(2008) described the short format, 'The brash new game represents
cricket after all the flabby bits have been liposuctioned away.' The
reason for the difference is television. The need to make the sport
televisual, structures both the form of Twenty20 cricket and the
experience of the spectator at the ground.

   The style of presentation of Twenty20, screened on Sky Sports in the
UK, is characterized by the more staccato paced editing and televisual
style of US televised sport production. Audiences are now highly familiar with the formal conventions of televised sport. Hyperbolic promotional trails, cross-promotion across channels and associated websites,
previews and montages of previous competitions, detailed analysis
with multi-angle slow-motion, statistics and virtual overlays and the
post-match interviews with expert post-mortem. Sport is increasingly
configured to fit inside this format, transforming itself for the television

viewer as much, if not more than, the spectator in the stadium. This dilution of the spectator experience has long been feared and criticized (Whannel, 2005), particularly by sports aficionados. But as the relationships between television and the governing bodies of sport have matured and rights fees escalated as competition between channels has opened up, sport is increasingly eager to bend their organization to suit televisual presentation. Cricket, a bastion of tradition and upper-middle-class authority, has not been immune to this process.

In trying to understand how this process has changed it is instructive to briefly look at the early history of producing televised cricket. The BBC first televised cricket in 1938 and in the immediate postwar period began to refine a production technique for covering the game. The emergent format of televised cricket was heavily shaped and arguably constrained both by technology and the MCC, the governing agent of broadcasting negotiations. The BBC's first established producer of cricket was Anthony Craxton who from an early stage in television's relationship with cricket understood how the medium transformed the game. He effectively developed the visual language of producing cricket for television.

In a pamphlet designed to help the viewer of cricket understand 'the problem of transferring a game played on an area some 150 yards [130 metres] in diameter to a screen a few inches square' (Craxton, 1958: 29) Craxton makes clear televising cricket was considerably more complex than simply pointing the camera at the action. To do so, he argued, would 'make for extremely dull viewing' (Craxton, 1958: 29). Entertainment values, then, were to foreground the positioning of cameras, and the use and mixing of wide, mid and close-up shots. Two cameras were ideally placed in line with the wicket, one directly behind the bowler the other slightly offset to capture the fielders. A third camera would be placed at extra-cover (to the side of the wicket) and would be used for close-ups, shots of the scoreboard and of the crowd. Craxton and his team of cameramen would create the standard format for covering cricket that influenced coverage for years to come. Even after the introduction of more cameras (including the switching of cameras after each over to continually show the bowler running away from the camera) and various presentational tools (such as 'Hawk-Eye') the format for screening the game remained by and large the same. For many years the BBC producers had to negotiate access to preferred positions on pavilions, often building temporary platforms for cameras to find their optimum position. However, even by the end of the 1950s the BBC were being consulted by cricket administrators in the redesign of cricket grounds with a view to accommodating television cameras and commentators.

This was an early sign of the power of television in sport: partnering, cajoling and sometimes manipulating the organization of sport itself. Although BBC producers were conscious they were transforming the viewers' perception of cricket – where an 'enthusiastic producer can undoubtedly make a rather dull match into enthralling viewing' – they were also conscious that the success of televised cricket depended on 'the players themselves no matter what tricks the producer may try in order to enliven the game' (Craxton, 1958: 39). Televised cricket, particularly Test and County Championship coverage, tried to keep an unobtrusive approach to the sport. In the 1950s and 1960s cricket authorities were vigilant of the effect television would have on the sport. The presenters of cricket – Peter West being most notable – were suited upper-middle-class men, much like the establishment figures that run the game. They were largely conservative in outlook, taking an establishment view of an establishment sport.

In contrast, contemporary cricket coverage belies this ideological view. Every game is billed as being exciting, every innings is a crucial one, the dramatization of individual cricketers and their performance is always prefigured and embellished in order to entertain and keep the attention of the viewer. Out of economic necessity one-day cricket transformed the game in the 1970s, spawned a host of competitions heavily backed by sponsorship and paved the way for the ICC World Cup. But even one-day cricket was slow by comparison to other sports and demanded an extensive commitment from viewers to stay tuned to the action through the day. Twenty20, with twenty over's per side, time restrictions for the bowling side and its unremitting speed of play is tailor made for television and lasts little more than three hours. This compression speeds up play and distils the dramatic content of the match. Furthermore, the structure of the event draws the spectators into the action, with fans encouraged to participate in the televisual presentation of the sport. BSkyB have been particularly attuned to the need for televised sport to generate an atmosphere. As well as Twenty20 they have reignited interest in other 'dead' sports such as darts whose heavily promoted BDO Premier League now fills large arenas as it tours across the UK (Waddell, 2007).

BSkyB's entertainment-driven style of rapid pace, music and action which characterizes much of its sports coverage and trailers structures not only the coverage of the sport but the whole organization of a Twenty20 match. Lurid coloured outfits, from deep bright pink to dayglo orange, add emphasis to the fact that the sport is designed to catch the attention of the spectator and viewer. Coloured outfits are nothing particularly new in limited-over cricket – having been introduced by Australian media mogul Kerry Packer in the late-1970s to contrast with the anonymity of cricket's traditional 'whites'. Packer introduced pastel shades so that teams could be identified more easily by television cameras under floodlights (Frindall, 2005). But, Twenty20 aims at direct spectator identification with the colours of competing teams, with an eye to the lucrative sale of replica shirts. Here, cricket mimics the commercial success of football and its successful partnership with the world's major sports manufacturers Adidas and Nike. The spectacle itself is neatly explained by the following report by *The Telegraph* sports journalist Andrew Baker who described the English 2008 final as follows:

> From the moment of arrival at the verdant amphitheatre, supporters of all four counties were bombarded with entertainment. Ra-ra girls combined cheerleading with handing out leaflets promoting a mobile phone service; youngsters were handed red plastic helmets to protect them from the 'rain of sixes'. And that was before the mascots got going. (Baker, 2008)

To English eyes this would all seem very American. But it is a formula that has worked for various – mainly team – sports on a global scale. As we have already noted in Chapter 3 the IPL in India has taken the format devised in England as an 'experiment' and turned it into a potentially global television phenomenon worth multiple millions of pounds. Twenty20 is about fast explosive action, both on and off the pitch, that builds drama and excitement. Some of the entertainment is structured into the event – such as dancers in the stands, the constant blare of pop music throughout the game and cavorting mascots.

While much of Sky Sport's cricket coverage owes a considerable debt to the established pattern of television sports coverage mentioned above, its mixing and editing approach is far more 'up close and personal'. Twenty20 is principally about the heavy personalization of cricket stars and a constant focus on storytelling. Battles between particular bowlers and batsmen – between personalities – is all important. All this razzmatazz is designed to attract new viewers to the sport which has classically been a turn-off for women, children and younger men who prefer fast-action sports like football or rugby. Another crucial aspect of the target audience for the sport is summed up by ECB director of operations John Carr: 'There was a tremendous support for a three-hour game in the early evening, after work and after school. There are a lot of people out there who are cash-rich yet time-poor' (Weaver, 2008). Twenty20 delivers fast-paced summer entertainment at a time and place people can get to or tune into at their leisure.

Sports commentary: codes and conventions

In 1995 BBC Television began a new comedy/sports/quiz programme entitled *They Think It's All Over*, hosted by the English actor and comedian Nick Hancock, with two team captains recently retired from their respective sports of football and cricket, Gary Lineker and David Gower. The programme was a hybrid of sports trivia and satirical comment, where the manner and style in which the game is played is more important than the final score. The title of the programme is of interest as an example of the familiarity of televised sports discourse, its transcendence into mythologized, structured narratives of sport as popular culture and the way in which it serves as an excellent reference 'to the ideological character of images and stories which naturalise and disguise the reality of the historical and the man–made' (Silverstone, 1994: 22).

The title of the programme is taken, of course, from Kenneth Wolstenholme's running commentary of the 1966 World Cup Final at Wembley (the complete phrase: 'Some people are on the pitch, they think it's all over [Geoff Hurst scores for England] it is now, it's four' is probably the most frequently repeated sports commentary in British broadcasting history). Wolstenholme's commentary has gained mythological status as it is the key signifying element of England's World Cup victory of 1966; specifically, it denotes England's fourth and final goal against West Germany at the end of extra time, and the moment when Geoff Hurst scored the only hat trick in the history of the World Cup final. As Whannel (1992: 148) suggests, television, consumed by millions, aids 'this instant production of myth'. According to the BBC's Audience Research Unit approximately 27 million viewers watched the 1966 final on BBC Television; several millions more have seen the image of Hurst's final raid and shot from the edge of the German penalty area, complemented by Wolstenholme's commentary.

Sporting drama

The moment is not only replayed as a significant part of English sports history (often to the annoyance of Scottish viewers), but often presented as a central element of British television's history (the broadening of the national nomenclature is also of significance here). In many respects, the event represents a transformative period in British television, both in its social and cultural importance and, more pertinent to what we argue here, in the codes and conventions of the communicative process of televised sport.

As we argue in Chapter 8, the coverage of such large sporting occasions connects with and inscribes a range of social relations and cultural meanings, which are both general and specific in any given time and space. Therefore it is the biography of such television texts – their production, distribution and reception – which is central to an understanding of the relationship between the technology of television and its mediation of sport. Similarly, in creating these links between mediated form and social process, television also produces a double movement of mediation by ingestion and projection: what Corner (1995: 5) has characterized as 'centripetal interplay' and 'centrifugal interplay'. By centripetal interplay, Corner suggests that television has a powerful capacity to draw towards itself and incorporate wider elements of society and culture.

This leans heavily on the idea of Williams (1974) who talked of 'Drama in a Dramatised Society', where much in culture bears a resemblance or relation to what is 'on the box'. Clearly, televised sport with its rhetoric of realism very much fits into this typology, with the key transformations centring upon a mix of commentary, edited highlights and action replays. By centrifugal interplay, Corner is alluding to the process whereby television projects its images, characters and catch phrases into broader aspects of the culture. Once again, Wolstenholme's commentary from the 1966 World Cup is an evident case in point, and is now verging on pastiche and satire, as illustrated by its use in the title of the aforementioned comedy/sports/quiz programme. The use of such 'golden moments' in television, therefore, becomes a contested site of a struggle for control over meaning and potency –the significance of Wolstenholme's commentary is clearly different for supporters of English football from the fans of Scottish, Welsh or Irish football.

There is a third dynamic to which Corner (1995) alludes which is important in understanding the mediation of sport by television; it is also a dynamic integral to the popularity of the game per se. This is the need to understand the contingency of sport and television: their uncertain variables, their conditional elements and incidental moments which, within televised sport, create narrative pleasures. In the early years of television there would have been doubts as to whether a television picture could be produced at all, which, as we suggested in Chapter 2, produced an institutional and promotional discourse (specifically within the *Radio Times*) preoccupied with the technology of the medium: the wonder of television. As we have already seen with radio broadcasts from sport, once the techniques, codes and conventions were established, this unpredictability changed and discourses preoccupied with the aesthetics of television and modes of address became more dominant. Therefore the expectations of the audience with regard to televised sport have changed with the development of new technologies. The relatively sophisticated institutional discourse of Wolstenholme, and the way in which it combines with the camera image of Hurst as he attacks the German goal (which is also institutionalized), refer not only to that moment in the game, but also take on their own significance through the unpredictability of what happens next and create their own powerful communicative poetics. The codes and conventions of sports commentary are social processes that have developed over time. In various ways, commentary as an institutional discourse of television has become the context for thinking, talking and writing about sport: in other words, television becomes central to our perceptual field of what sport actually means.

Presence at the microphone

There can be no doubt that the television coverage of the football World Cup, the summer and winter Olympic Games, world heavyweight boxing, the Super Bowl, the US Masters golf, Wimbledon and the Grand National has produced some of the most enduring images within twentieth-century popular culture. However, it is not merely the visual mediation of the athletic ability of Pele, Carl Lewis, Franz Klammer, Muhammad Ali, Joe Montana, Tiger Woods, Bjorn Borg, Steve Redgrave or Red Rum that is recalled in popular memory, but also the descriptive narratives of the commentator which provide the bases of such communication. As we outlined in Chapter 2 with regard to radio commentary on sport, this particular form of sports discourse had to be invented through trial and error and, as Whannel (1992: 26) has highlighted, by overcoming 'the conflicting aims of naturalism and construction'. This tension alludes to the fact that sports commentary is, as part of television technology, a social process, and employs specific techniques as a roundabout way of achieving a desired effect: that of realism and entertainment. The conventions for delivering a coded narrative of a sporting event with an economy of words was a process well underway within BBC radio commentary by the mid-1930s, under the guidance of de Lotbiniere. The level of economy of speech required by radio and television were, however, different, and were recognized as such by de Lotbiniere as he anticipated the arrival of television in 1937:

> The art of the 'sound' commentator is scarcely ten years old and it still has a long way to go. But there may not be much time left for its normal development, as television will soon be making a different demand on the commentator, and, I believe, a lighter one. (*Radio Times*, 4 June 1937)

The necessity for a mellifluous quality within sound broadcasting – painting a picture with words – seemed unnecessary and almost intrusive with the medium of television, and the notion of using the same commentary for radio and television was soon discarded after the 1938 Cup Final when the radio commentary was used for both broadcasts. With radio there was room for error. If there occurred 'a slip 'twixt eye and lip', the radio commentator could use little 'white lies' to get him out of a sticky situation.

For instance, one BBC producer advised radio commentators: 'If you make a mistake in identifying players, don't leave the audience in any doubt, don't let on that you're not infallible, make him pass it' (Kenneth Wolstenholme, interview with one of the authors, July 1995). However, television revealed – although selectively – the actual sporting performance and, therefore, continually opened up the possibility that viewers could recognize mistakes in the narrative and be reminded of the transformative nature of television, despite all the rhetoric to the contrary.

Creating the sports commentator

Another comparison is of interest at this point, that of the recruitment of new commentators by the BBC in the late 1940s and 1950s. Within radio, prospective candidates had been asked to perform under broadcasting conditions by providing a closed-circuit commentary to a 'blind' listener who would adjudicate his talent (or lack of it). According to de Lotbiniere the number of what he considered to be 'good commentators' was scarce, and anyone taking the test would have a difficult task in displacing the now familiar voices of George Allison, Teddy Wakelam and Fred Grisewood (all of whom shared a similar upper-middle-class status to that of BBC producers and directors).

In the shadow of radio, recruitment into television sports commentary appears even more ad hoc and circumstantial. Take, for instance, the movement into television by the BBC's first recognized football commentator Kenneth Wolstenholme. In an interview with one of the authors, Wolstenholme recounted how he had always possessed a desire to be a sports writer, and had been fortunate enough to meet the editor of a Sunday newspaper, Harold Mays, while on active service during the Second World War. Immediately after the war he met Mays once more at the FA Cup semi-final between Charlton Athletic and his home-town side of Bolton Wanderers in 1946, whereupon Wolstenholme was asked to write a small feature on cricket in Lancashire. At the same time he had written to the BBC informally applying for work, and was subsequently asked, upon the strength of his article, to provide an eye-witness account from a cricket match. He was then asked to do a full radio commentary on an amateur international trial match between Northern Counties and Southern Counties. As Wolstenholme describes:

> So that was sheer luck. Which I suppose is the short answer to how you become a football commentator. If you're cheeky enough to ask for a job, you're lucky enough for someone to ask you to do it. (Interview with one of the authors, July 1995)

Wolstenholme's move into television was due to a similar happenstance. Jimmy Jewell, who had refereed the first televised Cup Final of 1938, had taken over the role of football commentator for television immediately after the war. Wolstenholme had moved from BBC Radio in the North West to become Jewell's understudy when the ex-referee suddenly died of a heart attack, leaving Wolstenholme as BBC Television's principal football commentator.

Even as television began to cover sport in a more comprehensive fashion in the 1960s, personnel appeared to drift into working within the medium, for example Scottish football commentator Archie MacPherson. A school teacher by profession, MacPherson had written a series of short stories, a selection of which he had been asked to read for broadcast by BBC Scotland. Upon hearing the distinctive grain of voice and with the knowledge that MacPherson had previously had a brief spell with the Glasgow club Partick Thistle, the sports producer Peter Thompson asked the teacher if he was interested in giving eyewitness accounts of Scottish League matches for BBC Radio Scotland. MacPherson soon found himself promoted to BBC Television in Scotland after turning down a commentary post in London on the advice of another young BBC radio commentator, Brian Moore.

MacPherson continued to teach throughout his early years of commentary until he realized in 1965 that a full-time career could be made in broadcasting. The biographical backgrounds of Wolstenholme and MacPherson reflect wider connections of sport with both the military and education, rooted in a historical concern for disciplining and schooling the body (Hargreaves, 1986). The assumption that sport was morally and socially a 'good thing' lurked beneath the discourses of both commentators, as it had done for those early producers of televised sport.

Established voices of sport

Another route of entry into the role of sports commentary was sports journalism, traditionally a cloistered profession which was given a new lease of life by television. For instance, David Coleman joined the BBC in 1954 after an apprenticeship with the *Cheshire County Express* and several years as a freelance radio contributor; Barry Davies joined ABC TV in 1966 before moving to the BBC in 1969 after beginning his career with the British Forces radio in Cologne and a spell as a sports correspondent with *The Times*; John Motson worked for the *Barnett Press Weekly Newspaper* and the *Morning Telegraph* in Sheffield before joining BBC Radio in 1969 and making his debut for television in 1971; and Martin Tyler, now BSkyB's principal commentator, began as a staffwriter and subeditor for a publisher, before becoming an editorial assistant on LWT's *On The Ball* with Brian Moore, and moved to commentating for Southern TV in 1974. These career profiles sketch a more familiar pattern of entry into 'factual' broadcasting: from print, to radio and then television. In this respect, these commentators share similar career patterns with sports producers and editors.

However, as Wolstenholme and MacPherson testify, there is no clear-cut or straight-forward 'career-ladder' upon which the budding football commentator may climb. One thing is certain, it remains an exclusively male preserve, despite the few women sports journalists who have managed to cross over into broadcasting to stake a claim in an otherwise ubiquitously masculine domain (the BBC have developed a group of much-favoured female presenters rather than commentators – see Chapter 7). It is also worth noting the longevity within broadcasting of all the above practitioners. For the BBC Wolstenholme provided the commentary for twenty-three FA Cup finals before being replaced by Coleman in 1972, and for ITV Brian Moore had been the principal commentator from 1968 before retiring in 1999 and was preceded by less familiar men at the microphone, like Peter Lloyd and Ken Walton (once an actor) who had provided some of the earliest ITV commentaries, and a host of regional commentators, most notably, perhaps, Hugh Johns (of ATV in the Midlands region) who provided ITV's commentary for the 1966 World Cup final. Other sports reflect similar patterns: Murray Walker commentated on motor sports for over forty years with the BBC (mostly part-time as he also held down a lucrative career in advertising) before joining ITV Sport in 1997; Dan Maskell was for many viewers the essence of watching Wimbledon from the 1940s through to the early 1990s; Peter O'Sullivan, another BBC commentator who retired in his late 70s, had been reaching that familiar crescendo of description and excitement towards the end of a horse race since the 1950s; and Peter Alliss continues to be the calming and humorous voice behind the BBC's coverage of golf.

The commentator's address

One reason for such longevity is the need for familiarity by broadcasters to obtain and maintain an audience for their sports programmes. When a new commentator is introduced one can sense that a 'bedding-in' period is required for acceptability by the audience. As we have seen with radio, this requires a conversational style, building up sentences with a familiar lexicon of sporting phrases and idioms and weaving a narrative without losing shape. Here we see some congruence between radio and television commentary, although the need to be quiet and stop talking is one distinct golden rule of television commentary. The edict handed down from the BBC's first dedicated Head of Television Sport, Peter Dimmock, was always: 'If in doubt, leave it out' (interview with one of the authors, May 2008). The mode of address of the commentator is governed by the general mood of the programme and the professional ideology of the producers, directors and editors who structure it.

Autobiographies of commentators (such as Benaud, 2005, and Davies, 2008) and sports producers (such as Weeks, 2004, and Cowgill, 2006) attest to the working practices of television sport and in our interviews with sports commentators, professionalism and teamwork were heavily emphasized: from the background researchers who feed an endless supply of biographical and statistical data on sports women and men, managers, coaches and clubs, to the production engineers who enable the commentators' performance with television monitors, microphone equipment and 'lazy talkback' (which allows communication with the final team members: the producers, directors and editors who orchestrate the whole broadcast with their control of sound and cameras – again, operated almost ubiquitously by men). Although the tight production teams which used to operate within the pioneering years of BBC sport have disintegrated to a certain extent, partially due to advances in technology and a level of homogeneity of practices in outside broadcasting (many sporting federations now set strict guidelines on camera positions and editing), Wolstenholme's adage that 'any broadcast with commentary needs as much teamwork as on the field' would appear to substantiate claims to slickness and professionalism in production.

Whannel (1992: 60) illustrates how the professional ideologies of sports broadcasting are a fusion of journalistic practices of objectivity, entertainment practices grounded in the principles of 'good television' and dramatic practices which involve the audience in a narrative. These ideologies can be seen to govern the principles of football commentary and were clearly evident when the BBC began its first regular football highlights programme *Sports Special* in 1955, the residual effects of which can be seen throughout contemporary television coverage of football in Britain. Wolstenholme recalled how he utilized the general guidelines of de Lotbiniere: 'you've got to think of the audience as a pyramid', from the small cross-section of specialists at the top to the broad audience made up of occasional viewers at the bottom. The tensions between realism and entertainment are evident once more. The commentator has to explain why a player is offside without regurgitating the laws of the game. Technical or 'in' expressions need to be avoided but the commentary must be well informed and put over the significance of the event.

The description of play is required to be faithful to what is happening on the field, but must also avoid being overly objective and has to introduce human interest and suspense. Associative material in the form of pre-researched notes are frequently utilized, but the commentary needs to avoid the appearance of being scripted and requires a level of fluency and informality of address. Some commentators rely more heavily on notes than others.

For example, rugby commentator Bill McLaren drafted a complex

A3 sheet of information and small phrases before every commentary. In contrast, Peter Alliss does not take any notes with him into the commentary box and relies on his skills of memory and instinct to react to the play on screen. Sports commentary is very much part of a social process. It is also a crucial means by which television attempts to convey the dramatic form of expression which is intrinsic within sport. Television commentary both ingests from and projects into a public discourse on sport. As John Hargreaves (1986: 12) has suggested, these forms of public discourse on sport constitute 'some of the basic themes of social life – success and failure, good and bad behaviour, ambition and achievement, discipline and effort'. What television had to develop was a convenient discourse which addressed the need to inform and entertain both the fan and the family audience. Many of the techniques of addressing this tension had been adapted from radio, although it could be argued that as ex-players continue to proliferate behind the microphone the mode of address in television sport is increasingly specialized and conversational. To our knowledge, sport in Britain has never been televised without commentary.

Many fans criticize the often inane comments of the football commentator – seen most vociferously in the irreverence of many football fanzine skits on televised football (Haynes, 1995) – but, in order to escape this sports chatter, we are left with the inferior alternative of turning the sound down. Digital television may change the possibilities available to the 'armchair supporter' in this respect (see Chapter 11). Sport may still be mediated, but with more control as to what the viewer sees and, more importantly in this discussion, what they hear. Digital television may make it possible for viewers to individualize their consumption to the extent that choosing from an array of commentaries on any one particular sporting event may provide the ultimate means of identification with such a discourse: each competitor, team or nation involved could have a commentary biased in its favour, and a third could attempt to be impartial in the classic tradition. Movements in this direction have already occurred within football with dedicated broadband television channels on club websites.

Conclusion

We have argued in this chapter that there are a number of reasons, economic, cultural and social, that explain why sport matters to television and broadcasters. This involves a constant evolution of the transformation of sport into television sport, or sports adapted for television. While this evolution has been driven in the past largely by an institutional and technological impetus informed by notions of public service, this is no longer the case. Commercial and technological imperatives now drive this process of transformation and, when allied with the erosion of public-service broadcasting in a multimedia environment, have led to a blurring of the codes and conventions of terrestrial and satellite coverage of sport. There remain differences, but both increasingly borrow and innovate from each other in attempts to secure audiences, advertisers and, increasingly, subscribers. The ideological aspect of this process of transformation is examined in more detail in Chapters 6, 7 and 8 of the book; however, the next chapter sees us turn our attention to one of the core functions of the media's coverage of sport: the creation of the sports star.

Chapter 5

Who Wants to be a Millionaire?
Media Sport and Stardom

It is now possible not only to play your golf with Palmer clubs while dressed from cleat to umbrella tip in Palmer clothes (made in the US, Canada, New Zealand, Australia, Hong Kong, Japan, France or South Africa), but to have the Palmer image at your elbow in countless other ways.

You can buy your insurance from a Palmer agency, stay in a Palmer-owned motel, buy a Palmer lot to build your home on, push a Palmer-approved lawnmower, read a Palmer book, newspaper column or pamphlet, be catered to by a Palmer maid, listen to Palmer music and send your suit to a Palmer dry cleaner.

You can shave with his lather, spray on his deodorant, drink his favourite soft drink, fly his preferred airline, buy his approved corporate jet, eat his candy bar, order your certificates through him and cut up with his power tools. (Mark McCormack, sports manager and agent, writing about client and golfer Arnold Palmer (1967: 112))

Football commits an act of terrible treachery on young players when it over-rewards them too early. A foot comes off the accelerator, only to be applied to a tinted-window Porsche. (Sue Mott, *Daily Telegraph*, 20 November 2007)

Introduction

The pressures of success in sport are often all too apparent. At the Beijing Olympic Games in 2008 Liu Xiang, the Chinese 110 metres hurdler, defending his Olympic Gold medal from Athens 2004, limped out of the Games before the race began. A stunned stadium and tens of millions of Chinese television viewers were said to be emotionally destroyed and furious at the deception surrounding his injury – a chronic inflammation of his Achilles tendon – which had been covered up by the Chinese Olympic Team, his coach and the athlete himself. Xiang was the carrier of the nation's Olympic Gold hopes in the 'Bird's Nest' stadium and was set to earn a reputed 1 bn yuan from commercial deals if he successfully defended his Olympic crown (Watts, 2008). The athlete had starred in the much-hyped promotion of the Games in China, becoming the Chinese face for American global brands Nike, Visa, Coca-Cola and Cadillac. But the episode was fascinating for what it revealed about sport, media celebrity and national popular culture. It not only revealed the frailty of success in elite sport, but also how the commodification of sport depends heavily on the construction of sports stars, sporting narratives and their connection with national, sometimes global, media audiences.

If the media, and television in particular, have transformed the organization and economic importance of sport in the twentieth century, they have also dramatically transformed the relationship between sports performers and the public they entertain. Perhaps the most important aspect of media sport is the centrality of the star and the cult of celebrity that generates the contemporary fascination with the men and women who reach the pinnacle of their sport. This chapter reveals the processes that create sports stars and analyses some of the economic, social and ethical consequences such processes have for sport as popular culture.

We begin with an investigation of how new sports stars are constructed by the media, in particular reviewing academic research on sport stardom and celebrity culture by Garry Whannel (2002). Secondly, we investigate the origins of sports celebrity and the rise of the sports agent, perhaps one of the most influential additions to the business of sport. Thirdly, we draw on a case study of the new model of sports stardom represented by the synergy of the media, popular culture and merchandizing exemplified by the endorsement of leading manufacturers of sports apparel Nike and Adidas by global sports megastars. Fourthly, we analyse some of the key transformations in sports labour markets created by sports stardom and the increasing value of image rights in sport. In conclusion, we raise questions about the ethical problems posed by sports stardom, focusing on the mavericks of the world of sport who undermine the conventions of media celebrity.

Heroes, stars and celebrity

The rags to riches story is a familiar motif in the narratives society tells itself about sport. The rewards of elite sport – the wealth and fame – are key motivators for wannabe professional athletes. The myth of the noble athlete, persevering against adversity, playing for the love of the game and bonhomie of fellow competitors, while enduring, is not what drives people to excel in professional sport. Because of this, the stories the media tell about sport are increasingly cynical: about money and greed or corruption and cheating. Nevertheless, when new prodigious talent emerges the romantic discourses of sport invariably come to the fore. The effervescence of youth, the naivety of 'raw talent', the fun temperament, the comparison with sporting heroes of the past and the expectation of future 'greatness' are common traits in the language describing the birth of a new star.

The language commonly used by the media to describe the sudden 'rise to fame' of individuals is intrinsically tied to the fact that 'star performers are characters within a set of narratives' (Whannel, 1992: 121). In other words, the televisual and back-page blitz that greets new sports talent is symptomatic of the media elevation of sporting achievement as part of a wider story, connecting the individual with society. As Whannel has commented, sports performers hold a 'three-fold function' for broadcasters and the press:

> [A]s stars they are the bearers of the entertainment value of performance; as personalities they provide the individualisation and personalisation through which audiences are won and held; and as characters they are the bearers of the sporting narratives. (Whannel, 1992: 122)

Whannel (1992) has also argued there is an inherent tension in the star system of mediated sport caused by the increasing commercialization of the individual that eclipses any attempt to place sports stars in the national ideologies of representative sport. These tensions were certainly evident in the career of footballer David Beckham, but more especially in predominantly individual sports like tennis (think Andy Murray), Formula 1 (think Lewis Hamilton) or golf (think Justin Rose) where the lives of the highly individualized, professionally motivated sports stars do not necessarily adhere to the demands of the national media's expectation of success and national pride.

More detailed, longitudinal work on sports stars by Whannel (2002) analyses the historical relationship between the notions of sporting heroes, stars and celebrities. Focusing on the representation of masculinity of male sports stars in leading popular newspapers and magazines, he paints a series of biographical sketches of key male athletes positioned in the media and cultural environment from which they appeared. Tracing the unfolding crisis of hegemonic masculinity, drawing on a range of recent studies and popular cultural signposts Whannel suggests there has been a cultural shift in the construction of masculinity in the coverage of leading sportsmen reflecting changes in the perceptions of sport and gender relations in society. Taking philosopher Daniel Boorstin as one of his inspirations, Whannel reveals some innate differences between the conceptions of sporting heroes and sport stars in the age of celebrity culture. The fleeting status of celebrity, heavily equated with contemporary sports stars, is tied to the media imagery and narratives that produce them. Celebrity contrasts with the notion of the heroic, a far more organic form of sporting fame and less prevalent in a media age. The media construction of stars for a willing audience and readership is central to this process:

> Stardom is a form of social production in which the professional ideologies and production practices of the media aim to win and hold our attention by linking sporting achievement and personality in ways which have resonances in popular common sense. (Whannel, 2002: 49)

Whannel's most important theoretical argument is that sports stardom as part of the cult of celebrity is subject to what he characterizes as a 'vortextual effect'.

In the new media age of 24-hour news outlets, global communications and high-speed digital information, media outlets feed off each other with a rapacious hunger for news. This process is so overbearing that sports stars and sports events can come to dominate the entire media agenda to the exclusion of all else. One only has to think of 'Posh and Becks' to appreciate this idea. Indeed, Ellis Cashmore (2004) draws on some of Whannel's work to emphasize the media vortext into which Beckham has been received. He charts Beckham's trajectory to global stardom to suggest that Beckham, a player of his time, was not simply a talented footballer but also made by an economic and cultural revolution in football engineered by the Premier League and the satellite television service BSkyB. In the age of celebrity culture and magazines like *OK*, *Hello*, *Now*, *Heat* and *Closer* Beckham was presented more playfully both in terms of his masculinity and increasingly as a global brand.

Like Whannel, Cashmore's analysis is persuasive, particularly when he concludes:

Beckham, or, at least, the commodified Beckham, has profited from the same kinds of processes that create kings from fools, luminaries from dullards, It Girls from underachieving nymphets. All have been delivered to a vast audience courtesy of a media with a seemingly inexhaustible appetite for celebrities. (Cashmore, 2004: 192)

The question underlying this analysis is: why are we so enthralled by celebrity? What hold do sports stars have on their audience? One answer is certainly our desire for stories of fame and fortune, but in sport, it is also the underlying heroic narratives of trial and tribulation, victory and defeat, humiliation and redemption. This is why biographies of sports stars are so popular and, in everyday media, why their biographies are 'reinscribed' (Whannel, 2002) or retold almost on a daily basis. Sport stars are constructed and produced through the working practices of the media through complex sequences of selection and framing. We may never know the 'real' David Beckham or Tiger Woods.

Heroes and villains

A further tension in the social and mediated construction of sports stars stems from the various idiosyncrasies of sporting characters (Rowe, 1995: 115–18). As with any cast of characters, the sports star system sets up a range of 'heroes' and 'villains' in order to play out sporting narratives. Either through design or default the private lives of sports performers converge with their public personas to reveal sports celebrities as model citizens and family members or fallen idols and 'flawed' individuals.

Where the details of sordid private lives invade the public domain of sports performance, the favours enjoyed under the media spotlight can quickly disappear as the media, and the press in particular, take great pleasure in morally denigrating the crimes and misdemeanors of past favourites. Indeed, within the UK, and the English-based press in particular, the back-page 'gossip' and 'sleaze' of the sports press mirrors the political 'mud' used to undermine the political aspirations of MPs on the front pages of national newspapers (Leigh and Vulliamy, 1997). The desire for non-sport news about sports stars also saw the evolution of 'The Rotters' (rottweilers) a pack of tabloid news journalists hungry for sensationlism off the field and who preyed off any wrongdoing.

The moral vilification of sports stars who defame sport throws up one final quandary for our initial analysis of the theory of sports stars: the notion that sports stars are role models in society. Whannel heavily criticizes the popular notion that sports stars carry a significant cultural power as role models for others' behaviour. Sociological research by Gill Lines (2001) on the media coverage of a 'summer of sport' in 1996 emphasizes this point to suggest the media's readings of sports stars do not necessarily conform to the opinions of young people. This has broader implications for a critique on the way the media overtly sensationalizes the misbehaviour of sports stars and its supposed effect on young male fans.

In contradistinction to masculine sports stars women do not feature prominently as sporting heroes or villains, and are marginalized as cultural icons. This is reflected in the imbalance of reward between male and female sports (see Chapter 7). For example, in the 1990s Britain had two outstanding performers in athletics: Linford Christie and Sally Gunnell. Both were world champions, both had received wide television exposure at numerous meetings, but, in terms of prize-money and endorsements, Christie earned more than three times the income of Gunnell (Guinness Sports Yearbook, 1994).

The origins of the sports celebrity and the sports agent

The first quote at the beginning of this chapter is taken from a biography of the golfer Arnold Palmer by his friend, lawyer and business partner Mark McCormack, head of one of the largest sports-media management organizations in the world, International Management Group (IMG). It is a snapshot of the Palmer business empire that used golf as a launch pad for a fantastic array of enterprises. Golf was the medium through which Arnold Palmer became a global brand name known far beyond the field of sport.

The 'brand-name principle' through which Palmer and McCormack approached the business of sport was, in the early 1960s when they first teamed up together, the first attempt to transform the business activities of leading sports personalities. As noted in Chapter 3, it was not that sport and business were not previously related, nor that an individual sportsman or woman had not cashed in on his or her fame through endorsements and promotional activity, it was more the scale of the enterprise, the level of horizontal and vertical integration that made McCormack's promotion of Palmer unique for its time.

According to Stephen Aris (1990), McCormack invented what he terms 'Sportsbiz'. Where golfers like Sam Snead had used agents to handle endorsements and appearances, with Palmer, McCormack took this relationship further, overseeing contract negotiations, proactively seeking business opportunities and planning the sale of the Palmer brand on a long-term basis rather than the ad hoc promotion of earlier sports stars. McCormack set a precedent for selling people as marketable commodities.

Furthermore, in the game of golf the professional sport had a direct link to corporate America as the preferred pastime of the American middle class. Selling the Palmer brand to this audience made the transition from the business of sport to sport as a business remarkably smooth. Within two years Palmer's earnings had risen from $59,000 to more than $500,000 a year. By 1962 IMG was also the agent for Gary Player and Jack Nicklaus, presenting McCormack with a triumvirate of the best golfers in the world.

The demands of maintaining 'celebrity status' in order to fuel the sports stars' media ubiquity and mystique requires a constant vigil. Again, Palmer led the way in America, making numerous appearances on television shows, advertisements, celebrity golf tournaments and business events. While many of these activities are for direct payment, they also facilitated the promotion of both Arnold Palmer Enterprises specifically and the sport of golf more generally. However, such evangelical patronage of golf comes at a price when figures like Palmer are concerned. With his every move on a golf course potentially captured by television, Palmer, and those that have since followed him, realized that they are human advertisements. So when completing a round of golf a fresh bottle of Coca-Cola neatly placed in Palmer's hand would evade the expense of ad-spend on air-time, displacing a fraction of that money instead to the pocket of the golfer.

Spreading the gospel of golf

Palmer, along with his contemporaries Player and Nicklaus, has done more to spread the culture of golf on a global scale than any other professional. The extent to which new golf courses are designed and built has dramatically accelerated since the 1960s, where supply has struggled to keep pace with demand. As well as having severe environmental impact, the process of star-led initiatives creates a further supply of both ready-made golf venues and events made for television.

Of all the sports which respond to the demands made by television's insatiable appetite for sports 'product', golf is surely the master. In the contemporary world of televised golf, summer is perpetual, as the professional tours move from continent to continent to satisfy demand from global sponsors, advertisers and audiences. Pro-Celebrity tours and programmes (a long-running feature of golf programming on the

BBC during the 1970s and 1980s hosted by commentator Peter Alliss) add to the patina of superstardom many of the top golfers now enjoy. Breaking down barriers between sport and the entertainment industries has become a key feature sustaining the sports star system. While written over thirty years ago, the wider meaning of the contemporary sports star as performer is explicitly related in Palmer's biography by McCormack:

> At heart . . . Arnold is an actor. When he walks down a fairway, he seems to want everybody's eyes on him. There is something in the way he moves that almost says, 'Look, look, I'm Arnold Palmer, and aren't we having fun.' (McCormack, 1967: 184)

Sports stars, then, must perform in all manner of capacities, as skilled athletes and practitioners, interviewees and sometimes interviewers, ambassadors for sport and sports sponsors and celebrities in and of themselves.

This last point alludes to the fact that celebrity is a self-fulfilling process, where stars become famous for being famous. This enables stars whose moment in any given sport has passed to maintain a public presence.

Sport can also attempt to extend the longevity of a generation of stars through secondary tournaments and events. Golf's Senior Tour (currently screened on CBS) provides an opportunity for professional golfers to play on a competitive basis for the television cameras with all the peripheral promotional activity such a venture incorporates. The idea of 'Senior' sport is also maintained within other sports including tennis and football. While such events do not challenge the status of top professional sport, they do provide vehicles for further promotional activity that can be tied into the sponsorship activities of 'first-class' sport. Remarkably, in an era of contemporary multimillionaire golfers, in 2007 Palmer still earned $25 million through his various endorsements and fees to make him the fourth highest paid golfer in the world behind Tiger Woods, Phil Mickelson and Vijay Singh.

Michael Jordan and the NBA brand

> Basketball isn't my job. For me, my job begins the moment I walk off the floor. It's everything that surrounds the actual playing of the games. My job is being a product endorser, an employee of the Chicago Bulls,

trying to live up to the expectations of others, dealing with the media. That's my job. (Jordan, 1994: 43)

Basketball has become one of the prime examples of the interweaving of media–sport production and marketing interests that have transformed sports performers into global stars. Over the years the game has undergone numerous mutations to arrive at its current venerable status: the introduction of time-outs for television ad breaks; the twenty-four second rule to speed up the action; the three-point rule to increase the level of scoring; overtime to ensure a result when the scores are tied; and the erosion of the sovereign governing body of the sport to allow television a free reign in the choice of live broadcasts.

These changes have also had a profound effect on the performance of basketball players. After a slump in the popularity in the game during the 1970s a re-emphasis on the heroic nature of the sport, in the manner in which it was promoted, augured a new era of basketball superstars in the mid-1980s. Characters like Larry Bird and Magic Johnson epitomized the introduction of a new set of entertainment values that laid emphasis on display and glitz.

However, both Bird and Johnson would be eclipsed by the most prolific basketball player the game has ever seen, Michael Jordan. Jordan, apocryphal son of the modern NBA, in the 1990s came to be viewed as 'Michael the Marketed' or a 'post-modern sports commodity of truly heroic proportions' (Vande-Berg, 1998: 146). Jordan's commodification of sport was integrally related to his African-American origin tangibly linked to broader elements of black popular culture. His symbolic worth, as a highly successful black sportsman, was transformed from cultural to monetary capital. Jordan remains far more than a retired basketball star. His branded shoes – that helped build and sustain Nike as the world's leading sportswear brand – tell an important story in the origin of the hyper-commodification of sport and sports stars that many have since sought to emulate.

Be like Mike?

Through his agency Pro-Serv, Jordan capitalized on the 'sneaker' as an essential element of black urban street style through his promotion of Nike footwear under the signature of 'Air Jordans'. The 'sneaker' or 'trainer' universally represents youth, hedonism and the individualization of consumption. Indeed, in many respects, the contemporary style wars of the high street have been fought on the feet of millions of people for whom the trainer represents the ultimate in 'hip', 'cool' and 'chic'. How did Jordan fit into this process? And why did he emerge as the 'crown prince of Nike' before being superseded by a new generation of global sport stars including Tiger Woods, Roger Federer and Thierry Henri?

As Dyson (1993) has suggested, one element to Jordan's wide appeal is his ability with a basketball: his style and craft. Sport, for Jordan, has become a marker of his self-expression. Many quotes from Jordan on the playing of basketball eschew any mention of money and his monetary worth as a performer. As the above quote indicates, that part of his life, 'his job', is dealt with off the court. Rather, his status as a sporting hero stemmed from his basketball craft.

Dyson (1993) argues there are three elements to this. First, a will to spontaneity, expanding the 'vocabulary' of athletic ability and spectacle through innovative manoeuvres and plays. Second, a stylization of the performed self allows Jordan an aura and persona on the basketball court that sets him apart from other players. For example, his ability to hang in the air, in a specific manner, that ultimately led to the moniker 'Air Jordan'. Finally, allied to this last point, is Jordan's edifying deception, his ability to subvert the common perception of what is culturally or physically possible. All these elements combined to make Jordan an exceptional athlete and heroic figure.

This exposition of the relationship between the sporting body and culture has been criticized by Hoberman (1997) who argues that Dyson presents an essentialist view of African-American sports performance, conveniently forgetting the lack of political empathy Jordan had often showed to the politics of race in the United States. However, the discourse of African-American popular culture has generated some resonance with new audiences for the NBA. Post-Jordan black basketball stars like Kobe Bryant or Shaquille O'Neal continue to be paraded as the epitome of street credibility. The sports media and promotional activity that surround the game play heavily on such black cultural style, fusing elements of popular music (rap and hip-hop) and fashion (from sneakers to tattoos) with a guarded sense of racial politics. Nevertheless, work by Andrews (2001) and others suggests that, in spite of this commercial success in the realm of sport, Jordan also, paradoxically, remained a cultural site for neoconservative racial ideologies of black sportsmen.

Sport stars, then, are central to the political economy of media sport. In the next section we explore the exploitation of sports talent and labour is related to media interests. In particular, our concern is with the industrial relations of sport and the capitalization of image rights.

Stars and transformations in sports labour

A combination of factors have led to key transformations in the sports labour markets: the media focus on stars and the rise of sports agents; the increasing mobility of individual sports performers between teams, leagues and nations; and legal challenges mounted against antiquated administrative systems of sport.

We have covered the rise of stars and their agents in more detail above; however, in terms of industrial relations, it is quite clear that these developments have undermined the ability of sport administrators and organizations to govern the destiny and careers of leading sports men and women. This is chiefly due to the increased symbolic power sports stars now enjoy in comparison to their sporting ancestors.

As with the case of Arnold Palmer, sports stars are now marketable commodities and, like any product, they require legal support to maintain their value and protect their interests. As Steve Redhead has noted in the field of sports jurisprudence, the heightened intrusion of market forces in sport 'is posing all kinds of questions about legal rights and duties which have rarely been subjected so strongly to the judicial gaze' (Redhead, 1997: 27).

The negotiation of transfer fees and employment contracts has become an important domain where sport and the law have become synonymous. In an era of 'hyperlegality' (Redhead, 1997) we would not expect any elite sports man or woman to sign along the dotted line without first consulting their lawyer to fine-comb the small print. In football, and increasingly in other elite sports, the price, worth and wages of top players provides a staple diet of speculation and gossip for daily and Sunday newspapers, which have a salacious appetite for revealing the latest record-breaking fees.

Reviewing the transformations of domestic football in England during the 1990s, David Conn astutely captured the new era of industrial relations in sport to assess critically the impact the massive injection of money from television has brought to the game:

Football in 1992 was thrown utterly to the winds of market forces. The players, advised by their agents, now do their deals to a backdrop of anonymous stands, corporate sponsorships, knowing that flotation is making fortunes for the clubs' owners. The money has flooded in and much of the soul has been squeezed out, but the argument is hollow. The clubs have put no framework in place to show the players a more rounded way to think about football. They have led by mercenary example. (Conn, 1997: 225)

Given the 'mercenary' context sport now occupies, exactly what the 'rounded way to think about football' entails is not absolutely clear.

The confusion is born of the constant tension set up by the industrialization of sport between the socio-cultural meaning of sport and sport as business. As we argued in Chapter 3, the two have never been mutually exclusive, but sports business is no ordinary business.

Doing the business

In negotiating a new contract for a club, tour or federation, or in making the decision to join another, we can readily surmise that contemporary sports stars will consider the financial options before any other. This is not wholly surprising, but it is quite a departure from the origins of payment for play where one could equally argue that issues of locality and loyalty figured far more strongly. Even postwar football heroes Stanley Matthews and Billy Wright have given testimony in their biographical accounts of how wider recognition brought illicit financial reward but, more importantly, status and pride among their families, peers and communities.

This is not to suggest that emotional sentiment or the desire to win championships or titles do not play their part in motivating contemporary elite sports men and women; rather, we are merely pointing out that the financial capitalization of an athlete's star potential and worth are foremost in the development of their professional careers. In England, for example, organizations like the Professional Footballers Association (PFA) have lobbied long and hard to ensure that those from the professional ranks of sport receive fair reward for their talents and security once their careers in the top flight are over. The PFA, in particular, has maintained a strong media presence whenever the livelihood of its members or the sport itself are threatened. In 2001, when the Premier League clubs threatened to reduce the annual levy of television income to the players' union – its main source of funding – the PFA Chairman Gordon Taylor threatened strike action (Boyle and Haynes, 2003: 84–5).

Transformations in the legal status of sports professionals can, however, produce conflict in the aims of such organizations. The most important case in this respect has been that of Jean-Marc Bosman, where the European Court of Justice ruled in 1995 that the operation of the transfer system and the 'three foreigners rule' amounted to an infringement of European law under the Treaty of Rome.

One of the ramifications of the Bosman ruling was that players were free agents once their contract with a particular club had ended. This had severe ramifications for the old system of transfer fees because instead of money circulating between clubs (maintaining a flow of income within the game) cash windfalls moved directly to players on signing for their new club (rather than the money returning to the game). A further consequence was that players who originate from the EU are able to move freely between the various leagues of EU member states without the need for work permits. Hence, the contradiction for the PFA was the financial reward of domestic players given their new-found mobility at the expense of a flood of 'foreign' players plying their trade in the lucrative English Premier League.

The process was compounded by a further court case in 1999 by a Polish basketball player, Lilia Malaja, who successfully challenged EU work-permit restrictions on Eastern European athletes in a French court on the premise that Poland had an open trade agreement with the EU. On hearing reports of the case the PFA chairman, Gordan Taylor, announced:

> This could have serious repercussions. We could become a dumping ground for world football, since this is one of the game's honeypots. (Cited in Butcher, 1999)

In the same year the Home Office introduced stricter controls on the immigration of non-EU footballers but by 2004 Poland and other Eastern European states had become members of the EU and the flow of football talent to the Premier League and the Championship did not abate.

By 2007 there were 280 foreign players registered in the Premier League. The issue caused concern at UEFA and FIFA with both presidents Michel Platini and Sepp Blatter passing comment on the possible introduction of foreign quotas in domestic league competitions. In 2008 the idea of quotas also gained favour with the UK government's Secretary for Culture, Media and Sport, Andy Burnham, who vowed to lobby for change in EU employment law. Nationalist sentiment has also been redolent in the UK sports press, with the *Daily Mail* proclaiming:

[The] game is nothing more than an accommodating circus at which the footballers of the world arrive, pitch their tents and perform their acts for immoderate reward. ('The lost generation – how foreign players dominate the English game', *Daily Mail*, 4 August 2007)

For the time being the Premier League remains a 'honeypot' to the world's football community.

The boy done good – salaries and image rights

Revenue from television rights and sponsorship have certainly driven up the core salaries of elite sports stars. At the elite end of professional sport, stars are far removed from the average citizen in terms of wealth. In their 2007 annual round up of the world's top earning athletes Forbes.com revealed Tiger Woods earned an estimated $100 million that year. Woods, the exemplar of sporting excellence and mega-stardom, earned considerably more than Formula 1 racing driver Haki Raikkonen ($42 million) who came second in the rankings. As well as golf and Formula 1 the top twenty-five of the Forbes list was littered with multi-millionaires from American football, basketball, baseball, tennis and soccer (with David Beckham the top earner in the sport with an income of $33 million).

The only female athlete in the top twenty-five was tennis star Maria Sharapova ($23 million), laying emphasis once again on the dispropor-tionate way in which male professional sports stars are wealthier, obtain more television coverage and are considered more attractive to global sponsors and advertisers. How accurate these surveys of wealth are is anyone's guess, but they do reveal a fascination for wealth generation through sport and, perhaps more crucially, the global cache of sports celebrity. It is well recognized that elite sport stars are a product of the age in which they live. The organic connection of sporting heroes to their communities of the early twentieth century (Holt, 1989) has been gradually transformed into a distanced gaze at talent and wealth by more than fifty years of televised sport, tabloidization of the press and proc-esses of globalization and commodification of the sports industry.

Pay-TV and the money accrued through subscriptions to niche sports channels have increased competition for television rights, inflated the wealth of particular leagues and tournaments and seen a direct transformation in the fortunes of athletes at the end of the value-chain. This is most visible in English football where, according to the annual survey of English Premier League by accountants Deloitte, the average salaries of players topped £1 million in 2006 and the total wage bill for all twenty-two Premier League clubs in 2007 was more than £1 billion (Deloitte, 2008).

The gravy train of professional sport does not end with salaries and prize money. As the media coverage and celebrity status of sports stars has risen, so too has their ability to control and manage their image, its uses and commercial worth. For example, of the $100 million earned by Tiger Woods in 2007, only $13 million came from prize money, the remainder coming from appearance fees and endorsements. Sports stars are the focus of the dedicated sports media and of the wider cult of celebrity and it is not difficult to understand why athletes and their agents seek to control this particular aspect of their 'brand' value. One of the key tools in the capitalization of the individual sports star is what has come to be known as 'image rights'. In the UK there is no legislation that recognizes a right in one's image (Haynes, 2005) but there are legal mechanisms available to control how the images of sports stars are used in media and advertising. The most celebrated case involved former Formula 1 racing driver Eddie Irvine who in 2002 successfully sued radio station *TalkSport* for 'passing off' the use of his image in their promotional literature (Haynes, 2005: 106–9). The unsolicited use of his image was viewed as damaging his goodwill, reputation and name and has set a precedent in British case law in the protection of the commercial value of a sports star's image.

Image rights or rights in publicity do exist in various forms across the world. This means that global stars like David Beckham can rest easy in the knowledge that their movement into territories like Spain or the US where dedicated laws to protect private images exist will be commercially secure and respected (Haynes, 2007). But questions might be asked of why well-paid millionaire sport stars should be afforded further protection to enhance their wealth? Moreover, in football and other sports, we are witnessing what James Boyle (2003) has referred to as the 'enclosure' of information goods and ideas that maximalizes the control and value of media images at the same time as restricting and privatizing certain rights of access to the media and their audiences. Therefore trademarks in a sports star's name are not only considered acceptable but are strictly policed to the point where fan websites are restricted in their choice and registration of domain names (Boyle and Haynes, 2004: 89–92). Such controls seem zealous and contradictory at a time when the Internet and all forms of digital communication are affording new creative outlets for sports media and fans that add impetus more generally to the cultures of sport.

The sports star as celebrity is a global phenomenon, and local markets dictate which sporting heroes adorn billboards and television advertising. However, there are exceptions. In Iran, the Western commodification of sport stars has been challenged by state intervention. In the lead-in to the Beijing Olympic Games in 2008 the Iranian superstar weightlifter and double gold medalist Hossein Rezazadeh, known as the 'Iranian Hercules', was caught up in a furure over the use of sporting icons in commercial advertising. In an effort to dampen overt commercial intrusion in sport the Iranian government banned sports stars from merchandizing and endorsements because 'athletic role models should be promoting chivalry not consumerism' (Arabianbusiness.com, 8 July 2008). Yet challenges to the commercial status and wealth of global icons of sport remain rare, in spite of a common criticism for the inflated egos and the inflated wallets of some sports stars. However, even in some of the largest sporting leagues in the world artificial checks and balances are put in place to ensure fare competition and the distribution of wealth. We now return to the nature and structure of US sport.

Stars in control: the battle in American sport

In a wider context, what image rights and the other cases we have highlighted above represent is a transformation in the level of power exerted by individual athletes over the control of their performance, both in the sports arena and its representation through the media. This mirrors the rights of other individuals and groups in other realms of the entertainment industries: from pop stars to Hollywood actors, everyone has their price.

The power of some sports stars can seriously undermine the authority of the organizations they work for, and the gain or loss of a sporting hero can dramatically affect the share price of a sporting plc.

The governing bodies of the four main North American team sports, the NFL (American football), Major League Baseball, the NHL (ice hockey) and the NBA (basketball), have attempted to allay some of these financial and legislative threats to their administration of sport through the collegiate draft and some element of wage capping. The philosophy behind such collective bargaining between the player unions and the Leagues is to maintain competitiveness through the distribution of talent. This ensures that no one team can dominate the entry of new sports talent by buying up all the best players.

The draft enables competitive equality and impedes aggressive bidding for amateur players, thus keeping a check on the cost of sports labour. It also places great importance on the selection process, and the ability to spot future potential becomes acute. For example, in the NBA draft of 1984 the Chicago Bulls were given the third pick in the first-round draft of rookie pros after a disastrous performance in the previous season. Luckily, for the Bulls, Jordan had been passed over by the Houston Rockets and the Portland Trailblazers leaving the road free for them to negotiate a deal for the NCAA player of the year. The rest is history as far as the Chicago franchise is concerned, which, propelled by the leadership of Jordan, went on to win six NBA titles during the 1990s.

The draft system is indicative of the extraordinary business of sport, where a tension arises between the need for team success and meaningful competition. This state of monopsony in North American sport (Scully, 1995) allows teams to perpetuate 'their special need to be rivals and partners simultaneously, since they must act as partners to carry out the conditions that make rivalry possible' (Koppett, 1994: 284).

However, in order to maintain a worthy product, Leagues, operating collectively on behalf of the franchises, must negotiate with players who collectively bargain the parameters of their salaries through player unions. One major problem with this collective bargaining is that the transformations in the sport–media nexus mean that salaries may not be proportionate with the rapid rise in television rights' fees filling the coffers of the clubs and the governing bodies of sport.

During the 1990s this has become a familiar scenario for North American professional sports markets. Player lockouts, or strikes, driven by breakdowns in contractual negotiations between Leagues and player unions seriously disrupted the seasons of Major League Baseball in 1994 and the NBA at the start of the 1998/99 season. Long spells of inaction have significant consequences for the ancillary businesses of professional sport, in particular television and sponsorship. NBC and the cable network Turner had signed a $2.6 billion deal over four years for the combined television rights to the NBA and the lockout was a clear threat to their advertising revenues as basketball was 'off the box'.

The NBA star players, who had headlined the push to increase player salaries, had also threatened the excellent public relations they had built up during the reign of Magic Johnson, Larry Bird and Michael Jordan, at a period where sports merchandise was experiencing a grave downturn in sales (*SportBusiness International*, February

1999). Disputes of this kind can seriously undermine the status of stars who run the threat of betraying the trust of the sports fan and the television audience. This fine line between hero and villain is the subject of our final section on sports stars that investigates instances where sport stardom can be as much of a burden as it is a boon.

The trouble with fame

The use of sports stars to promote various products and services of sponsors, advertisers and communities can be a potentially risky business. Media sport frequently has the ability to reveal the human nature of the heroes it produces. That sports men and women are open to the vagaries of everyday life is hardly surprising; however, as the financial stakes in sport spiral to unprecedented levels, the cost of a fall from grace becomes more pronounced.

Very little research has been done on the what we would call 'sports sleaze': the public scrutiny of sports celebrity and morality. The exception to this is David Rowe's (1997) review of the 'anatomy of a sports scandal' where he reflects critically on three case studies: the drugs scandal of the Canadian sprinter Ben Johnson; the 'bad boy' image of the American basketball player Magic Johnson; and the murder trial of American footballer and actor, O. J. Simpson.

All three cases, Rowe argues (1997: 219), reveal how the 'media are key conduits in the communication of the meaning of the sports scandal', setting the parameters of acceptable behaviour by 'switching between official and popular discourses and private and public domains in a relentless quest for the "truth" of the day'. These are extreme cases where sport grabs the headlines of newspapers, radio and television news. On such occasions sport jumps from the news enclave of the 'sports page' into a wider public domain, carrying a wider resonance with societal concerns and general interest.

British sport is no stranger to claims of drug taking, corruption and cheating. As wealth in and through sport has increased so too has the media attention on malpractice and irregular commercial behaviour in sport. In 1994 allegations of match fixing against goalkeeper Bruce Grobbelaar by the *Sun* newspaper focused attention on the place of sport in society and the place of the media in the coverage and reporting of the sport. The allegations were built on video evidence that revealed Grobbelaar willingly receiving money for a fake bribe set up by the Sun. In a staged publicity stunt, footage of the transaction was publicly delivered to FA Headquarters by the Sun's two investigative journalists to reveal the newspapers' role in 'cleaning up the game'. Grobbelaar won a libel case against the *Sun* in 1999 only for the Court of Appeal to overturn the verdict in 2001 due to a 'miscarriage of justice' in favour of the newspaper. Bankrupt and broken the footballer returned to his native South Africa and disappeared from the spotlight of the British media for good.

The issue of bribery strikes at the heart of sporting ethics, and in football has a history as old as the sport itself (Inglis, 1987). The question of fairness and the notion of a 'level playing field' underwrite all competitive sport. Moreover, the ideals and moral rhetoric of sport have a wider resonance with moral codes in many Western cultures, based on various notions of social democracy.

It is the transgression of these codes that propel match-fixing allegations into a wider public domain. When South African cricket captain and national hero Hansje Cronje admitted taking money from a bookmaker for information and forecasting in 2000 it sent a wave of panic through the sport and shattered the public perception of cricket as a 'pastoral redoubt' (Whannel, 2000: 52). However, throughout the 1990s and early twenty-first century the distinct realms of 'hard news' and 'sports news' has approached the issue of corruption in sport in quite different ways. This is most pronounced in television sport programmes, where tensions arise between the sports pundits' peripheral role of passing comment on the violation of the sporting order and their promotion of the sport as a televisual spectacle.

Television sport strives to maintain its distanced sense of objectivity in the coverage of scandalous events. Rarely is sport itself brought into question. Rather, ex-stars of the game, in their role as pundits, pass judgement on transgressive behaviour in sport by ultimately 'closing ranks' on the sport that feeds their careers. Television's protection of the culture of sport serves to maintain the hegemonic position it enjoys with sport, for it knows that it must not kill the goose that lays the golden eggs.

King Eric and that kick

When in January 1995 Manchester United's star Frenchman Eric Cantona lunged kung-fu style at a Crystal Palace fan, having just been sent from the field of play, it produced a slightly different scenario of how the media treat illegal behaviour in sport. The case is interesting from a media perspective as it illustrates the often fickle and contradictory nature of press reporting of sports stars. The immediate aftermath of the event saw the demonization of the player in both broadcasting and newspaper reports.

The largest-selling newspaper in Scotland, the *Daily Record* (27 January 1995), printed a blown-up picture of a Nike football boot, Cantona's sponsored footwear, with the headline 'lethal weapon', a particularly sensational pun on the flying kick that led to the player being convicted of common assault. The knee-jerk judgemental reaction to Cantona's violence also fell back on stereotyped language based on the Frenchman's history of transgressive behaviour on the pitch.

For example, the BBC2 programme *Sport on Friday* (27 January 1995) carried a feature introduced by former professional Garth Crooks that used an extended montage of Cantona's past misdemeanours as evidence of his uncontrollable Gallic temperament. As an extensive review of the 'Cantona Affair' by Simon Gardiner (1998) has illustrated, much of the media rhetoric that poured scorn on the player was premised on a wider cultural animosity of the English for the French. As with the demonization of other sports 'anti-heroes', such as Mike Tyson, the media reporting of the Cantona incident produced a set of essentialist discourses that conflated narratives of race and ethnicity with deviant or criminal behaviour (Sloop, 1997). In spite of an initial media backlash on his return in September 1995, Cantona reinvented himself, ironically capitalizing on the event, where he was viewed as a victim of abuse rather than a perpetrator of violence. Most notably, in three advertisements for Nike, Cantona's complex persona was articulated both politically and symbolically to advocate the products of the global sportswear company.

In the first advert Cantona reflected on his image as the 'enfant terrible' of sport; in the second, the player challenged those who denied his right as an individual to play football in an ethnically and racially divided society; and in the third, he exorcized his demonic alter ego by shattering the image of the devil by driving a ferocious shot towards goal causing the devil to implode. The dialogue and the images of the adverts clearly drew on the paradigmatic elements that combined to construct Cantona's media persona, as well as drawing on the mythological status of the sporting hero.

Conclusion

Cantona's complex characterization in the media illustrates some of the ongoing problems contemporary sports stars now face when they are elevated to iconic status and lauded as role models. However, the stereotypical roles prescribed to stars are rarely lived up to.

While the sports star dates from the earliest commercial moments in sporting history, few generations have had to deal with the level of interest which the media, now the main sponsors of sport, currently focus on the stars of the contemporary sporting stage.

The pressures that star status bestows on any athlete (who is often inexperienced in dealing with matters of business, law and public relations) ensure that the nuances of everyday life and private interrelationships are in tension with the fictionalized persona constructed by the media. It appears that fame does come at a price.

Chapter 6

The Race Game:
Media Sport, Race and Ethnicity

I wonder if there will soon be a separate entrance for Jewish supporters at Manchester City, or if they will be allowed in at all? The club's new owners [Abu Dhabi Royal Family] wish the team to play exhibition matches and hold training sessions in Abu Dhabi, but it is expected that not all the players will be invited to attend. Tal Ben Haim is an Israeli national and therefore not allowed to enter the horrible little country, so it is almost certain he will be left behind. (Rod Liddle, 'Awkward questions that haunt new owners', *Sunday Times,* 14 September 2008)

Introduction

As a central component in popular culture, sport and its mediated versions operate within a terrain heavily laden with symbolism and metaphor. As we have argued earlier in the book, the issue of representation remains central to any study of media sport. Mediated sport is saturated with ideas, values, images and discourses which at times reflect, construct, naturalize, legitimize, challenge and even reconstitute attitudes which permeate wider society. It should come as no surprise that a cultural form which has narrative and mythology at its core can also become a vehicle for what Cohen (1988) calls 'rituals of misrecognition'. What these next three chapters examine is the extent to which mediated versions of sport play a role in the larger process of identity formations of race, ethnicity, gender and national identity.

While we focus our attention on a specific area in each chapter, we are aware that often these strands interact, so that at a key moment issues of race will apparently be subsumed within the larger framework of national identity (such as when black athletes are representing Britain), while at other times the differing fault lines which run through society are also clearly evident within a sporting context (when Celtic play Rangers in football). However, we make the separation over the next three chapters to allow us to focus on some of the specific issues involved with each area.

In this chapter we look at the media's treatment of black (using the political term here to refer to those of African, Caribbean and southern Asian origin) and Asian (those of Indian subcontinent descent) sports people. Later we also briefly highlight the issue of ethnicity as it relates to sectarianism and media sport in both Scotland and Northern Ireland.

Sporting and media representations of race

Issues around media representations are fundamentally about power and status in society. A community's or individual's ability to feel themselves represented accurately in media discourse is in part related to assumptions about the power of the media to shape and change public opinion. In the areas of television comedy or drama this can often be about using stereotypes and stereotyping as a type of cultural shorthand for comedic or dramatic purposes.

This often reduces diffuse and complex groups into simple and straightforward characters with distinctive characteristics. Jarvie (1991: 2) notes also that discussions of issues relating to race and sport have in the past ignored the diversity and differing experiences of various ethnic groupings and also largely removed gender difference from the discussion.

In their overview of media coverage of African-American athletes in the US, Davis and Harris (1998) note how particular stereotypes of the 'natural' black athlete have been used to explain the apparent over-representation of black people in sports. This explanation, rather than the more materially rooted one which links it to class and deprivation, has also been echoed in work on British and North Amercian black sports people (Cashmore, 1996; Hoberman, 1997). Regester (2003) notes how early twentieth-century screen images of black athletes constructed a myth of 'danger and desire', while Wilson (1997) has also demonstrated how such images have also been replicated, with some variation, in the Canada experience.

Martin Polley (1998: 158), writing about the interface between race and sport in postwar Britain, argues that racism has been a large part of sporting culture in this country. He notes that racist abuse suffered by black and Asian sports people has often gone uncommented upon by the media. He argues that:

For black Britons, sport has remained a double-edged sword in post-war society, offering both advancement and obstacle, acceptance and crude stereotype. That many individuals have excelled must be read both as a sign of a growing tolerance – particularly when national representation is at stake – and as a sign of perceived limited opportunities in other walks of life. (Polley, 1998: 158)

There is an argument which suggests that the changing media profile of black people in general and their centrality within the realms of mainstream popular culture has diminished or undercut negative racist stereotyping. But empirical research on black and Asian sports people, such as Burdsey's work on Asian footballers (Burdsey, 2004), suggests there remain very real conditions of prejudice.

Jarvie and Reid (1997: 218–19) alert us to the need to be wary of applying universal theories of sport, ethnicity and racism. They argue that this 'is not to deny different theories of race relations but to caution against their universality as ways of explaining different situations throughout the globe'. This could be extended when media coverage is added to the equation; in other words, the particular social, cultural and historical context becomes important when examining the production and consumption of media representations of sport, race and ethnicity.

Big Ron's and other racist outbursts

. . . he is what is known in some schools as a fucking lazy thick nigger. (Ron Atkinson, comment on French defender Marcel Desailly by ITV football pundit captured 'off-air' after a Champions League match between Chelsea and Monaco, April 2004)

The former Manchester United manager Ron Atkinson's racist outburst in 2004, which went beyond the kind of faux pas commonly delivered by television football pundits, was an exceptional instance of racism that betrayed the more familiar social and regulatory checks on extreme prejudice and racism in the media. Atkinson's comments were not heard in the UK where the ITV Champions League broadcast had ended but was heard across Middle Eastern channels where the television feed continued. The global reach of televised sport on this occasion tripped up a very parochial sports broadcaster passing a very personal judgement (or so he thought) on a black international football star. Atkinson's media career was stopped in its tracks.

He left ITV and withdrew from writing his football analysis for the *Guardian* newspaper.

It had ended his reign as the UK's most prominent sports media pundit. He was clearly sorry for the remark – at least, sorry he had been caught making it. His denial of being racist was to be expected and he pointed to the fact that as a manager in the 1970s and 1980s he had been in charge of England's emerging black talent. As he remarked: 'I have worked with more black players, I would think, than any other manager in the country and I bet none of them has ever heard me say it to them' (BBCi, 2004). One thing the episode reveals, among many things, is that casual racist remarks remain commonplace in everyday circles, in football as elsewhere. The remarks may not be delivered with deep malice or with political intent, but nevertheless hint at continued social divisiveness along the cleavages of race and ethnicity and resistance to the multiculturalist ambitions of postwar Britain.

One response to the Atkinson case would be that to eradicate the incipient racism that creeps into casual conversation in the context of sport there should be a more diverse ethnic mix of sports broadcasters. Throughout the 1990s it could still be argued that there was an almost complete absence of black and Asian sports presenters and commentators working within the mainstream. It has not been until the early 2000s that this situation has begun to be remedied in terms of black pundits and summarizers, although the core roles of lead commentary and studio anchor noticeably remain the province of white middle-class broadcasters.

Whannel (2002) notes how former professional footballer Garth Crooks represents the 'embodiment of the dream of liberal assimilation' – articulate and middle-class in style and tone and a polished media performer – but even after many years with the BBC he has not advanced beyond a minor role as interviewer. There are exceptions such as ex-athlete and Olympic gold medalist Colin Jackson who has been preened for the screen, but it does seem a strange state of affairs when the visibility and profile of black sports people within Britain has been extremely high since the mid-1990s.

Other former black sports stars, such as Ian Wright, have become pundits and wider media celebrities – famed for their 'street' attitude and, much like Jackson who appeared on the BBC TV genealogy series *Who Do You Think You Are?*, take pride in their Afro-Caribbean ancestry. Gilroy (1993) has noted the increased visibility of black and ethnic 'cool' in Western popular cultures, but he suggests this doesn't mean that racism or other forms of political and economic discrimination have disappeared or been eradicated.

What is clear is that, while the range of media images associated with black and Asian sports men and women has expanded, and is often more positive than it may have been previously, this is not necessarily an indication of a less racist and more tolerant society. Much like the Atkinson comment, the complexities and contradictions of the multiple identities people have are often brought into focus only in specific contexts. Thus it is not uncommon at football matches for fans to abuse a black or Asian player on the opposing team in a racist manner, while praising a black or Asian player who is playing for their team.

A similar scenario occurred in February 2008 involving the British Formula 1 racing driver Lewis Hamilton who was subjected to racist abuse by a section of Spanish fans during the pre-season testing of cars in Barcelona. Hamilton had been engaged in both a professional and personal battle with former Spanish teammate Fernando Alonso in the driver's championship the previous year. The spat had clearly rankled some of the Spanish fans of Alonso, but the racist taunts of 'puto negro' (fucking black) and 'negro de mierda' (black shit) reported in the Spanish sports newspaper *Marca* – including a much-publicized troupe of fans with blackened faces and afro wigs – showed that in the global age of sport national rivalry brings to the fore quite entrenched racist cultural beliefs. The FIA's response to Hamilton's abuse was lacklustre. According to *the Guardian* sportswriter Richard Williams the FIA appeared to miss the point:

> Hamilton is known as formula one's first black driver, although he is actually of mixed race, with a black father of Caribbean parentage and a white English mother. His youth, intelligence and good looks make him the best thing to happen to motor racing since Ayrton Senna left the scene. Demographically speaking, he is a marketing man's dream in an international sport rapidly conquering distant territories. So, whatever its own private opinion on racial issues, you would think that it might have been in the governing body's own interest to offer him the best possible protection and to inflict the sternest possible punishment on those by whom he is threatened in such a rebarbative manner. But no. (Williams, 2008)

Similar outpourings of abuse had fallen upon English black footballers during an international match against Spain at the Bernebeu in 2005. In that instance the European governing body UEFA were more proactive in their stance against racism and ultimately fined the Spanish FA £44,750. Small change in the world of football perhaps, but it sent out a signal that racism is not tolerated in the sporting arena.

Unfortunately this does not mean such racist chants go away. September 2008, for example, saw the English FA make a complaint to FIFA about racist chants directed at England's Emile Heskey during a World Cup qualifying game in Croatia.

Great white hope: representations of Amir Khan and the discourse of Britishness

> Not that I know much about the sport of boxing but I would be tempted to say that travesty was fixed! Did you hear the tune that was playing whilst Khan walked into the arena? Only Land of Hope and Glory. For Fuck Sake! After the terrorist outrage committed by Khan's Pakistani Muslim brothers, I call that taking the bloody piss and rubbing our faces in it! (Quote from a person calling themselves Brentwood Racist, Stormfront.org, 2005)

The bombings and attempted bombings of London in July 2005 prompted an outpouring of commentary and debate on the nature of Britishness and the meaning of multiculturalism. The attacks not only brought disruption, fear and paranoia among London's population, but also instigated a crisis in the majority (white) population's understanding, and perhaps tolerance, of immigrant communities from Southern Asia and other ethnic minority communities. In what follows we analyse one instance of this crisis over ethnicity and national identity taking our cue from the realm of sport, in particular the media coverage of the British boxer Amir Khan.

Khan rose to national fame during the 2004 Olympic Games in Athens. Trailblazing his way to the Olympic lightweight final Khan gained recognition for being the only British boxer to qualify for Athens 2004. By sensationally fighting his way to the silver medal at the relatively young age of seventeen Khan secured wide media exposure in September 2004 and received a hero's welcome on returning to the UK when his home town of Bolton in North West England held a civic reception in his honour. Fast forward to 9 July 2005, two days after the London bombings, and Khan fought his first professional bout. In the short interim period between the bombings and the fight, the Metropolitan Police had announced that the four London bombers were British citizens of Pakistani origin. As a second-generation

British teenager of Pakistani origin, the context of Kahn's fight took on new significance. The media coverage of the fight fused discourses of a rising sport protégé and celebrity with the language of nation-hood, ethnicity and patriotism. In such instances the media coverage of sport frequently problematizes the construction of nationhood.

In many ways Khan's story of local boy made good followed famil-iar narratives of sporting success that the media churn out with regular-ity. But what made his rise to fame of interest were the complexities of his national identity and ethnic origin and the manner in which his pro-fessional debut coincided with a specific conjuncture in the history of ethnic minorities in the UK, pulled into crisis by the events of 7 July.

Khan represents an incredibly complex figure in British contempo-rary popular culture. The media coverage of his first professional fight was delivered in the context of the London bombings and the wider crisis in the ideology of multiculturalism that exists in the shadow cast by such horrific events. The events in 2005 caused fissures between perceptions of Britishness (and more specifically Englishness) and the inclusiveness of various ethnic minorities in the UK's wider civil society. Reports of increased racial confrontations and attacks up and down the UK, the introduction of expedient legislative measures to tighten up national security and immigration combined with wider public debates on British citizenship and its conduit responsibilities. Khan's reaction to this crisis – and of the media coverage of his com-ments and boxing display – represented something of an enforced public display of Britishness (and perhaps, northern working-class Englishness). He made several public statements affirming his British Muslim identity and his family and entourage followed suit with Union Jacks stitched together with the flag of Pakistan. It all seemed like an immediate antidote to the derailing of any confidence in the concept of multiculturalism and the multiculturalist ideal. In many respects, Khan's emerging career in boxing had come at a critical con-juncture in identity politics in the UK and coming from the arena of sport opened up interesting vistas from which to analyse how the play of historical events and the processes of inter-cultural exchange impact on debates of race, ethnicity and national identity (Burdsey, 2007).

British Boxing's 'Golden Boy'?

In a study of Latino boxer and world middleweight champion Oscar De La Hoya, Delgado (2005) provides a fascinating case study on the complexities of media narratives of boxers as sports stars. In particular, in relation to the trajectory of Khan's own story, Delgado unpicks the construction of national identity, focusing on the ways in which representations of De La Hoya problematize the narrative of national hero due to the tension created by two competing discourses: ethnicity and mainstream white American sport. In other words, De La Hoya's public persona, as constructed by the mainstream US media, has been constructed in a way that suppresses his Latino and Mexican roots in favour of how he has become the 'model professional', assimilated into some perceived notion of what an all-American sports star should be. As Delgado notes, this view of the boxer contrasts with the media that addresses a Latino audience:

> Despite his roots and his success both in and out of the ring, De La Hoya occupies an interesting position as a subject constructed by and reflected in both the sports and entertainment media as well as the Latino community. (Delgado, 2005: 199)

As a successful multi-millionaire boxer – with all the luxurious trappings – De La Hoya is 'located at the crossroads between ethnic and cultural pride and assimilation' (Delgado, 2005: 199). Does Khan's rise to prominence present a similar divergent crossroads in identity politics? Or are media representations of Khan settled in his self-proclaimed dual identity of British Muslim?

Khan's initial moment of fame and notoriety came in September 2004 during the summer Olympics in Athens. As each stage of the tournament passed, the BBC's focus on the seventeen-year-old intensified as one by one he carved out convincing victories against far more experienced opposition. Khan did not appear on the scene without his own reputation. He had become the World Junior Champion earlier that year and as Britain's only boxing entry into the Games carried the medal hopes of a nation with a long history of success in amateur boxing. Media attention on Khan grew exponentially with each round leading to extensive coverage before, during and after the Olympic semi-final. His new success prompted BBC correspondent Gary Richardson to find out more about the 'golden boy' from Bolton, specifically focusing on the role of his family in supporting his sporting achievement.

Although there is nothing unusual in television's search for a wider cast of characters to help embroider the narrative of sports stars, the BBC's story behind the story took a deliberate approach to reveal Khan's father's British patriotism for his adopted nation. Mr Khan wore a Union Jack waistcoat, an important nationalistic motif, in a very public display of Britishness, but this symbolic gesture was placed in a wider context of references to the Pakistani diaspora with many of Khan's supporters waving Pakistani flags or wearing the deep green cricket jerseys of their ancestral home. As Khan made his way to the Olympic final to face the Cuban gold medallist Mario Kindalan, the dual identities of the boxer's entourage was writ large, parading with pride their South Asian and Muslim identity at every opportunity at the same time as supporting a British boxer competing for gold in the spotlight of the entire British sports media.

Violent and ethnic masculine identities in boxing

To understand how Khan's identity has been interpreted and constructed by the media, it is valuable to note points raised by both Delgado (2004) and Woodward (2004) who highlight the various audiences or constituencies interested in boxing. On the one hand, media coverage is clearly aimed at the sports fan, the aficionado. The journalist's codes of factual reporting and the sports broadcaster's conventions of realism cope adequately with this element. More nuanced is the media's construction of masculine discourses to appeal to either the voyeuristic desires of a wide, predominantly male audience or the 'blood lust' of a particular community of viewers who enjoy the celebration of violent masculinity. Boxing clearly represents a form of sanctioned violent masculinity, and even though women's boxing has grown since the 1990s (Hargreaves, 1997), its appeal remains staunchly masculine and part of male sports subculture.

The prescribed masculine values of boxing are made a little more complex when the main protagonists are African American, Afro-Caribbean or South Asian. African American boxers are classically characterized as either the 'dark menace' by the majority white population of America and Europe or held up as fantastic examples of racial harmony in spite of overwhelming social evidence to the contrary (Sugden, 1996). Ever since Joe Louis broke the colour bar on boxing in the 1930s black boxers have dominated professional boxing, particularly at the heavyweight division, and have been accepted as occupying this terrain of popular culture. South Asian sportsmen occupy a slightly different terrain and do not as easily find themselves placed on such a prominent cultural platform as their black counterparts. Although Khan could, and did, position himself in the context of other successful Muslim boxers – notably the brash British boxer Naseem Hamed (of Yemeni descent) and the more globally prominent

Muhammad Ali (his 'hero') – the kind of masculine traits associated with Khan's South Asian ethnic identity are more likely to conjure stereotyped images of passivity and cultural compliance.

Although Khan's trade as a boxer inherently meant he had to display his own brand of violent masculinity, it had been notable that his performances, both in and out of the ring, were marked by a calm, considered professionalism. This mirrors Delgado's analysis of De La Hoya who, like Khan, during his meteoric rise from the amateur ranks to professional boxing was Knicknamed the 'Golden Boy' and was viewed as eschewing the dominant practices of Latin boxers with a dogged, bruising and battling style for a more precise, clinical, tactically reserved style of fighting. Like De La Hoya, Khan occupies a complex position – 'the crossroads' mentioned by Delgado above. Both boxers embody a professionalized violent masculinity that restricts their ethnic and racialized roles.

Post 9/11 and in the context of the Western world's 'War on Terror' there has been a very pronounced demonization and, in some quarters, virulent hostility and suspicion of Muslim communities and the Muslim faith. In the UK this has manifested itself in a deep questioning of the loyalty of British Asians, in particular Muslims, to the British state and their role as citizens. Protagonists of such prejudicial and racial hatred point to a series of conflicts associated with the British Asian community from the Rushdie affair to urban disturbances in Oldham and Bradford and latterly the bombings in London in July 2005. As Modood (1992) has noted, British Asians have often had to confront racism on two fronts, in terms of colour and culture, and this has made positive public expressions of dual identities – in Khan's case Britishness and Pakistani – all the more difficult and contentious. Khan's entry into the world of British professional sport and the media attention it garners has, arguably, led him and his family towards anglicization and cultural assimilation in their attempts to gain wider public acceptance. Overt displays of Britishness by Khan and his entourage may be deeply meant and felt but, as the overtly racist comment cited earlier in the chapter, which appeared on a Far Right bulletin board indicate, such displays can be viewed with suspicion by some sections of the dominant white population. As Lewis (2008: 300) has noted, post 9/11, although diversity and difference are to be celebrated, 'at what point does difference become a separation that is predisposed to hatred, social fragmentation and political violence?'

Sport, in this sense, becomes a site of cultural and political conflict. On the one hand it can become a conduit for social cohesion and consensus and, by and large, is represented as such in the discourses of mainstream sports journalism and broadcasting. On the other, it becomes a site for ethnic stereotyping, overt exclusionary nationalism and outright racism, increasingly present on the margins of the media, particularly the Internet.

Sectarianism, sport and popular culture

John Brewer (1992: 353) has noted the parallels and differences between sectarianism and racism. He argues that, unlike racism, sectarianism remains a relatively undertheorized area of study, partly because of the supposedly declining importance of religion in Western societies.

> Instances where religion remains a potent social marker are usually marginalised by being seen as a third world problem (India) or as an aberration of modernity (the Lebanon, Northern Ireland).

He goes on to argue that sectarianism, like racism, operates at three interrelated levels: in the domain of ideas, in individual behaviour and when its values become embedded in the social structure of any society. There is obviously a linkage between these levels. For example, in a country where there are discriminatory laws this is liable to both reinforce and legitimize individual personal prejudices.

The symbolic and material support for either Rangers or Celtic offers the possibility of sectarianism operating at all three levels described by Brewer above (the domain of ideas, behaviour and a set of values which have become naturalized in social structures).

Sectarianism then can be viewed as a system of beliefs through which a social group differentiates itself from a perceived other, primarily through religious difference. In their study of the role of sport in a divided Ireland, Sugden and Bairner (1993) argue that:

> Sectarianism can be best understood in two overlapping ways: first as a symbolic labelling process through which community divisions are defined and maintained, and second, as an ideological justification for discrimination, community conflict and political violence. (Sugden and Bairner, 1993: 15)

They argue persuasively that religious labelling becomes part of a wider semiotic system through which, in revealing one's sporting preferences, at the same moment one marks out a position for oneself on the complex terrain of political/cultural/religious affiliation in Northern Ireland.

Being labelled Catholic or Protestant also identifies one with a range of political and cultural positions which are triggered by having a religious label attached to oneself or one's support for a particular sport or football club highlighted. For example, for someone from Northern Ireland to show support for the games of the GAA (Gaelic Athletic Association) immediately identifies them as having nationalist and possibly republican sympathies.

To play cricket in Northern Ireland would place one as a middle-class Unionist, to support Linfield FC as a working-class loyalist and so on. Cronin (1997) has argued that even in a sport such as boxing, which at first glance may appear to straddle both communities, the wider political and cultural conflict ultimately impinges also.

In addition, the centrality of religious labelling in collective identity formation and its attendant connection with support for either Celtic or Rangers is still very much a part of everyday experience for many people. To know which team (Celtic or Rangers) a person supports becomes 'an oblique mechanism for determining a person's religious persuasion' (Sugden and Bairner, 1993: 16).

Brewer (1992: 360) suggests that in Northern Ireland your religious persuasion is also triggered by, among other things, the name of the school you have attended, your place of residence and even your name. While Scotland is obviously not Northern Ireland and has suffered none of the violence and political upheaval associated with that part of the world, a combination of the proximity of the north of Ireland to Scotland and the close historical and cultural links between them – not least in terms of shifts in population which have occurred across the Irish Sea – have resulted in religious labelling and aspects of sectarianism (both at the symbolic and material level) having an impact on Scottish society and sport.

The residual legacy of this relationship provides a specific sport–media environment which doesn't exist anywhere else in Britain. It is simply unimaginable that England's largest selling newspaper would lead with a story about the alleged extreme Loyalist paramilitary links of an international football player. Nor is this type of story uncommon in the Scottish media. When former Celtic and Northern Ireland international Neil Lennon (now on Celtic's coaching staff) was attacked as he walked home after a night out following an Old Firm game in 2008 it made front-page news across Scotland. Strathclyde police confirmed that the attack on Lennon – a Catholic who stopped playing for Northern Ireland after death threats – was motivated by sectarianism.

It appears that religious labelling or affiliations associated with these clubs play a key role in attracting a specific kind of support, while at the same time this process reinforces a distinctive identity between supporters and their club.

Sport, ethnicity and media bias

The extent to which the media play a role in their treatment of sport in either reinforcing, challenging and perhaps at times even illuminating the issues around sporting identity and conflict is in fact quite underdeveloped in studies of sport. Research carried out by one of the authors in Glasgow and Liverpool found a wide perception of bias among supporters of Celtic against the club and its supporters among sections of the media, the press in particular. The issue of media bias was also an issue widely commented upon by the interview groups in Glasgow.

The 'Old Firm' link with sports journalism in Scotland is interesting and highlights some of the geographical problems faced by journalists working within a relatively small sporting environment (see Chapter 9). The degree of attention devoted in the press and broadcasting to the 'Old Firm' is a source of constant irritation to football supporters outside the west of Scotland.

Of course, this does not necessarily mean that a wider systematic bias based on a wider discrimination against Catholics exists. However, it does point up how perceptions and issues of sporting and ethnic identities (Catholic/Irish Protestant/Scottish), often assumed unimportant elsewhere in Britain, are played out in part through the interaction of media discourses and individual and collective experiences.

Conclusion

Issues of race, ethnicity and national identities are, of course, deeply interwoven, at some times and in specific contexts more so than at others, for example when Cronin (1997: 144) argues that the more general principle that sport can bring people together is only useful when placed within the specific wider political and cultural context. Thus in a politically and culturally divided Northern Ireland, we see a wider sectarian culture impact on the image of even such a sport as boxing.

Until there is a strategy that addresses and resolves the competing traditions of Loyalism and Nationalism, sport generally, and sports men and women specifically, will always have a confused and problematic identity thrust upon them.

This wider argument for structural change also finds an echo in some commentators looking at the media profile of black and Asian sports people: that, while positive images are better than either being ignored or treated negatively, they do not guarantee deeper or more structural shifts which would facilitate a less racist society.

However, the situation is both complex and fluid. Bairner (1999: 14), in his work on the relationship between the media and sport in Northern Ireland since the Good Friday Peace Agreement (1998), suggests that the changing print media treatment of sports, historically divided along sectarian lines, 'far from being ephemeral in terms of the politics of the north of Ireland reflects, contributes to and . . . at times challenges influential social and political trends'.

What is being suggested here is the role that the media can play in creating climates of opinion, within which wider and more deeply rooted political and structural change may occur, or at least suffer from less opposition. We suggest that this is one possibility held out by a more accurate and sensitive treatment by the media of the issues centred around race and ethnicity in sport. This may remain difficult to achieve given the at times too cosy relationship between the media and sporting industries.

In the past the media's treatment of black and Asian sports people in various contexts has been either absent or stereotypical. As John Hoberman has argued:

> Such ideas about the 'natural' physical talents of dark-skinned peoples, and the media-generated images that sustain them, probably do more than anything else in our public life to encourage the idea that blacks and whites are biologically different in a meaningful way . . . The world of sport has thus become an image factory that disseminates and even intensifies our racial preoccupations. (Hoberman, 1997: xxiii)

As a starting point a greater scrutiny by the media of areas of discrimination in sporting culture and a willingness to connect this with society at large would be useful. Media should also expose the reluctance which some sports governing bodies appear to display in either acknowledging or dealing with any problem they may have. This was precisely the attitude of journalist Richard Williams (2008) when reflecting on the racist abuse aimed at Lewis Hamilton. 'What this proves', he suggested, 'is that if you really want to put a stop to something, you have to take real action.' He went on to warn, 'there will be no surprise if Hamilton is in for similar treatment when the Spanish grand prix takes place at the same circuit on April 27.' In the end, the race appeared to go on without incident – perhaps because of the intense media focus on the issue and in spite of 'toothless warnings' issued by the president of the FIA Max Mosley.

Chapter 7

Playing the Game:
Media Sport and Gender

Victoria Pendleton's Secrets
She's a world champion and favourite to win an Olympic gold medal in
Beijing, so why has Victoria Pendleton had to resort to posing in a black
dress with a spanner in her hand? (*Sunday Times*, 6 January 2008)

Introduction

Sport has always been a sexual battlefield. The issue of gender and
the representation of biological difference between the sexes have
long been central to our perceptions of sport in society. The media
representation of sport is no different and, as this chapter sets out
to argue, no analysis of media sport would be complete without an
understanding of how patriarchal structures are constructed through
media institutions and their coverage of sport.

Equally, no understanding of how patriarchy is reinforced in capitalist societies can ignore the importance of sport in communicating
familiar stereotypes of men and women and their physical abilities.
Indeed, the historical tendency towards the invisibility of women in
media sport has suggested a whole field of public life in which women
have been marginalized. To what extent is this critique still valid as we
move towards the end of the first decade of the twenty-first century?

Playing the game

Women's participation in sport has been blocked on several levels
throughout the history of modern sporting practice. Whether as
athletes, coaches, administrators or sports journalists, women have
found it difficult to establish the right and recognition of their place
in the sporting world. The notion that there are favoured or permitted

sports for women to participate in has been well documented by feminist sociologists and historians of sport (see Williams et al., 1985; Hargreaves, 1997) while the work of Messner (2007) has demonstrated that despite growing participation rates in sport by women, this change has not been reflected in attendant media coverage of women in sport.

Political struggles to gain equality in sport have been fought and won since the turn of the nineteenth century, most visibly seen in the painstakingly gradual gains women have made in the Olympic movement. The social movement for gender equality in sport has proved a valuable terrain for liberal feminist activity and reform throughout the twentieth century. However, serious feminist critiques of sport did not gain any momentum until the 1970s and 1980s, when challenges to the hegemonic dominance of men's sporting structures and cultural practices emerged from feminist critiques of Marxist sociology (Hall, 1985) and cultural studies (Willis, 1982; Hargreaves, 1986).

What the various contemporary feminist studies of sport reveal is that sport remains an incredibly conservative domain for the representation of men and women. Moreover, feminist scholars of sport have repeatedly confirmed that differences in sporting chances are a matter of power, not only across genders but within them. It has been argued that the sex/gender system as it is reproduced in sport is one site where patriarchal cultural hegemony can be challenged and that it is important to address the possibility that transforming sport may help to break down stereotypical representations of the sexes as they are framed by the media.

The key to the political challenge to male dominance and female subordination in sport has been the deconstruction of biological values and principles formulated and articulated in sport. The Victorian legacy of modern sport has ensured that concerns about women's medical vulnerability, emotional nature and social limitations have endured at a very banal level. Essentialist notions of men and women are manifested more frequently through sport than in any other public domain and this differentiation of physical prowess is confirmed by the disproportionate media treatment of men's sport over women's sport (Creedon, 1994; Bernstein, 2002).

This chapter sets out to examine the role of women in media sports' institutions and the representations of women in sport. We are also interested in integrating the study of male patriarchy in media sport, and in particular the importance of violence in male sport cultures and the media celebration of masculinity and manliness.

Representing female sports and sportspeople

Women who wish to stake out a career in professional sport often face more obstacles than their male colleagues. The idea of women being actively involved in sport, either as participants or spectators, appears to remain unacceptable for sections of the male-dominated sports industry. This is more directly evident in some sports than others. Broadcaster Beverely Turner's (2004) book documenting her time working in and around the F1 motor racing circuit is both a compelling, and, from a journalistic perspective, brave account of the strident sexism that pervades that sport and much of its attendant media coverage.

In his examination of sport in postwar Britain Martin Polley has noted how this period

> has seen sport continue to act as a location for the display and negotia-tion of gender politics. In line with changes in the political and economic spheres, sport as a physical activity has provided women in search of equality and recognition a cultural sphere in which to test traditional assumptions based on physical difference, and the popularity . . . of women's rugby, football, cricket, athletics and even boxing demonstrates a change in the wider discourse of gender relations. (Polley, 1998: 109)

While there have been broader social shifts in gender relations, resist-ance to women's sport is still evident, and as often as not it takes place off the actual field of play and is embedded in the mostly male subcul-ture which still surrounds many aspects of the sporting industry.

It is also not only athletes who can suffer discrimination. In 1998, for example, Rachel Anderson, the only female football agent working in the English game, was banned from attending the Professional Footballers Association's award ceremony in London after being invited by a number of the players she represents. The PFA stated that for twenty-five years the ceremony had been a men-only evening! Despite the advances made over the years, it is still routine in 2008 to find women golfers having difficulty in being granted the facilities and rights offered to male colleagues.

Despite negative attitudes from some quarters, significant changes are taking place. Backed by a FIFA initiative in 1995 to both recognize and encourage the development of women's football, participation rates in the game have grown dramatically. Simmons (2007) notes how the numbers of registered women football teams in England grew from

55,500 in 2001 to 147,302 in 2007, with 1.1 million girls and 250,000 women playing the sport. The Women's FIFA World Cup has gone from strength to strength since its inception in the 1990s. Indeed in some countries such as Germany, World Cup success has seen very healthy television viewing figures, with 12 million watching the 2007 World Cup final held in China between the Germans and Brazil.

More women are also watching sport on television, with the dedicated subscriber sports channel Sky Sport 1 recording a 30 per cent female viewership in 1998 (BSkyB Annual Report, 1998: 29). These women who are watching sport on television are significantly watching male sport, as female sport remains dramatically underrepresented on television in the UK. As Pam Creedon (1994: 172) has noted:

> In sports, more often than not, underlying the 'importance' of an event and its audience 'interest' is how much money the sport earns for the athlete or team and the media institution itself. The more revenue the sport and sporting event produces, the more likely it is to receive more significant coverage.

This appears to be increasingly the case in American television. In the States there is a developing awareness among television sports executives of the potential advertising revenue to be gained in targeting a female sports audience. In the UK coverage of female sport on television remains limited – estimates put Sky's coverage in 2008 of female sport at about 4 per cent of its sporting output (Women's Sport and Fitness Foundation, 2008), although the women's FA Cup Final is now regularly covered on BBC television with audience figures ranging from 2.1 million in 2006 to 1.5 million in 2008.

In the US, Val Ackerman is president of the Women's National Basketball Association (WNBC) and has been at the forefront in driving the television profile of that sport in the US. Building on the success in television rating terms of the women's game in the 1996 Atlanta Olympics, they rescheduled their season for television and in the process gained good rating figures which in turn have attracted major sponsors keen to access an audience which accounts for 50 per cent of the retail sports dollars spent in the US market (*SportBusiness International*, February 1999, p. 10).

It is important to recognize the differing roots of the game in the US and the UK, with the game being deeply embedded in the American college system. However, other sports such as women's golf are also enjoying a higher profile in the US, again in part driven by the economics of the sports business with sponsors keen to gain access to a potentially underdeveloped female market.

When the World Cup was held in the US, corporate sponsors from, among others, Adidas, Coca-Cola and MasterCard showed little hesitation in getting involved. In addition, since 1997 in America there has existed a professional women's football league, while almost 40 per cent of the 8.5 million Americans playing football are women (*Guardian*, 10 December 1998). As a result, a growing number of women who wish to play the game professionally are being lured to the US on scholarship schemes.

There is also the issue of the financial rewards which flow from sporting success. Even in sports such as athletics which allow a substantial degree of media exposure for female performers, it appears that male sportstars are better rewarded than their female counterparts. In part this becomes part of a circuit of promotion which we outlined in Chapter 3, where sports which fail to attract television exposure find difficulty in getting sponsors on board, which in turn make it less likely that 'stars' will be created and given the media exposure which generates the accompanying lucrative endorsement portfolio (see Chapter 5).

Gendered accounts of sport

In the UK the explosion in print media coverage of sport during the 1990s (examined in Chapter 9) has not resulted in a growing profile for female sport on the back pages. The cultural capital (Bourdieu, 1988) of women sports performers is considerably less than that of men on the back pages of daily newspapers. In research carried out in 1995, Samantha Smith (1995) demonstrated that on average about 3 per cent of the space devoted to sport in both national and Sunday newspapers during November of that year was given over to sport involving women. Over a decade later, while the volume of sports coverage has grown, a survey in 2008 indicated that just 2 per cent of articles and 1 per cent of images in the sports pages of the UK print media were found to be devoted to covering female athletes and women's sport (Women's Sport and Fitness Foundation, 2008). While this is likely to increase during the track and field athletics season or the Wimbledon tennis fortnight in July each year, it remains an extremely low figure.

While this trend was also commented on by Biscomb et al. (1998), who examined the differing trends in treatment by the print media of women in sport between 1984 and 1994. They also identified an increase in print-media coverage of sport, but an actual decrease in the percentage coverage devoted to women's sport. They did, however, note that 'the type of description [given to female athletes] was directed away from appearance [and] towards [their] performance' (Biscomb et al., 1998: 145). They also noted the ways in which men's and women's sport are treated differently in terms of the language used to describe and make sense of them. While they also argue that the language used in coverage of men's sport has also changed since 1984, the notion of a gendered treatment of sports coverage remains valid. More recent work by King (2007) has examined this area in British newspaper coverage of the Olympic Games from 1948 to 2004. He also argues that there has been a lessening of the sexism evident in the coverage, more specifically in the 2004 coverage from Athens, and concludes that at these Games:

> It was shown that female athletes received more article, headline and photographic coverage than their participation rate of approximately 44 per cent. Although negative commentaries were found, the majority of the coverage celebrated and applauded their female athletic achievement. (King, 2007: 198)

From a US perspective Tuggle et al. (2007) have argued that in television terms, NBC's coverage of female athletes in the 2004 Games was more than fair, in volume terms, given their medal success and participation rates. However, they also suggested that:

> Further analysis reveals a pattern that observers of sports coverage have noted for decades. Typically, for female athletes to garner media coverage, even in the Olympics, they must be involved in socially acceptable individual sports rather than in team sports. Women who take part in sports that involve either power or hard body contact are particularly unlikely to receive media coverage. (Tuggle et al., 2007: 67)

Debates about gender and sporting representations can also be more complex than they appear.

Wensing and Bruce (2003) examined media coverage of the female athlete Cathy Freeman during the 2000 Sydney Olympics. They found that in this case gender was not the overriding frame of identity in media coverage suggesting that:

> Coverage during international sporting events such as the Olympic Games may be less likely to be marked by gendered (or racialized discourses) or narratives than reporting on everyday sports, at least for

sportswomen whose success is closely tied to a nation's sense of self.
(Wensing and Bruce, 2003: 393)

In this assertion they echo earlier arguments to this effect made by
Blain et al. (1993) and by ourselves when we examined the intersection of ethnicity, masculinity and nationalism evident in coverage of
the British boxer Frank Bruno (Boyle and Haynes, 2000), although,
as we argue below when we briefly examine coverage of the 2008
Wimbledon tennis grand slam tournament, narratives built around
national identity and gender can also sit equally side by side in particular forms of coverage.

It is clear then that there is a highly gendered treatment given to
female athletes – and, as we see below, sometimes even by female
journalists – when they do appear in print. While this appears to be
improving, the overarching maleness of sporting culture in Britain still
clearly comes through in a number of ways.

Examples are not difficult to find. Tennis has also been a field of
sport where the attractiveness or 'lady-like' temperament of women
players is central to media narratives. From Chris Evert Lloyd to
Martina Hingis, grace and finesse in the women's game have been
courted with more praise and deemed more feminine than the power
games of Martina Navratilova or Venus Williams. The emphasis on
women's bodies is also used to question the legitimacy of muscle tone
and evidence of classically 'masculine' body traits such as big shoulders
and biceps. Vincent et al. (2007) examined British newspaper narratives
around the Wimbledon tennis grand slam tournament in 2000. They
concluded that the mostly male journalists 'devalued, marginalized
and trivialized the athleticism of the female players'. Another example
of the unreceptiveness to women changing their bodies is given by *The
Times* sports feature writer Simon Barnes in this review of Mary Pierce
after the French tennis star transformed her physical appearance:

> Now she has changed tack. She has grown a set of quite terrifying masculine appendages. Phwoar, look at those muscles! Suddenly, bursting
> out of her skimpy tennis tops, we have a pair of arms like Boris Becker's
> thighs. It is like the Incredible Hulk in drag and slow motion. (*The
> Times*, 5 May 1999)

The point is that often female athletes find the frame of reference
within which they are positioned relates to their sexuality and their
appearance in a way male sports people are rarely defined. Another

trait is to relate women athletes to their domestic/family environment; while this may be important in some cases, it clearly represents a gendered approach in the treatment of male and female sports people.

British female boxer Cathy Brown is clear that sports women do not compete on a level playing field with men in terms of commercial sponsorship and media coverage. She also argues that:

> Women are pressurized into doing sexy media shots and dressing in a way that will encourage media attention and make them more appealing to the male eye (men constitute the majority of sporting audiences, we cannot get media coverage simply because we are brilliant at our sport. [...] Anna Kournikova, who in all honesty was not great at her sport, managed to get sponsorship. Why? Because she is beautiful, sexy and prepared to show half-naked images of herself. (Brown, 2004: 3)

Brown was making this argument about the body image role in the wider media representations of women in sport in 2004. In the Olympic year of 2008, have things changed?

On your bike . . .

The case of British sprint track cycling world champion Victoria Pendleton illustrates some of the dilemmas still confronting female athletes, in particular those competing in sports which do not always enjoy the high media profile of, say, football or tennis. Pendleton is one of Britain's most successful female athletes. In 2005, the track sprint cyclist won the gold medal at the World Championships and followed this with two further medals at the 2006 Commonwealth Games, three more gold medals at the 2007 World Championships and a further two medals at the 2008 championships. Despite being named *Sunday Times* and Sports Journalists Association Sportswoman of the Year in 2007, she was not even nominated for the BBC Sports Personality of the Year award. In part this reflected the skewed nature of such an award and the importance that mainstream media profile usually plays on promoting the winner of the BBC award.

It also raised the issue of whether undoubted athletic prowess and world-class achievement is enough to move your profile into the mainstream media if you are engaged in a sport that lies on the periphery of television's interest. Pendleton then in part set about raising that profile through a set of promotional glamour shots where she posed in a black dress, heels and in one shot with a spanner over her shoulder.

When asked by Paul Kimmage in a *Sunday Times* interview why she had a spanner, she replied, 'I was fixing my wheel' (*Sunday Times,* 6 January 2008).

She then appeared naked on her bike for the front cover of the *Observer Sports Magazine* in March 2008. For Pendleton, who saw the photograph as mimicking Annie Leibovitz's famous photogragh of the Tour de France winner Lance Armstrong, she was clear about why he choose to do the shoot. Speaking in a pre-Beijing 2008 interview in the *Observer* newspaper she noted how:

> Some people were disappointed in me, like my dentist, but I did think about it. I spoke to my mum and dad first, and I thought it would raise my profile and the profile of cycling as a consequence, let alone all the other reasons – positive body image, doing it because I have already achieved something wonderful, doing it because I can. I'll look back at it when I'm 70 and think, 'I was in good shape'.

She went on to discuss the importance of the relationship between body shape, sports and perceptions of femininity.

> For me, all the women seen as successful in track cycling had a masculine image, which was what you have to be if you want to be successful – you have to become androgynous or beefy and slightly aggressive. It doesn't have to be that way. It's almost like it's not considered very feminine to be competitive. No one encouraged me to consider sport as a career option. It wasn't like it was avoided, it never even came up. I enjoy it, I tried hard, and it was important to me, but the boys were encouraged to do county cricket or athletics. (*Observer,* 27 July 2008)

Subsequently, it would not be uncommon to find Pendleton referred to in the press as the 'golden girl' of the British Olympic Team GB. Indeed, on her return from Beijing as Olympic Champion, Pendleton noted how being 'constantly highlighted as the golden girl' brought with it an extra burden and pressure to succeed (*The Times,* 13 September 2008).

Some commentators such as Richard Williams, sportswriter of the *Guardian* newspaper, felt it was a pity that a hugely successful female athlete needed to play 'the fame game' through selling aspects of her sexuality through media imaging. What it did highlight was the important role that champions like Pendleton and other top cyclists such as individual pursuit athlete Rebecca Romero have in encouraging women into the sport. Romero has appeared in media as diverse as the *News of the World* newspaper (in a bikini shot) through to BBC Radio 4's *Women's Hour,* in attempts to raise both her individual and the sports profile. Interestingly it was Romero, rather than Pendleton, who appeared on the front cover of *The Times* magazine (12 July 2008) under the headline 'Girl Power: Why Women are Britain's best bet in Beijing'. This feature focused on eleven of Team GB's best female medal hopes, with pen pictures and a double-page photo shoot of the athletes in their sportsgear. Amazingly, Romero then appeared in an almost identical pose (naked on a bike) for an interview with *The Times* (2 August 2008) newspaper the week before the Beijing Games started ('Romero body language suggests that she was right to accept ticket to ride').

What these examples highlight is that for those female athletes from sports who do not enjoy a high media profile then managing their media profile and playing the image game remains one way to increase your earning capacity. Pendleton is now managed by the Professional Sports Partnership agency and as long as success continues on the track, away from the sporting arena she will clearly use her increased media profile as a way of entering the media mainstream and possibly extending her career in this area when her elite sports career comes to an end.

Meanwhile at Wimbledon . . .

When fourteen-year-old Laura Robson won the Junior Wimbledon tennis title in 2008, she became the first British winner of this tournament since 1984. The media coverage of her win was extensive in the UK and offers a brief example of the interplay between discourses of national identity and gender that get articulated through sports coverage. The British media are largely indifferent to tennis for most of the year. Newspaper coverage is at best patchy of major tournaments around the world, athough the recent rise in the profile of Andy Murray has increased the level of coverage somewhat. Free-to-air television also largely ignores a sport that is increasingly played around the year and across the globe. However, for two weeks every summer the Wimbledon grand slam tournament dominates the BBC schedules and its various platforms and begins a seemingly annual discourse about the state of British tennis and the lack of credible home-grown talent to challenge at the elite end of the game.

The media discourses surrounding the success of Laura Robson captured both the heightened status given to Wimbledon as a marker of British national identity (although given its London location and its organization by the All England Lawn Tennis Association, this identity has always been bound up with more specific aspects of English identity) and the media's fixation with a home-grown success story. From the broadsheet *Sunday Times* (6 July 2008) front page ('At Last! A Brit wins Wimbledon') to the popular end of the market and the *Sunday Mirror's* (6 July 2008) back-page splash, 'Wimbledon SHOCK: Brit Wins Single Title (Honest)', the coverage was extensive.

The fact that Robson was born in Australia and only recently acquired a British passport proved little hinderance in the media classifying her as a 'Brit'. *The Sunday Times*, with no apparent irony, could tell us that she may be, 'Australian-born but [is] very much a British citizen after moving to England as a six-year old and getting a UK passport last year' (6 July 2008), while at least the *Independent on Sunday* had the good grace to acknowledge the irony of the situation. David Randall wrote:

> Of course, there are some who have looked at Laura's genealogy and suggested that there may be grounds for some doubt about the extent to which she is totally British. They say her parents are Australian, her birthplace Australian, her early childhood was spent in Singapore, and her coach is Dutch. But we're claiming her. She lives in Wimbledon, can walk to the All England club, trains at the British National Tennis Centre, and represents the UK. Besides, we need her. So there. (*Independent on Sunday*, 6 July 2008)

This was in marked contrast to the media comments made during this same summer about the inclusion and performance of Darren Pattinson for the English national cricket team in a Test match against South Africa.

Pattinson, born in Australia, was a surprise inclusion which led to various commentaries from, among others, the BBC's cricket correspondents and a former England captain to lament in various ways his lack of passion in playing cricket for England given that he had been brought up in Australia. It was left to former England captain and now *The Times's* chief cricket writer Michael Atherton to bring some semblance of reflection on what became a heated media debate. It is worth quoting at length. He argued:

> That background, rather than personal and professional pride, is at the heart of performance is an old argument and one that has been levelled at any number of supposedly 'non-English' players. In its most extreme

form, the question of national pride, performance and being 'unequivocal Englishmen' was asked by Robert Henderson years ago in an article in *Wisden Cricket Monthly* in 1995 titled 'Is it in the Blood?' Devon Malcolm and Phillip DeFreitas sued, successfully.

The idea that an English upbringing makes for greater commitment in the middle has never struck me as having one grain of truth in it. It certainly did not strike me as particularly relevant when Robin Smith, who was brought up in South Africa, was being carried down the stairs on a stretcher at Old Trafford in 1995, his cheekbone bloodied and smashed to bits by a bouncer from Ian Bishop, the West Indies fast bowler. England were subsiding at the time; from memory, we were four down chasing a smallish target and Smith refused to be taken to hospital until it was clear that victory had been won and that he would not be needed to bat again. That was commitment of the deepest, most desperate kind. [. . .] The question is not one of upbringing but commitment. If Pattinson stays for a short time with Nottinghamshire, returns to Australia with his England cap, never to be seen again, his selection will leave a sour taste. But opportunity and choice should never be frowned upon. If he makes a commitment here, he should be welcomed.

On the basis that it is where you are brought up that counts, England have assimilated South Africans (Allan Lamb, Smith, Pietersen), Zimbabweans (Graeme Hick), Australians (Ambrose, the Hollioake brothers, Geraint Jones) and any number of West Indians (Gladstone Small, Ellcock, Roland Butcher) over past decades. That is not a roll call of shame, but a list of which to be proud. (*The Times,* 24 July 2008)

No such concerns regard a *successful* sporting athlete such as Laura Robson, or 'Laura, Princess of Wimbledon' as the *Independent on Sunday* (6 July 2008) titled its front-page photo story of her win. Across much of the coverage, although most of the journalists covering her success were male, there were notable exceptions, including Eleanor Preston in the *Guardian*, a paper which also carried a column by former child tennis star Tracy Austin in which she urged the British to leave Robson alone if they really want to nurture a long-term success story.

Women taking control?

There are changes taking place, slowly, in what is perhaps the key battleground in the struggle over representation and role models: the news room. The last decade or so has seen the welcome growth in female sports journalists in both the print and broadcast media, although it is generally accepted by female journalists that the former remains a more difficult arena for women to establish themselves in. It is also true that they remain a minority among media workers who produce sport across media platforms.

BBC Radio 5 Live, the news and sports station, has also proved to be an important media outlet in promoting female journalists who deal directly with sports coverage and there remains a substantial difference between women working in broadcasting and the more closed world of male sports journalism. While there is a growing number of female journalists working in sport in both broadsheet and popular newspapers, competition for women remains particularly fierce at the tabloid end of the market, where sport has traditionally been characterized as being a male preserve, covered by men, talking to a male audience. In her 1995 survey Smith (1995: 37) suggested that 'it would appear that the acceptance into the male-dominated field of sports journalism largely depends on the type of newspaper the female reporter works for'. It is also clear that, as the number of female sports journalists grows, however slowly, they in turn will act as role models for a new generation of female journalists who previously may have viewed sports journalism as out of bounds.

Research in 2006 (Boyle, 2006) indicated that while the number of female sports journalists remained low in the UK, those who did work in this sector, by and large, had not felt discriminated against. However, women journalists in this section of the industry are aware that any mistakes, which may be allowed to pass for a male colleague, will be seized upon by others. There is also a strong recognition that, as long as female sports do not gain more television exposure, they will remain under-reported by the print media, which assume that there is not a readership for them.

Interestingly, across the various media profiles about Victoria Pendleton (discussed above) that appeared in 2007/2008, only one, the *Observer* article that accompanied the controversial photo shoot, was written by a female journalist while the article on Rebecca Romero was written by sports journalist Owen Slot and opened with a paragragh that almost certainly would not have been written by a female journalist. His opening to the piece began:

> For the next three weeks these pages will be packed with legions of extraordinary althletes, but be assured of this: there are few you will find as arousing as Rebecca Romero. And that is not because she looks good naked on a bike. (*The Times*, 2 August 2008)

A breakthough in television sport appeared to occur in 2007 when Jacqui Oatley became the first woman commentator on the BBC's *Match of the Day* highlights programme, covering the Premiership League match between Fulham and Blackburn Rovers. However, mainstream female sports commentators remain someway off. Indeed the reaction to Oatley's appointment included remarks by former manager and now Sky TV pundit Dave Bassett which signifies the barriers that still may exist.

> I am totally against it and everybody I know in football is totally against it. The problem is that everybody is too scared to admit it. I knew this would happen eventually. The world of football is so politically correct these days. I'm completely relaxed about women presenting football shows. Women like Clare Tomlinson are very good. But commentating is different. You must have an understanding of the game and the tactics and I think in order to do that you need to have played the game. Maybe the BBC are trying to be innovative and ground-breaking but I think it undermines the credibility of the programme and when she commentates at the weekend I will not be watching. I never really agreed that we should have women officials and I don't think we should have female commentators. And my wife agrees! (*Daily Mail*, 18 April 2007)

The idea that you will have had to play the game (one assumes he means to a certain level) will be news to most male football commentators such as John Motson (BBC) or notable commentators of the past such as Brian Moore (ITV), neither of whom rose above the level of the odd kick-about in the park.

It remains the case that, until we can treat female presenters of sports programmes as simply television presenters and journalists, then much work – despite the advances being made – remains to be done.

Masculinity and sport

During the 1990s there was a concerted effort among researchers of sport to draw on critical feminist analysis in order to understand the position and representation of men in sport and the media. Increasingly attention has been placed on both the construction of male hierarchies in sport and media institutions and on the dominant discourses of men and masculinities in media representations of sporting achievement.

The focus on men has not only maintained an interest in the various disadvantages faced by women as athletes and media professionals,

but also looked more closely at the structural contexts in which 'hegemonic masculinity' (Connell, 1987) is constructed and maintained.
In particular, work by Messner and Sabo (1990), Messner (1992)
and Whannel (2002) provide historical and empirical examples of
how cultural and symbolic power in sport has been used to define
and substantiate wider beliefs about manliness. Moreover, following
Connell (1987), such studies have shown that any particular definition of masculinity in sport exists in relation to other masculinities
and notions of femininity. The problematizing of male identity, then,
has the potential to produce new avenues of research for sport–media
studies that bring together interdisciplinary concerns for the production, distribution and consumption of sporting texts and wider issues
of power in popular culture.

As we have noted above, media sport is a powerful context for the
representation of gender identities, and men's place in the world is
often framed, one way or another, by their interest or lack of interest
in sport. As this binary social code suggests, sport is heavily laden with
values of maleness. Men who abstain from male sporting subcultures
can be stereotyped as being effeminate in character, in a context where
a feminine trait is viewed as a negative, less empowering, attribute.
Male sporting subcultures, therefore, operate twin dynamics of misog-
ynist and homophobic behaviour.

As discussed in Chapter 5, the concentrated media attention on
male sports stars does much to consolidate the belief that men's physical prowess in sport has a positive and worthy function in society.
Lack of ability in sport can, where male familial and peer pressure
exists, lead to low self-esteem and a sense of failure. Similarly, if
determination to succeed in sport is found wanting, athletes may be
criticized in the media for not showing enough grit and courage to
achieve their goal.

Masculine traits, such as strength and toughness, are celebrated in
the media coverage of sport and operate to reaffirm the myths of male
prowess. Where a sportsman's masculinity is brought into question, as
by the heterosexist gesture by the Liverpool footballer Robbie Fowler
towards the Chelsea defender Graham Le Saux in March 1999, the
abuse gains its power from society's wider prejudice against gay and
lesbian groups.

Le Saux is not gay but was viewed as being effeminate because of his
middle-class origin and, what some might call more refined, cultural
tastes than the average footballer from a working-class background.
In this instance, the complex relations between gender, sexuality and

class were revealed to exemplify how masculinity is perceived differently by different socio-economic groups. Le Saux may conform more closely with the gentility of the marketing industry's middle-class 'new man', whereas Fowler, whose bravura could be said to have been born of the similarly media-constructed 'new laddism', was clearly displaying the homosexual fears of traditional male working-class culture. Once retired from the game, Le Saux reflected on the persistent rumours about his sexuality including a taunt of 'You fucking poof' from an unexpected source, David Beckham. Beckham's status as a 'gay icon' seemed contradictory to his behaviour on the pitch. As Le Saux commented:

> I could produce endless lists of players who threw a line at me about being gay, or entered into whatever level of homophobic abuse, but with him it made me stop and think, 'Wow', even somebody with his understanding doesn't get it. (Samuel, 2007)

Le Saux's recollections were published in his autobiography *Left Field: A Footballer Apart* and serialized in *The Times* in 2007. Beckham denied making the comment and Le Saux's career as a television pundit seemed to evaporate soon after.

The meaning of masculinity is also fought over in the spectating of sport. Men's conspicuous consumption of sport, in particular of football in Britain, has gone hand in hand with more varied images of men and masculinities. This can be seen during the 1980s and 1990s by the proliferation of men's 'style' magazines (Nixon, 1996) and some specific transformations in football as popular culture (Redhead, 1987, 1991).

Young male fans are not merely continuing the male secular ritual of supporting a particular football club, as their fathers and grandfathers had before them, but bring to this profane culture more promiscuous, consumerist lifestyles, where preoccupation with fashion goes hand in hand with passion for the sport. The development of 'style wars' at football grounds had their roots in the crossover between football and popular music in the late 1970s and early 1980s, but would go on to draw from a wider male popular cultural desire for designer clothing.

The shifting patterns of young men's consumption, with heavy emphasis placed on 'the look' and style of appearance, may not, however, suggest a wider transformation in sexual politics. Sport, again, plays a key role in controlling masculine relations. While fashion at the football ground may provide status and recognition among peers, it is still the assertion of hegemonic male relations through pride, honour and a sense of superiority that binds men to their particular community.

Sport and violent masculinity

Football fandom lies at the heart of the historical fear of sport-related violence (Dunning et al., 1988). Any resurgence of spectator violence in sport is often viewed through the eyes of a media moral panic. However, violence in the playing of sport is an important carrier of wider meanings of violent masculinity. Many sports are predicated on aggressive values, where competition demands violent physical contact and often the deliberate infliction of harm or injury.

The display of violence in sport is further legitimized by the voyeuristic gaze of the television camera. As Sabo and Curry Jansen (1998: 209) have observed: 'Within the commercial imperatives of television, the blood sacrifice of the athlete performs the same function that it does in dramatised violence.'

The ritualized expression and linkages of sport, masculinity and men's violence are most startlingly realized in the television coverage of boxing. Emphasis on male physical power and strength are frequent motifs of media narratives on male sport. As Connell (1997: 52) states: 'In our culture, at least, the physical sense of maleness and femaleness is central to the cultural interpretation of gender.'

The legitimacy of violence in sport, therefore, balances upon the axis of power in the gender order, where physical combat, blood and bruises are considered 'natural' for men and alien to women. As Connell and others have further concluded, the media accounts of 'natural masculinity' based on biological determinants are scientifically unfounded and fictional.

Boxing and being a man

Nowhere is the metaphor of the male body as weapon or fighting machine more evident than in the sport of boxing. Boxing has received a new level of critical analysis with interest from sociology (Wacquant, 1995; Sugden, 1996), psychology (Oates, 1994; Beattie, 1997), cultural studies (Sloop, 1997; Baker, 1997; Jefferson, 1998), feminist analysis (Hargreaves, 1997) and new sports journalism (MacRae, 1997). A theme that runs through all of these studies is the centrality of masculine identity as it is embodied through boxing.

Any critical study of boxing, then, demands an analysis of the construction of gender difference and development through sport. Boxing as an 'iconic embodiment of masculinity' can tell us much about the 'representations of the masculine body and their psychic underpinnings' (Jefferson, 1998: 78–9). Jefferson also notes that boxers, in particular Mike Tyson, came to be identified with a level of 'hardness', in terms of both 'mental' and 'physical toughness'.

This characterization of boxing as an exclusive, essentialist masculine domain, is dominated by metaphors of power, strength, ferocity of the competitive spirit and courage. These discourses are retrieved, circulated and reinforced in the media coverage of boxing. In February 1995 one of the most brutal fights to be screened on British television was fought between Nigel Benn (UK) and Gerald McLellan (USA) for the World Boxing Council (WBC) version of the 'Super-Middleweight' Championship of the World.

In the week before the fight Benn was considered the underdog, his challenger, McLellan, a man the *Observer* (19 February 1995) sports writer Kevin Mitchell proclaimed to be 'a fighter of distinctly pit-bull tendencies'. However, it was further observed that 'Benn is at his most dangerous when in trouble'. The British boxer, known as the 'Dark Destroyer', conjuring up images of 'blackness' and 'hardness', was well known for his ability to come back from the brink of defeat, having previously had well-publicized and bloody battles with the other British Super-Middleweight champion Chris Eubank. It also illustrates the complex interplay between discourses of masculinity, race and nationality. The media epithets that are frequently used to promote boxers before big fights set the scene in a gladiatorial fashion, laying emphasis on the destructive capabilities of the men involved.

In the event, Benn suffered a series of heavy blows that knocked him out of the ring in the opening round. The British boxer was continually buffeted about the ring, only denying defeat by literally scrapping for his life. McLellan appeared to be moving towards an inevitable victory until a clash of heads in the ninth round clearly distressed the American, turning the advantage to Benn. Spurred on by the partisan crowd and the injury to his opponent, Benn delivered some crunching blows that overwhelmed McLellan, causing him to drop to his knees and accept defeat by a technical knockout. As Benn celebrated his victory with the crowd, McLellan slipped into unconsciousness, ultimately to be left in a coma from which he later suffered brain damage.

Nearly 13 million viewers watched the fight live on British television on ITV, witnessing the destruction of two men – Benn was also hospitalized for observation suffering from exhaustion. The atmosphere in the arena was intense and the commentary by Reg Gutteridge and ex-professional boxer Jim Watt was equally charged with emotion after an incredible turnabout in Benn's fortunes. The fight was subsequently celebrated in the sporting press as one of the most exciting fights of the modern era. Some journalists did reflect on the brutality of the fight and struggled to equate their dependence and engagement with the sport as 'the manly art' with the concern that the horrific consequences of boxing could not be justified or legitimated.

Reflecting on the fight a year and half later, in a postscript to Benn's last fight and defeat by Steve Collins, the *Independent* boxing correspondent Harry Mullan (11 November 1996) admitted that the fight with McClellan was 'the most savage 10 rounds I have ever seen'. When Benn prematurely admitted defeat against Collins, the reaction from the crowd in the Nynex Arena in Manchester was to boo what they saw as an uncharacteristically 'unheroic' performance. Another sports journalist, Kevin Mitchell of the *Guardian*, also witnessed the McLellan fight from ringside and some years later concluded:

> At ringside, we had the luxury of reflection, however brief, and could wonder about the morality of seeing Benn and McClellan risk dying for money and a title. There are moralists who will say that is a question we should be asking before rather than during a fight. But we don't. We surrender to our weaknesses. (Mitchell, 2001a)

Gary Newbon, who presented ITV's coverage of the fight later, expressed his horror at the unravelling events and the difficulty it presented him as a professional sports broadcaster:

> My director wasn't really aware. Not his fault. So I'm saying, 'This is serious, this is really serious.' Everyone got a bit het-up and then we all realised there was a problem. We went into long-shot to get off the air. (Quoted in Mitchell, 2001a)

The media hype that framed the contest clearly prescribed a set of inflated expectations for the audience. The 'blood lust' that often generates the excitement of the crowd can at times be seen to be more harmful and destructive to the boxer than the fighter's own wilful intent to injure and be injured. The following quote from Mitchell's reflections on the fight capture the pathos of boxing quite startlingly:

The energy in the ring has travelled through the night like electricity to the crowd, who, collectively, could probably provide the material for a very acceptable orgy or riot, so high are they. This is what they paid for, this is why they came to Docklands when they could have watched the fight at home on television. This is why we fight and why we watch others who fight. At the moment of victory, you do not have to ask the question. In fact, the question is never asked. We just know. (Mitchell, 2001a)

Wacquant (1995) and Sugden (1996) have illustrated in their ethnographic studies of boxers and the culture of boxing that many pugilists are fully aware of the damage they can cause their bodies, but continue with the 'fight game' because it socially and psychologically 'inhabits' them. The sense that boxing is 'in your blood' is a common descriptor by boxing pundits to explain the self-destructive urge that appears to motivate them – self-evident in the media characterization and narratives that celebrated a 'scrapper' like Nigel Benn.

Masculine bravura and entertainment

A more cynical outlook on the profession would view it as a means to a financial end, a way out of poverty, an opportunity to enter the media spotlight. Similarly, as long as boxing entices large enough audiences, it will continue to enjoy the televisual spectacle it currently enjoys on satellite and cable networks around the world. As Bryant et al. (1998: 253) have observed with regard to world heavyweight boxing: 'violence in sports "sells"'.

Benn's fight with Collins was part of a ten-hour feast of televised boxing orchestrated on both sides of the Atlantic by the promoters Frank Warren and Don King. Promoted as 'Judgement Night', the evening comprised six world title fights, three in Manchester and three in Las Vegas. The three British fights were available to Sky Sports subscription holders. The three American fights were available on pay-per-view (ppv) on Sky Box Office for a standard price of £9.95 (rising to £14.95 on the day). An estimated 420,000 ppv customers watched the event, bringing BSkyB's 50 per cent share in the revenue to more than £25 million.

'Judgement Night' augured a new experience for fans of boxing, packaged and glossily delivered by television. The hype that surrounded the event had more in common with World Federation Wrestling, with its hybrid of showmanship and sport, than the era when boxing was soberly screened by the BBC. The 'master' showman of contemporary boxing at this time was World Featherweight Champion Prince Naseem Hamed. Hamed ritually entered the boxing arena in an extravagant manner: lasers, lights, dry ice and thumping dance music leading to his 'trademark' somersault over the ropes to the ring. This show of bravura was for the crowd and the cameras, and signalled what *the Guardian* sports writer Gavin Evans (8 November 1996) called 'the trappings of the ersatz gladiatorial arena of modern boxing'.

In the run-up to 'Judgement Night' Evans argued that Hamed thrived on the adrenaline rush of 'putting on a show' as much as he appeared to relish 'the pleasurable anticipation' of knocking out his opponent. Hamed was acutely aware of his own identity, and this did not only apply to him being a British Arab Muslim. His physical ability and exhibitionist performance were also part and parcel of the relationship boxing fans carried with the man. As Hamed put it in a pre-fight interview before 'Judgement Night':

> It's not about boxing is it? It's about watching this little guy on the telly tonight. He's so flash, so cocky that you want him to take a right lesson but somehow he always wins. A lot of people tell me that. (Interviewed in the *Financial Times*, 9 November 1996)

But boxing is not just about the characters and star performances.

Evans's considered feature article in the *Guardian* (8 November 1996), revealing a more reflexive attitude of the 'dirty reality' of boxing than is familiarly raised in the banal reports of tabloid newspapers, picked up on the immediate, tangible experience of boxing 'behind the glittering facade':

> Boxing has a smell coming off it, and a feel, that the camera is not designed to detect. Unless you have boxed, or at least watched from ringside, it is hard to glean a true picture of what happens in there: the taste and sometimes the stink of sweat, snot and blood as bodies clash and clinch; the surprise of how small most boxers are and just how hard they hit; the excruciating thud of a hook to liver, the sharper shock of a fist or head in the mouth or nose, the momentary haze from being caught on the side of the jaw, the exhaustion, the concentration and the exhilaration of getting it all to flow just right. There's nothing more intense for the participants in the mainstream sporting world.

What the juxtaposition of hype and glamour on television and the 'reality' of the sport described above illustrates is that the processes of mediation, from ring to screen, detracts from the brutality of the sport, celebrating instead the manly endeavour and bravura of the stars involved.

The ritual of the pre-fight weigh-in, the menacing eye-to-eye stares, the courage and competitive spirit that winners and losers display are the dramatic elements that constitute the sporting narratives of boxing. The pain, destructiveness and occasional death from boxing are glossed over to preserve the civility of the sport. Emphasis is placed on manliness and machismo and not violence in its rawest sense.

Conclusion

There have been changes in the manner in which women's sport has been treated. By 2007, for example, Wimbledon, after years of wrangling, had finally followed both the US and Australian tennis opens by paying both male and female players the same amount in prize money. Meanwhile, as research by Bernstein and Galily (2008) in Israel around basketball and television coverage has shown:

> A crucial thing to be learned from this Israeli example is that a television channel can raise awareness of a women's sport if, like Channel 5, it seriously commits itself to promoting that sport; but that there is no way it can single-handedly change the surrounding reality, including deeply embedded inequalities and attitudes. (Bernstein and Galily, 2008: 190)

The marginalization of women's sport is perhaps the clearest manifestation of patriarchal ideologies in sport. The gendered values of sport are acutely realized when the physical capital ascribed to men and women's bodies differs so greatly. Female muscularity is viewed as distasteful and inhumane. Masculine strength and bravura are celebrated and viewed as heroic.

Success and power in sport come to represent the iconic symbol of manhood. Women's boxing, for example, clearly disrupts and challenges such stereotypes, attempting to co-opt the quintessential male sport for its own celebration of women's power and physical ability. However, after a century of women's prizefighting, the professional sport remains a long way from attaining wider recognition. Until women's boxing is seriously courted by television it will continue to be viewed as a minority sport, and the dominant image of women and boxing will be one of titillation, from the 'Playboy girls' in the ring to the occasional boxing symbolism of topless Page 3 models in the *Sun* newspaper.

Chapter 8

Games Across Frontiers: Mediated Sport and National Identity

It is a stark dichotomy that sport, the battlefield where casualties are measured only in bruised egos, is also asked to be a healing agent. It is supposed to unite disparate cultures, religions and political regimes, and sometimes it does. But, more often, it does no more than temporarily bring them together, allowing for the possibility that enemies might understand each other a little better, or at least stop hating. (Sports writer Kevin Mitchell, 'Why I fear the dragon's claws at my throat', *Observer Sport*, 3 August 2008)

Introduction

With its visibility and focus on symbols, winning, competition, partisan fans – and in team games the necessity of collective struggle – few other cultural forms lend themselves as easily as sport to being used as an indicator of certain national characteristics and, by extension, of being representative of a national identity. Examples include examining how the Gaelic games of hurling or football typify Irish character (Humphries, 1996, 2007); contrasting English and Italian cultural life through an analysis of their differing footballing cultures (Vialli and Marcotti, 2007); noting the integral position of football in Scottish culture (Cosgrove, 1998; Giulianotti, 2005a) or the extent to which sports such as cricket or rugby have come to symbolize a particular aspect of Englishness (Paxman, 1998; Marqusee, 2001; Tuck, 2003). The ritual and ceremony of sport – particularly national and international sport – carry with them a symbolic significance which far outweigh sport's importance as organized play. Much of that symbolic importance is inherently attached to sport and its sub-cultures; however, as noted in Chapters 4 and 5, crucial ideological work is also carried out in the way that sport is both represented, constructed and transformed through its contact with the various forms of media.

Newspapers, magazines and books, in conjunction with the visual and online media, help define the social and political position of sport in society. They also act as the interface between sporting, political and ideological discourses of identity and meaning. Examples of this are not hard to find. The success or failure of the British Olympic team appears, according to sections of the media, to act as a direct barometer of the position and state of Britain in the world. A sporting crisis for national teams or individuals representing the nation are often linked and connected with wider political or cultural shifts, so the abject failure of the Scottish national team at the football World Cup in 1978 is used to help account for the failure of nerve among the electorate in the subsequent devolution referendum a year later while the 2001 doping scandals at the Nordic World Ski championships in Finland and the World Ski Championships in Italy two years later that saw seven Finnish skiers testing positive instigated a wider debate about Finnish national identity and 'national shame' in the media (Laine, 2006).

In Britain, sports coverage with a national dimension appears often not to be about sport. As Blain and O'Donnell (1998: 41) suggest, often it 'seems rather to be an obsession with corporate national self, to which sport is virtually incidental'. However, before we begin to read sporting character and success or failure simply as attributes which can be easily influenced by or indeed can determine wider political and cultural characteristics, we need to examine the relationship between sport, media and national identity and outline and highlight some of the central issues. We then look at particular case studies that bring into focus some of these issues, before finally broadening out the debate to examine the increasingly important relationship between global trends in media sport and collective identities, an issue developed in more detail in the final chapter of the book.

Media, discourse and identity

Organized sport has been viewed by governments of all political persuasions as an important sphere in the forging of 'national character', with this project often serving specific political ends (Cashmore, 1996: 235–57). This particular point is well made in the work of Houlihan (1994), which examines the relationship between sport, politics and international relations. He notes:

sport has always been a resource within the international system available primarily to governments, but also to other non-governmental political interests and, while it has, on occasion, been the primary tool of diplomacy and policy implementation, it has more often been an element of a broader and more comprehensive political strategy. (Houlihan, 1994: 209)

Examples are readily available. Duke and Crolley (1996: 24–49) document the politicization of football in Francoist Spain during the period between 1939 and 1975. Franco was not alone in attempting to align sport and, due to its universal popularity, football in particular with specific political regimes (Hoberman, 1984). This process takes place most notably at the level of international sport, and worldwide sporting competitions such as the Olympic Games or the football World Cup. The Beijing Olympics of 2008, for example, were clearly viewed by the Chinese government as part of its strategy to attempt to shift the global image of China, while sending a powerful symbolic international message about that country's dramatic economic rise within the world economy.

In the past countries such as the former Soviet Union and the German Democratic Republic have directly linked the health of the state to its ability to perform successfully in the international sporting arena (Houlihan, 1997). This linkage of political discourse with that of sport is still evident throughout contemporary Europe and beyond (O'Donnell, 1994). In recent times the winning of the rights to stage major sporting events – such as Euro 2004 in Portugal (Boyle and Monteiro, 2005), the 2010 FIFA World Cup in South Africa, the London 2012 Olympics and the 2014 Commonwealth Games in Glasgow – have become increasingly important both politically and economically in raising the external image and profile of a city or country, and signalling the key role that politicians now believe staging sports mega events play in programmes of economic and cultural regeneration (Roche, 2006; Newman, 2007; Panagiotopoulou, 2007).

To view this use of sport as some form of simple political manipulation by powerful interest groups in society to which people readily succumb is both simplistic and patronizing, and ignores the contradictions, tensions and struggles that exist within all supposedly national cultures. Sports can be an arena of cultural struggle, which oppressed groups use as a form of symbolic resistance. The turning of that most imperial of English games, cricket, by the West Indies (and other former British colonies) into an expression and celebration of indigenous culture is one such example (Malac, 1995).

Political scientists such as Hoberman (1984) argue that sporting activity in itself is not intrinsically ideological. However, sport as a cultural form based on competition is uniquely open to political and ideological manipulation. In contemporary societies this process is mediated through the media's close link with elite sport. This media relationship with modern sport has also helped transform our understanding of this particular area of popular culture. Mediated sport can be an important cultural arena in which ideas about various aspects of social relations can become naturalized. Today most sporting cultures are to some extent mediated through television, radio, print or online media. As has been argued elsewhere, in this process of transformation not only are discourses of identity mediated or simply transmitted, but in many instances they can be constructed or even at times invented, if the political or economic climate is suitable (Whannel, 1992; Blain et al., 1993; Brookes, 2002; Blain and Boyle, 2009).

This is particularly true in the field of international sporting competition, where sport can become a symbolic extension of various collective identities. International media sport can also become an arena in which the supposed superiority of one country, or ethnic group over another is celebrated. As Hugh O'Donnell has noted in his study of the construction of international sporting stereotypes:

> [Sport can] function on an international level as a site in which advanced countries can and must act out their preferred myths through self – and other – stereotypes, and celebrate those qualities which, in their own eyes, make them more modern, more advanced, in short superior . . . This process routinely involves downgrading other national groups. (O'Donnell, 1994: 353)

While much of this process of myth reinforcement is conducted in the media's transformation of sport, a note of caution regarding the origins of many of these discourses needs to be introduced.

Firstly, media institutions are themselves subject to a range of economic, cultural and political pressures which in turn heavily influence how they choose to frame or make sense of events. For example, the *Sun* newspaper in England may report a riot involving England supporters differently than the edition of the same paper aimed at a Scottish readership, as they address different culturally defined markets.

The popular press's at times overtly racist treatment of, say, a German motor-racing driver may differ from that found even on a commercial broadcasting channel such as ITV (where any racist overtones will be much more subtle). In other words, the mobilization of particular discourses of identity is partly determined by a range of factors such as the audience being targeted, the specific media institution and how it is funded, as well as current political and social attitudes. In this context Rosie et al. (2004) have argued that such is the importance of national (Scottish, English) 'frames of reference' for the newspaper industry in a politically devolved UK that the diversity of stories about differing parts of the UK have in fact declined, as increasingly newspapers aimed at specific media markets speak only to their immediate constituents.

Secondly, it is worth emphasizing the point made by Schlesinger when he argued: 'not to start with communication and its supposed effects on collective identity and culture, but rather to begin by posing the problem of collective identity itself, to ask how it might be analysed and what importance communicative practices may play in its constitution' (Schlesinger, 1991: 150). It can be misleading to place the media at the centre of the process of identity formation. While they may be a key site in constituting and reconstituting various discourses (and indeed in many instances both legitimizing and marginalizing ideas and value systems), they are not necessarily the primary definers of either discourse or aspects of identity.

Thirdly, while the internationalization of the media in recent decades has meant that global sporting events are given even more exposure than ever before, the reporting and framing of such events is far from universal. More often than not, international events are made sense of through a national media lens that is attuned for specific commercial and cultural markets (Boyle and Monteiro, 2005).

Finally, while the symbolic nature of these international media events can be important, in certain circumstances reinforcing or even challenging national and cultural myths and narratives of identity, they can't be divorced from broader political or economic context (Alabarces et al., 2001). An example of the overt linking of sporting activity to political rhetoric was evident with the re-entry of South Africa into the world sporting community, and in particular its successful staging of the 1995 Rugby World Cup. President Nelson Mandela explicitly associated himself with the Springboks team, projecting it as a symbol of the 'new' multi-racial democratic South Africa (this despite the fact that there was only one black player in the team). As one newspaper noted:

'One team, one country,' is the adopted motif of the Springboks' World Cup campaign. For once it seems to be more than just a PR gimmick. President Mandela spent three hours with the squad on the eve of the match and delayed his intended departure from the match yesterday so that he could be sure that 'his boys', as he calls the team, hung on for victory. 'Our loyalties have completely changed,' said the president. 'We have adopted these young men.' (*Guardian*, 26 May 1995)

Throughout the tournament, which South Africa would win, Mandela lost no opportunity to use the team's success both as an indicator of the positive and dynamic political changes taking place in that country and as a vehicle with which to project a positive image of the country to the world through the international media coverage of the event.

However, Steenveld and Strelitz (1998: 625) in their examination of this media event caution against ascribing too much long-term power to the images of unity generated by the success of South Africa. They suggest, 'if there was a coming together during the tournament, it was a temporary phenomenon and in no way laid the foundation – as the media and the government politicians would have us believe – for the creation of a collective self identity.' Twelve years later, when South Africa defeated England in the 2007 World Cup final, the team contained only two black South Africans (one more than in 1995), emphasizing that in modern South Africa white and back citizens 'still largely inhabit separate worlds' (Russell, 2007). Yet the 2007 victory was celebrated in the black towns of South Africa, much to the surprise of many commentators, suggesting that the cultural power of sport to offer highly symbolic moments, however transitory, remains compelling.

When the Iraq national football team defeated Saudi Arabia in the final game of the Asian Cup in Jakarta in July 2007, there was an outpouring of Iraqi nationalistic celebration on the streets of that country that is rarely seen (not least given the internal ethnic tensions within the country). However, this celebration of a unified Iraqi national team that saw Shia supporters chant the name of the Sunni goalscorer Younis Mahmoud was short-lived (*The Economist*, 4 August 2007). A few days later sixty people were killed in two bombings in Baghdad and despite a very brief respite to rally behind the football team, political deadlock and strife returned to the county.

However, it can also be argued that to deny the possibility that such events, in some contexts, can both shape and reflect broader shifts in the related social, political and economic arenas is also wrong and is to underestimate the power of the symbolic in a material world.

At the very least, in specific contexts they may contribute to creating what we have called in an earlier chapter a 'climate of opinion' within which more deeply rooted structural changes can more readily occur. What is argued is that it is important to situate media coverage in detailed contexts of interpretation. This does not negate the power, importance and role that the media can play in helping to make sense of a group's collective identity (usually by a process of boundary marking), but simply alerts us to the fact that this influence will vary depending on the specific influence of a range of other factors at particular moments in specific social circumstances. We concur with Adrian Mellor when he argued:

> People make their own cultures, albeit not in circumstances of their own choosing. Amongst these circumstances – within and towards which their activity is directed – are structures of representation; but so too are structures of class, ethnicity and gender, along with deliberate economic and political strategies that bear upon these. These things are real. They do not merely exist in discourse. Their reality and their consequences exceed their representation. But people are not merely constructed by them. (Mellor, 1991: 114)

Sport, media and identity in devolving UK

Within the UK's sporting environment, there exists the problem of mediating the complicated political and cultural relationship between the different component parts of the UK (for example, Scotland and England) – a situation which a decade after the establishment of a Parliament in Scotland and Assemblies in Wales and Northern Ireland has become acute in the reporting of news and current affairs (BBC Trust, 2008; Fraser, 2008).

Due in part to the universality of sporting activity, sport has been an important cultural arena through which various collective identities have been articulated within the UK. Richard Holt (1990) has documented how the political history and economic relationship of Scotland and Wales with England has been mediated through sporting occasions:

> Sport acted as a vitally important channel for this sense of collective resentment . . . Football gave the Scots a way of fighting the 'old enemy', whilst addiction to rugby came to be one of the major ways in which

the English defined the Welsh and the Welsh came to see themselves. Cultural identity was a two-way process. (Holt, 1990: 237)

This viewing of cultural identity as a continuous process that is subject to political, economic and cultural constraints and pressures is important. It also emphasizes how the concept of localism is relative. Within Scotland, for example, the national press can mean the Scottish, not the London based UK press, and the idea that the British media's coverage of sport unproblematically reproduces the British 'nation' is dependent on how that nation is defined and from what cultural and class position the viewer/reader is engaging with this discourse.

This is not to argue that television's transformation of sport as a cultural form does not have a role to play in cultural identity formation. What is being suggested here is that to view this process as unidirectional is to underestimate the other factors that shape collective identities and the degree of resistance that may exist among certain groups to any 'official' discourse.

While discourses of sporting national identity do differ across sports, depending on whether they are individual or team games, what class connotations are attached to individual sports, and their profile within the media arena, the contradictions and tensions that exist in any 'national culture', are rarely articulated at the international sporting level. As Schlesinger comments:

National cultures are not simple repositories of shared symbols to which the entire population stands in identical relation. Rather, they are to be approached as sites of contestation in which competition over definitions takes place ... It may also reproduce distinctions between 'us' and 'them' at the intra-national level, in line with the internal structure of social divisions and relations of power and domination. (Schlesinger, 1991: 174)

Thus it appears useful to view the media as one important part of the process of identity formation, but not to start from a media-centred view of society.

Sports fans and national identity: Scottishness/ Englishness

In the first edition of *Power Play* we examined how an evolving political relationship between Scotland and England was being mediated through media coverage of the Euro 96 football championships that had been held in England. It is worth revisiting this relationship twelve years on from this sporting event.

In 2008 we have a Scottish National Party minority government in power in Edinburgh and very real political tensions between a Westminster Labour government committed to maintaining the union (and, under PM Gordon Brown, keen to stress the ongoing importance of 'Britishness' in the political identity of the country) and the Scottish Parliament and Welsh and Northern Irish Assemblies. Much of this tension is played out through a symbolic media landscape which focuses on the apparent increasing differences that exist around health, education and economic well-being depending on what part of a devolved UK you live in, and the balance of power between those decisions reserved to the London parliament (for example, broadcasting) and those within the gift of the parliament in Edinburgh (health, education).

Against this highly political backdrop how do media representations of sports and sports culture both play into this wider cultural arena and in turn how are the discourses around sport themselves shaped by wider political and cultural shifts in the relationship between Scotland and England? Throughout the book we have argued that it is simply impossible to keep politics with a small 'p' out of sports discourse. Any sports media culture is rooted in a particular society whose attitudes, fears, prejudices, hopes and expectations are articulated through the language of sports. In this context, what happens on the field of play is of course only part of the story and representations of sports fans, for example, also can become important boundary markers in various forms of individual and collective identity formation.

To this end the portrayal in both the Scottish and European media of the supporters of the Scottish national football team who travel abroad as the increasingly self-styled 'Tartan Army' is not simply a media construct, but highlights the complex relationship between media discourses and audiences.

The Scottish national team supporter who travels abroad constitutes part of perhaps the most image-conscious footballing group in Europe. Many of the images of the 'fun-loving' internationalist Scottish supporter are juxtaposed by the media with the dour aggressive xenophobic English supporter. This is a point which is not lost when Scottish supporters travel abroad and are faced with reporters and television cameras and realize that, by adopting particular dress codes (the kilt, tartan and such like) and cultivating a friendly attitude towards the local population, they clearly differentiate themselves in the eyes of the media as being Scottish and not English (Giulianotti, 2005a).

We would argue that the mediation of national and international sport can only be understood by locating it within the specific economic, political and historical contours which shape societies. Often mediated sport will reproduce, reinforce and even normalize attitudes and values which exist in other spheres of political or cultural life. Blain and O'Donnell (1998: 51–3) have argued that football, as mediated by the press, has three kinds of relationship with society.

> Football is a sign of society: in other words footballing success or failure is one part of a country's overall sense of identity. It can also be an extension of society: here sporting failure is viewed as a wider failure of society as a whole. And finally football may be a simulacrum of society: where, for example, the Scottish national team is 'at least partly presented as referring only to itself'. (1998: 53)

They argue that these categories of coverage reflect to varying degrees the level of political and economic modernity in each country, so that a country such as Spain or Germany treats football as one part of its overall identity, while in less well developed countries (in terms of modernity) such as England/Britain, English sporting failure is mediated as an indicator of national decline.

We would agree that these categories are useful when examining media (the press in particular) treatment of international sport. However, one has to take into account the complexities of the media industries, all mobilizing sporting discourses for differing commercial and/or ideological reasons aimed at a range of audiences, readerships and viewerships. In other words, we would suggest that the boundaries between these categories are perhaps less rigid and well defined than they initially appear.

At any one time aspects of all three categories may be used in differing sections of the press or media. While we would argue strongly for the important link between a country's political and economic development and its cultural confidence and sense of judgement, often this can also be quite specifically linked to significant changes in the health of the economy.

Thus images and imaginings of a country's past and present and projections of its future come together to underpin the mediation of sporting discourses. Put simply, at certain specific political, economic and cultural moments these can come together around one sport or sporting event and be evident across both sports and media institutions (such as the South African Rugby World Cup discussed earlier). At other times they may be more diverse and even contradictory, but are always rooted in the tensions between change and continuity which characterize societies. In some instances sport will carry the burden of national expectation, at other times, depending on the political and economic climate, it won't.

A sporting nation: Scotland, May 2008

We want to briefly examine a particular moment relating to the media coverage of two Scottish sports related stories, the 2008 UEFA Cup Final involving Rangers and Zenit St Petersburg held in Manchester, and the death of Tommy Burns, the former Celtic player and manager announced a day later on 15 May. Both stories received extensive media coverage in the Scottish national, UK national and international media and we argue that the discourses surrounding these stories illuminate and reveal deeper aspects of the public mediation of cultural and national characteristics through sporting discourse.

The way the narratives around these two events gets constructed also tells us much about the changing nature of information gathering and dissemination in a 24/7 media news culture, as well as the role and importance of news management and PR in contemporary sports media culture (Boyle, 2006).

While on the pitch, the sports story for the British media was the defeat of Rangers by 2 – 0 by the Russians of Zenit St Petersburg, the story that would dominate headlines for days after was the violent clashes between police and Rangers fans that took place in Manchester on the evening of the game.

Panic on the streets

Police estimates put the number of Rangers fans that travelled to Manchester for the final at between 100,000 and 200,000. The scale of the 'invasion' of the city was quite unprecedented in British football history with the relatively close proximity of Glasgow and Manchester meaning that convoys of fans travelled without tickets for the match. Versions of what happened on the evening of 14 May vary. For some fans the failure of the big screen on one of the fanzones just as the game was due to start acted as a trigger for the violence; in other fan accounts, fighting between Rangers fans helped to fuel an atmosphere in which the riot police were forced to intervene. Much of the support-ers, post-mortem on events was debated through websites and online discussion boards or through comments that directly responded to journalistic pieces about the events.

What is beyond dispute was that shocking scenes of violence involv-ing Rangers fans, riot police, police dogs and the wanton vandalism of various vehicles was captured on a mixture of police video, CCTV footage and mobile phone video which was broadcast or uploaded to the Internet and witnessed around the world. Specifically the attack on the police officer PC Mick Regan by a group of supporters in which it initially appeared that he was about to be beaten to death became one of the defining media images of a night of violence. The media followed up this story with a subsequent television interview with the police officer and the person who helped him escape the mob. Like many of the narratives that surround that night, initial reports regarding the person who saved the officer proved to be simply wrong and inaccurate. It wasn't as reported a Rangers fan that saved him, but rather a passer-by, Tom Bardsley, who was in fact from Greater Manchester. Rangers fans from Scotland wearing club colours were involved in a number of the incidents despite protestations that the violence was perpetrated by a small number of hooligans who were neither Rangers supporters or indeed Scottish.

As the *Scotland on Sunday* (18 May 2008) journalist Tom English reported: 'So many myths. So much hypocrisy [. . .] So many assump-tions, so little evidence'. He noted how many of the initial accounts of the events given by Rangers' Chief Executive Martin Bain and those carried in some newspapers such as the *Daily Record* (15 May 2008) that 'none of the ringleaders wore colours or spoke with a Scottish accent' could immediately be disproved by simply going online and watching some of the numerous video postings of the events on YouTube of Rangers fans fighting with themselves and police. In an age of the 24/7 news culture that demands instant explanation and comment and reaction, accounts from the 'frontline' were simply carried and picked up by other news sources without any systematic checking of the accuracy of the facts.

Here on public display and transmitted around the digital world were damaging pictures of violence associated with Rangers football fans that also reflected back on images of Glasgow, Scotland and Scottish identity. For some fans the media amplified the scale of the violence given the volume of people visiting the city (both Rangers and Strathclyde police severely underestimated the number of fans who would travel). Yet as the video footage of attacks and violence circulated in the media, for some commentators a few home truths regarding the relationship between these events and aspects of Scottish national identity needed to be addressed.

The Sunday Herald (18 May 2008) in its editorial saw the core of the problem centred on Scotland's booze culture and the role that binge drinking plays in Scottish cultural life. In addition it recognized the very real problem that violence on the streets of Scotland's towns and cities often perpetrated by young males fuelled by alcohol posed in modern Scotland. For other media commentators such as Ian Bell writing in the same paper under the headline 'Flower of Scotland? Let's think again', what the events in Manchester exposed was something that is rotten at the core of a brutalized culture in Scotland that has in some way lost touch with aspects of its imagined civilized past.

> They tell me, and I believe them, that this is an ancient and therefore mature democracy. Some advise that, after the Athenians, we did more for the demos than most. That's nice. So what am I supposed to conclude when I see some fat get in a sweaty jersey with a big stick threatening the peace of the dull and decent city of Manchester? Something has gone wrong. We raise our young men badly. We obsess over things that could never possibly matter to grown-ups. We misunderstand nationhood as a kind of puerile revenge. And we never, ever say: enough, no more, not in my world. (*Sunday Herald*, 18 May 2008)

Thus what you see here is the very public profile given to certain sporting events allowing, often not in the sports pages, some reflection on how the narratives of sporting culture illuminate wider social attitudes and national characteristics.

Given the reputation for violence among English football supporters over the years, it was unsurprising to see English journalists drawing a comparison between events in Manchester and Moscow, the venue a week later for the all-English Champions League final between Manchester United and Chelsea. Jim White writing in the *Daily Telegraph* about the 'invasion' of Moscow by English fans noted that:

> Unlike last week's Glaswegian assault on Manchester, this was an invasion that was almost entirely peaceful, quiet, relaxed even. There were one or two reports of skuffles, of English fans being set upon by local hooligans. But there was no responding in kind. (*Daily Telegraph*, 22 May 2008)

The national flipside of the representations of the violent drunken Scots presented to the world via Manchester was the media coverage and public reaction to the death in that same week at the age of fifty-one from cancer of Celtic Football Club's first-team coach Tommy Burns. Burns had played for Celtic from an early age and also managed the club for a period in the 1990s. He was also an assistant manager to the Scotland national team serving under both Berti Vogts and Walter Smith. Burns was a man defined by his love of family, his Catholic faith and his passion for Celtic and football. The scenes as his funeral cortege passed by Celtic Park with the streets lined with thousands of supporters offered a salient reminder of the role that heroes such as Burns played and continue to play in the lives of ordinary supporters.

It was not simply empty rhetoric that saw both the Celtic chairman John Reid and chief executive Peter Lawell speak about the importance of Burns to the 'Celtic Family' and how is early death meant that this family, around the globe, was in mourning for a much loved son. The open emotion with which Celtic manager Gordon Strachan spoke at a news conference about the last hours he spent with his friend, and the very public grief of his friend and Rangers assistant boss Ally McCoist, demonstrated in a highly symbolic manner how at key moments sport has the power to transcend the rivalries that are deeply embedded in its culture and speak to the dignity and the honour that still resides in aspects of the wider society that sustains the sport. Here was by way of contrast to events in Manchester a public representation of the dignified, tolerant nature of the Scottish character, articulated through its sporting heroes and the reaction of Celtic and, indeed, many Rangers supporters to the death of Burns. It was also a salient reminder that sports culture and its extensive mediation remains a compelling public arena through which various aspects, however contradictory they may appear, of national character get constituted.

Forever England

Richard Weight (1999) has argued that the proliferation of St George's Cross flags among English supporters at Euro 96 and at France 98, coupled with the equally marked decline in fans carrying the Union flag, is another significant indicator of a shifting awareness among the English about changes in their cultural identity and political position within Britain (the English having often had little reason to differentiate between being British and English). Garland (2004) has noted how the relative success of the English national football team at the World

Cup in 2002 was represented in the tabloid media as an example of a multicultural country pulling together behind the national team. Others such as Tuck (2003) have commented on the rise of a distinctive 'populist' English discourse around the English national rugby team and its associated marketing through key sponsors such as Nike, while others such as Robinson (2008) have argued that sports such as international football have become increasingly important public media arenas through which the anxieties of Englishness and English national identity are being articulated. All agree that the English have finally woken up to the fact that their identity is not simply interchangeable with Britishness and as a result sport has taken on a growing symbolic importance as one of the cultural forms through which a particular form of English identity is given public expression.

There is a certain irony in this, given that traditionally it has been the Welsh, Northern Irish and the Scots who, when politically impotent, have burdened sporting discourse with national sentiment. At the end of the first decade of the twenty-first century, the English are beginning to grasp the complex realities of living in a politically devolved UK. Indeed, as we predicted ten years ago or so, mediated sport has become another arena in which a growing English resentment of perceived Scottish political influence gets articulated, and as we suggest in the conclusion below the inability of the media to report the complexities of political life in twenty-first-century Britain is exacerbating this process.

Globalization and the new age of sport

One of the major changes in the sporting landscape in the last decade or so has been the growing centrality of debates around the relationship between sports and globalization (Andrews and Grainger, 2007; Andrews and Ritzer, 2007; Giulianotti, 1999, 2005b; Miller et al., 2001; Rowe, 2003a). In this section we want to make a number of points regarding the relationship between the forces of globalization and how they are impacting on sport and identity. The extent to which sport is being increasingly reshaped by forces of globalization, by which time–space relationships are being altered with political and cultural implications, has been addressed directly elsewhere (Jarvie and Maguire, 1994: 230–62). As we have argued, while football World Cups and Olympic Games appear to offer examples of global cultural events, the impact these may have on national and cultural identities is complex (Blain et al., 1993).

Ultimately any impact on the process of identity formation of such events is determined by the specific historical, economic and political circumstances within which they are made sense of. As Houlihan (1997: 135) notes: 'The picture painted of sport and its relationship with global culture and with ethnic and state notions of identity creates an impression of a highly malleable source of cultural symbolism.' He argues that the impact of a sport or an event may be intense and powerful, but have a relatively short shelf life.

Rowe (2003a) has argued that ultimately sport, with its inherent national frame of reference and its competitive dimension, is ill-suited as a cultural form to fulfil the larger cultural characteristics that the globalization of cultural practice might initially suggest. Other critics have taken Rowe to task on this (Andrews and Grainger, 2007; Andrews and Ritzer, 2007), arguing that Rowe draws a dichotomy between the local and the global within sporting discourse and institutional and cultural practice. Some sociological linguistic contortions around the terms local and global (globalization, grobalization, localization, glocalization, glocality and so one) are used to argue that the interplay between global and local aspects of sports is more complex than any dichotomy suggested by Rowe (2003a).

There has always been an interplay between local, regional, national and international sporting discourse and practice. Culture has never come in neatly heremetically sealed compartments, and sports have been no different in this respect. Rowe (2003a) has always recognized this interplay and the key point he is making, with which we concur, is that as the pace at which international media systems and networks have grown has increased, and the importance of sports as media content has developed, particular national frames of reference have not gone away. What has changed – and Andrews and Grainger (2007) outline this process – is the extent to which in some sports, not all, the global commercial interests have successfully extended their influence, while ostensibly maintaining the local and specifc elements that give sports culture its purchase with fans and supporters. Our argument is that this is not a new process, but what has changed in the last decade or so is the pace at which what were specific local models relating to sports organization and media marketing transfer around and across differing sports in differing parts of the world.

So in 2007, the marketing techniques the English FA Premier League use gets cited as an influence by those setting up a new cricket tournament in India. As noted earlier in the book, the commercialization of media systems (as a result of political and economic decisions) has seen sports commercial value continue to escalute as communication platforms carrying sports content (often any sports content!) have boomed. Elite sport has benefited hugely from the move towards demand-led media and the end of the dominance of supply-led systems of provision. With this growth and the establishment of the Internet as a means of communication has been the consolidation of a network of interests around an international *business of sports culture.* Part of this has been the proliferation of agents, brokers, sports marketers, public relations organizations, media sports consultants, players and commercial sponsors, all selling their expertise, knowledge, business models and wares across continents and even across sports. This is the international process that is shaping sports culture and influencing the governing bodies of sport at national and international levels.

However, this process does not negate the fact that in terms of identity formation, the role that sports play in the process remains rooted around local, regional and national concerns, essentially Rowe's (2003a) argument. For in the age of 'globalization' more paradoxical patterns of identity and media knowledge around sports and information more generally are also emerging.

While much has been made of the process of globalization standardizing cultural habits and eroding others, this presents a partial picture. In a small country such as Scotland what you see are external European and global pressures impacting on both the football and media industries in that country, but this has not necessarily led to some sort of cultural erosion or standardization in Scottish sport (Boyle and Haynes, 1996; Haynes and Boyle, 2008). What has happened has been a resurgence of interest in what might be called the local or regional; however, this is often taking place within boundaries which are determined by global media interests.

Arundel and Roche (1998) in their detailed examination of British (actually English) rugby league convincingly argue that the interplay between global media and the sport is changing the localized traditions of the game. What is being suggested is not on one hand the overly optimistic resurgence of local traditions and difference, but neither is it 'some kind [of] simplistic cultural homogenisation' (p. 84) driven by global media forces.

In Scotland, for example, this process or interplay between the global and more rooted forms of sporting culture is being driven in part by a realization of the economic benefits that media organizations can accrue from focusing on issues specific to Scotland which are not covered in other media. Both BBC Scotland and its main commercial rival in the Scottish market, Scottish Television, have been keen to promote themselves as being distinctly Scottish in their output, with sport, and football in particular, a crucial part of their portfolio.

Yet in the age of demand-led media, and the loosening of the rights and obligations that regulators once imposed on broadcasters, most of the elite Scottish sports content is increasingly to be found on private pay-TV platforms (Haynes and Boyle, 2008). The nature of media sport in twenty-first century Britain is that to see the elite games and matches you often have to pay extra. The centrality of the market in this process is only curtailed if these events are deemed to be of such national importance that they are protected for free-to-air television. However, in a politically devolved Scotland, with its own parliament but no power over communications policy, this UK 'national' list does not include, for example, Scotland international 2010 World Cup qualifing football games (live on Sky and Setanta Sports).

The advent of a Scottish National Party government in Edinburgh has positioned such anomalies centre stage within their political discourse. In the process they have highlighted one of the paradoxes of information in the market-driven digital age. More and more mainstream media within the UK speak to very particular audiences, so Scottish sport is invisible in London-based UK newspapers (it appears in the regionalized editions printed in Scotland), and the BBC in London covers little Scottish-based sports news, or indeed Scottish news from within a devolved UK in general, other than through its regional/national outlets (BBC Trust, 2008; Fraser, 2008; Rosie et al., 2004). If you want to hunt around the web you can find more information about such specific Scottish sports such as shinty than you previously could (in the same way that you can follow American sports via the web from, say, the UK) but you are not going to stumble across this information in more mainstream media outlets.

It remains the case that even at global international events such as the Olympic Games or football's World Cup, it is how these events are made sense of at the local level that is important (in this instance the local may mean an entire country). Our broader point is that in some instances (and certainly within a politically and institutionally diverging UK), the local is becoming more local, and at the same time international information can be tracked down, by those motivated to do so, on the web. It remains useful to treat with caution some of the claims being made about the role of the media in eroding distinctive cultural characteristics at some transnational level. Certainly you can argue that sports specific to, say, Ireland, such as Gaelic football and hurling, have increasingly been influenced by international sports marketing and organizational techniques (the influence of globalization?) but remain intrinsically recognizable as Irish sports, rooted in particular regional identities and rivalries.

Subsequent research (Boyle, 2006) merely serves to reinforce the earlier observation by Blain et al. that:

> In fact sports journalism, albeit very unevenly, is as likely to produce a turning inward towards national concerns, and a buttressing of a sense of difference, as it is to operate ideologically on behalf of a harmonious world, even, as we have seen, at that mythic habitat of the familial, the Olympics. (Blain et al., 1993: 196)

While the debates around globalization over the last decade have not altered our belief in the importance of reiterating Schlesinger's earlier discussion of national-identity formation when he argued:

> It is more accurate (but less provocative) to suggest that it is a site of contestation and inherently an object of transformative practices. In any case, to assert that national cultures might, indeed, do, exist does not by any means exclude the reality of there being a transnational or global culture as well . . . To insist upon 'either . . . or' makes for good polemics or political sloganeering, but poor analysis. (Schlesinger, 1991: 305)

The Scottish media's interest in, say, for example, the Celtic/Rangers rivalry is as pronounced as ever, emphasizing that, while media and sporting organizations are subject to global economic pressures, this is in some instances accompanied by a resurgence in the local and the different. This is not some rarified 'local' context of course, but one that has *always* interfaced with international (or even global forces) in the same ways as societies have never been sealed off from a continual process of external cultural influence. This is particularly true where specific marketplaces and political and cultural spaces coincide to some extent.

Conclusion

Debates around the global and the local cannot simply be framed in the context of individuals or groups being located in either one space or the other. As Schlesinger notes when he argues for an actionist perspective on identity formation:

Such a perspective requires us to see identity not as a prior condition of collective action but rather as a continually constituted and reconstructed category. (Schlesinger, 1991: 173)

It becomes necessary in this perspective to be aware of the position that the media occupy in such a process, and to be alert that at particular times in specific circumstances their importance will vary considerably.

There is also the extent to which that, given the pace of political change in Scotland and in the UK as a whole over the last few years, sporting and broadcasting institutions at times appear to lag behind. The lack of control over communications policy for, say, the Scottish parliament has implications that extend to international sporting events and their media coverage. In the digital age, sports remain deeply embedded in local, regional, national and international identities. The globalization of the sports business creates its own tensions, as we noted in chapter 3, between these identities and the more global fan base that some organizations, such as the FA Premier League, want to speak to.

However, we would argue that against a backdrop of increasing political change and the growing competition for audiences in an increasingly competitive sports-media marketplace, the hyping of national rivalries as one way of appealing to and attracting an audience is, we would suggest, as likely to increase as disappear. We remain convinced that as the globalization of the media industries (in all their complexities and contradictions) continues apace, sport will continue to be an important cultural, political and commercial marker of boundaries, identities and markets.

Chapter 9

The Sports Pages:
Journalism and Sport

After more than thirty years of writing on sport it is still possible to be assailed by doubts about whether it really is a proper job for a grown person. But I console myself with the thought that it is easier to find a kind of truth in sport than it is, for example, in the activities covered by political or economic journalists. Sports truth may be simplistic but it's not negligible. (Hugh McIlvanney, *sportswriter*, *Arena*, BBC TV, 1991)

Murdoch tells WSJ execs: 'Shorter stories, more sport'. (Headline of news report on Rupert Murdoch's first meeting with *Wall Street Journal* bureau chiefs, *Press Gazette*, 17 January 2008)

Introduction

Despite living in a highly visual media culture, the print media remain an important source of information, gossip and insight for the sports fan. Reading about sport remains a pleasure for millions of newspaper readers and during the last decade or so, as media sport has expanded, so to has the interest in sport among newspaper editors keen to find a new audience. This chapter examines how sports journalism is changing in the age of digital media. As the political, economic and cultural importance of the sports industries continues to increase it asks how has journalism reacted to this new environment? It is also interested in outlining some of the key challenges faced by those working in those communications industries associated with journalism and sport. For example, how is the rise of online journalism changing existing print and broadcast sports journalism practice and to what extent is the increasing 24/7 media news agenda altering the nature of journalism about sports? Also, does the rise of user-generated content signal the end of more traditional forms of journalistic practice?

This part of the book also looks at how major sporting organizations and corporations are changing their media strategies in the digital media era of sports and examines some of the implications of these changes for sports journalism in general and sports journalists in particular. It also argues that many of the issues faced by journalists working in sport are also evident in a range of other fields of journalism and these challenges are often driven by the broader forces of globalization, digitization and marketization which are restructuring many media industries and their journalism. To this end, this article updates and develops a number of areas that have been addressed in previous research (Boyle, 2006).

Sports journalism: professional ideologies

As we have already observed in Chapter 2, the introduction of televised sport had a profound effect on the role of sports reporters as they found themselves passing on second-hand news. The sporting press had been central to the rise of modern commercialized sport and sports journalism had done much to promote and service the various organized sports that established themselves in the nineteenth century.

Sport gave newspapers a constant source of news and gossip as well as a new corps of journalists who specialized solely in the field of sport. Historically, the sports scribe often had to work in extreme conditions, from cramped press boxes to suffering the vagaries of the British weather. Moreover, in the newspaper hierarchy, sports reporters battled against a stereotypical image of the failed journalist, their status in the newsroom often suffering from the perception that sport was a trivial matter in the wider scheme of news values (Boyle, 2006; Rowe, 2005; Steen, 2008).

Often underpinning these assumptions were issues related to social class. Journalists covering working-class sports such as football were often viewed differently from those associated with more middle–upper-class sports such as cricket. In Britain a particularly literary approach to cricket or rugby writing was deemed acceptable, while no such pretensions would be allowed to inform coverage of mass spectator sports such as football.

The flipside of this slight to the sports journalist's trade was the increasing allocation of resources for foreign travel to cover the growth of international sport. More often than not, the sports correspondent would travel incognito with British teams on foreign jaunts around the world (Wooldridge, 2007).

Before the introduction of scheduled long-haul flights this invariably meant spending weeks away on board a ship filing reports back via telegraph or, in the case of an Ashes cricket series from Australia, via a courier service to North America and then on to Britain via transatlantic cable. With the global scale of contemporary sports events the demand on resources has continued to increase. Even in the difficult financial climate of 2008, a number of the UK's London-based national newspapers were investing heavily in their coverage of the Beijing Olympics. As we note later, much of this resource would be focused on their online operations and also the use of video content to be carried on their sites. This was particularly important given the substantial time difference involved which could result in print editions covering events already almost twenty-four hours old. *The Times* had a fourteen-strong team in Beijing, while the *Daily Telegraph* sent nineteen journalists and the *Guardian/Observer* sent fifteen journalists (*Press Gazette*, 1 August 2008). By way of contrast and signifying the growing financial crisis in the Scottish print sector, the Scottish-based newspapers sent their smallest cohort ever to a major sporting event, with only four staffers attending Beijing (Allmediascotland.com, 31 July 2008).

Different sports have developed their own formal practices, assigning reporters to particular organizations or events. 'The beat' is a method of providing a predictable supply of information from reporters in the field. It is rare, therefore, for sports journalists to cover more than two or three sports and, in many instances, journalists will report on the same sport throughout their careers, never seeking or being required to broaden their horizons into other sporting fields. This places severe restrictions on material and human resources. Furthermore, it dictates the breadth of coverage any newspaper can give to the varied environment of sport.

In the British daily and Sunday press professional sport has dominance over amateur sport, team sports get more coverage than individual sports, men's sport receives more attention than women's sport, heavily commercialized sport will gain a privileged status over large participation sports, urban sports are covered to the virtual exclusion of countryside or 'outdoor' sports, and new or imported sports are subordinate to historically traditional sports.

Some of these distinctions and formalized conventions of the sports page operate within sports as well as across them. For example, championship athletics will gain more coverage than paralympic athletics in spite of the widely acknowledged achievements of disabled athletes within the sport itself.

Similarly, as noted above and in Chapter 7, there is a marked gender bias in favour of men's professional sports that impacts on the comparative status of women in the same field (particularly noticeable in the virtually myopic coverage of women's team sports). In spite of the prejudicial parameters set by the sports press, there never appears to be a shortage of sports news itself. The routines of the sports reporter are such that there is always a daily supply of items, regardless of the extent to which sport is in the wider public eye.

The emphasis on which sports are reported, when and from where, clearly depends on seasonal changes, although the ubiquitous nature of football on the back pages of newspapers fifty-two weeks of the year belies the traditional division between winter and summer sports. This process, accelerated by the increasing role that television plays in sporting development, is likely to increase as the global commercialization of sports such as football, tennis and golf continues.

Indeed, the intrusion of the football season into the months of June and July during World Cup or European Championship years has somewhat distorted the cycle of sports news in favour of football and to the detriment of cricket, tennis, golf and athletics. There is now no rest from the latest hearsay regarding transfer deals and the latest exploits of stars, which places more strain on the ability of sports journalists to sustain the newsworthiness and exclusivity of their columns.

Constructing the sports page

As Hugh McIlvanney's reflection at the start of this chapter on the fortune of the sports journalist suggests, sports news is perceived as a trivial matter. News organizations, journalists and readers place sport in the wider news media environment and there is undoubtedly a hierarchy of importance given over to different fields of print journalism. Sport occupies a contradictory position of being placed low down the professional ranks of journalism – at times called the toy department – but enjoying a high status in the daily circulation of newspapers.

On taking over a newspaper, media mogul Rupert Murdoch will focus on the organization of the sports department and the level of sports coverage carried. He believes that getting this section of the newspaper quickly in order and offering extensive coverage of sport are crucial in both delivering readers to advertisers and increasing circulation. This philosophy has also held true in the growth of his television interests both in the US and the UK, which have been primarily driven by their sports programming.

Within the print media, a distinction is made between the 'tabloids' and the 'qualities', a split that is replicated in the typology of 'sports reporters' and 'sports writers'. The 'writer-driven' style of the quality papers is routinely contrasted with the assumed opposite, the reader-driven tabloid paper seen as cynically exploitative of sport and its personnel according to the demands of market-based profit maximization.

This often has an impact in the type of language used in sports reporting. Specific to British journalism, the issue of social class runs through the divisions in the newspaper market and the sports historically covered by differing newspapers. Although this is changing, vestiges of this system remain, as sports journalist Brian Glanville has pointed out:

> My thesis was that both the 'quality' and 'popular' writer were in some sense failures. The first because, although he could largely write as he pleased, about mass-interest sports, he reached only a fraction of the public. The second, because although he reached the public at large, he was rigidly confined to a highly stylised, ultimately patronising, form of journalism, which treated the readership with contempt. (Glanville, 1999: 257)

He notes that, unlike in the US, France or Italy, the British-based sports writer is locked into a particular quality–popular dichotomy which still exists today. What emerged in interviews with football journalists working in the broadsheet market in the UK was the main constraint they felt they worked under wasn't pressure from editors, but rather gaining access to players and managers.

Models of sports news

However, the manner in which issues of commerce and political affairs are dealt with by the sporting press is distorted by the various frames in which sports journalists operate. The clearest analysis of these different frames is given by Rowe's (1992) four typologies of sports journalism. Just as the wider field of journalism has its various modes and frames, sports journalism operates by producing 'hard news', 'soft news', 'orthodox rhetoric' and 'reflexive analysis'. Hard news may be characterized as the flipside to the current affairs dealt with at the front of the paper.

The sports headline mirrors the lead story of the front page, to create virtually a second headline that may attract the reader to buy the paper. Here, sports photojournalism also plays a distinctive role in the character and layout of the back page, not only as a pictorial representation of an event, but as part of the narrative that helps the abbreviated description of the action.

Hard news, then, records events, including match analysis, score-lines and results, in an apparently objective description of what has occurred. As Rowe argues, this invokes an air of authority to the serious business of sports reporting and will be constructed in the third person, with rare exception. However, in the British press the pretence to objectivity is masked by the subjective interpretation of events and, as Blain and O'Donnell (1998: 45) in their analysis of English tabloid coverage of Euro 96 reveal, interpretation of events is frequently framed by language that is 'restricted, adolescently masculine, and idiomatic, often deploying spoken modes and mixing them with what have now become codified tabloid habits'. This markedly contrasts with the specialized sporting press of continental Europe, where the analysis offered is more focused and technically sophisticated (Blain and O'Donnell, 1998: 46).

Reports on the latest commercial deals in sport will play a marginal role in the hard news of tabloid and broadsheet coverage, but will enter the more 'soft news' focus of the sports page. Soft news trades in the star gossip and biographical focus of key individuals within sport, whether they be athletes, managers, coaches, directors or administrators. Working within the realms of 'infotainment' soft news produces the latest 'scoops' or exclusives and, as mentioned above, provides the mainstay of the 'beat' reporters' daily routine. The emphasis here is on hero worship and, as we discussed in Chapter 5, it is the main vehicle for the construction and reaffirmation of celebrity status.

Star athletes may be placed in wider cultural terms, as reflecting the age in which they perform, but rarely are they situated in the political matrix of sport and, if at all, only in the context of representing the nation and thus causing it to resonate with some wider 'feel-good factor' (as in the pride engendered in the triumphs of Lewis Hamilton or Chris Hoy). Star profiles may also be an occasion where cross-promotion of sponsors and advertisers can piggyback on the focus on their star man or woman.

This may be a competition to win sports equipment used by the celebrity athlete or, as is more likely the case, a chance to reflect on the riches sport can bring to its elite, including a catalogue of endorsements and prize money from lucrative sponsored events.

Sport does not always get an easy ride. A high degree of critical comment is chewed over on a daily basis by a range of lead writers and

sports columnists. A third category Rowe alludes to is that of 'orthodox rhetoric', where the authorial subjectivity of the sports journalist
comes to the fore. The trade of the sports columnist is to develop a
distinctive voice that adopts a form of advocacy. This mode of writing
deploys a different form of authority to that of 'hard news' that stems
from the experience or celebrity status of the columnist.

It is not unusual for ex-professional sports stars to continue their
sporting careers by becoming the adopted pundit of any given paper.
With their inside track to the business of sport they can often reveal the
latest comings and goings in their specialized field or pass comment on
a particular issue without fear of accusation that they lack knowledge
or experience.

Orthodox rhetoric may also come from the seasoned sports journalist to pass judgement on the health of sport, casting a critical eye over
the latest scandals and transformations. This form of reporting does, at
least, admit the politics of sport. Revelations over irregular payments or
administrative procedures in sport, such as the bribery scandal involving members of the IOC and bidding Olympic cities, tangibly reveals
moments where the political economy of sport is of direct consequence
to a sports readership and judgement has to be passed.

Yet, rarely are such moments of criticism acutely problematized in
any sociological way. Issues often appear clear-cut and polemical. The
moral order of sport, historically embedded in the philosophy that
sport is a socio-cultural good, is often imposed or reasserts itself to
protect sport from wider political pressure for change.

The final mode of sports writing, involving what Rowe terms
'reflexive analysis', addresses the problematics of sport head on,
eschewing any simplified celebration of sport. The reflexive analysis of
sport critically questions the phenomenology of sporting practices and
discourse reconciling the celebration of sport with the particularized
subjective position of the writer.

Before looking briefly at the growth of sports print publishing,
we want to provide an overview of some of the significant challenges
facing sports journalism.

The political economy of sports journalism

We argue that it is globalization, digitization and marketization that
are the forces that are setting the parameters within which contemporary journalism is being produced and consumed. As noted in the
previous chapter, there is no doubt that many sports have become

increasingly global in the contemporary mediated age (Miller et al., 2001). The fusion of sports and media, and television in particular, has helped propel and transform major events such as the FIFA World Cup and Olympic Games. It is also a process in which sports journalism is deeply implicated.

The nature of modern communications, allied with sport as a cultural form and the global nature of sport, often appears to offer the possibility of some form of shared global identity or collective moment. However, the reality that is often associated with these shared sporting moments and a global cultural form is that they can also act as a vehicle for the expression of conflict, tension and a range of deeply rooted local identities. These tensions are often informed by economic, cultural and ethnic factors, and can often be reinforced by sports journalism as the sporting arena becomes a very public platform for the expression of a range of identities.

Sports journalism and the discourses it generates as a result remain a fascinating case study in how global and local media interact in contemporary societies, as sport itself can be at times global and outward looking, and also local and intensely domestic in its concerns and outlook.

Related to globalization is digitization. As we have noted above, digitization has clearly impacted on journalism in various forms. Within the arena of sports journalism, it has seen the emergence of an increasingly sophisticated battle for control of sports and how they are delivered, reported and made sense of for readers, listeners and viewers.

Previous research (Boyle and Haynes, 2004) has examined the ways in which sports clubs and organizations attempt to use the new media platforms of the Internet, digital TV and mobile telephony to deliver exclusive content and journalism to spectators. In so doing, many are seeking to bypass the traditional journalistic communication structures and speak directly to their audience. In the digital age the sports industry increasingly attempts to police its image through the control of its intellectual property (IP) and the growing use of public relations and other aspects of media management.

For sports journalists, issues of access to players and information has become more difficult as the commercial stakeholders in the game attempt to use the digital landscape to usurp and bypass journalism. There seems little doubt that over the next few years the battle lines will continue to be redrawn as sports seek to extract commercial value from all their assets, while media institutions (in particular those not holding specific coverage rights) will argue for the importance of continuing to journalistically report on all aspects of the sports industry.

Marketization has impacted both on the sports and media industries in the UK and around the globe. The intense commercial pressures that exist in the news market, particularly in a print sector that in the UK is viewed to be in long-term decline, can unduly shape sports journalism in negative ways. Phil Townsend, Director of Communications at one of the largest football clubs in the world, Manchester United, has argued that the pressure to deliver copy related to the club was leading to the most minor stories about the club being exaggerated and this helped fuel a 'cycle of mistrust' between footballers and journalists (*Press Gazette*, 30 January 2008).

At another level, the reporting of the political and economic dimension of sports has become more important in recent years as the commercialization of sport across the globe has developed. The sports industry now regularly involves major political, media and financial institutions. It forms part of public policy debates, and touches on areas of commerce such as sponsorship and marketing while remaining a potent cultural force in terms of national and regional identity formation.

In the UK press there has been a marked increase in the number of journalists reporting on and analysing this aspect of sports, with the 'quality' end of the market expanding its sports coverage dramatically. Sports journalism and writing is now seen as a key element of the wider branding of more and more newspapers as they reposition their appeals in attempts to attract new readers. A combination of the global expansion of sport, the new opportunities offered by digital media and the growing commercial value of sport have helped to extend the range of opportunities for those university graduates seeking to break into sports journalism. And of course the expansion of the sports industry and the range of commercial and political stakeholders involved also mean that rigorous, uncomplicit journalism is required in this area as never before. This presents a major ethical challenge for sports and journalism.

Journalism: wider challenges

Of course media institutions within which they work always shape journalists. This appears obvious but is actually quite important as increasingly the media marketplace within which media institutions operate plays a key role in shaping the scale and scope of the type of journalism that appears in print, on television or on the web. Recent damning critiques of the state of journalism in the UK by Alastair Campbell (Campbell, 2008), journalist and former communications advisor to Prime Minister Tony Blair, and investigative journalist Nick Davies (Davies, 2008) both cite the commercial constraints within which news organizations operate as having a negative impact on journalistic standards. In other words, while there are generic issues faced by all journalists there are particular constraints dictated by the specific media organization within which you as a journalist work.

We would also argue, certainly in the UK that many of the issues faced by sports journalists are actually similar to those increasingly faced by journalists working in other areas of the trade, such as politics and business (Boyle, 2006). Yes, there are particular aspects of reporting on the world of sports that are unique, yet equally there are more similarities with other branches of journalism than has been previously acknowledged.

Of course many of these issues are now driven by the broader forces of globalization, digitization and marketization. While these are generic terms, how they come to interact with each other and get played out in particular countries and journalism markets is dictated by the specific cultural and economic context within which sports journalism is located. In other words, the forces of globalization, digitization and marketization influence journalism in many countries, but often in different ways and within differing contexts. So there are similarities in the practised trade of sports journalism in, say, the UK and the US, but also significant differences in journalistic cultures. Sports journalists across the world are the same, but they are also different.

Sports journalism in digital media environment

A central feature of sports journalism in the UK is that it is part of a process that is seeing the extension and growth of the news journalism arena. Twenty-four hour rolling news channels now carry live media conferences involving sport and sporting issues in a manner unrecognizable ten years ago. In addition, rolling radio news means that another source of information is also being made available both to fans and, importantly, other sports journalists. The impact of these changes is to quicken the pace at which information gets circulated across media platforms, something discussed in more detail later in this article.

Another characteristic of the digital age is the growing synergies taking place across previously distinct media outlets. For example, while there is a history of links between some areas of the sports print and the broadcasting sector, digital technology, combined with a more market driven media system, is facilitating ever closer and often more commercial links. In an increasingly competitive multi-channel digital television environment, the brand exposure that the print media can bring to a fledgling television sports channel is important. It also allows various economies of scale to be enjoyed across journalistic resources and costs, while facilitating the cross-flow of news and editorial from print to both broadcast and online outlets.

One of the issues these kinds of editorial relationship raise is the extent to which sports journalism becomes complicit with a range of relationships that extend across newspapers and broadcasters, with the latter being rights holders to a number of sports. Will these events be promoted above others? Do these networks alter and impact on news values? Is there room for critical uncomplicit sports journalism that may be critical of other media partners? It would be naive to suggest that such commercial developments do not have an impact on editorial decisions.

In the UK, as a combination of both the digital landscape and a more lightly regulated broadcasting market allow a growing number of such synergies to develop, these editorial issues will have to be worked through. For sports journalists they suggest that some of the wider ethical dilemmas faced by their colleagues at the so called 'hard news' end of the journalistic spectrum about reporting on issues that are commercially sensitive to media organizations are becoming more difficult to avoid. As we have argued throughout the book, the digital age of sports journalism is characterized by elite sports that have become increasingly financially dependent on media organizations. Sports journalism now operates in a highly competitive environment where the speed of information flows and a multitude of often competing media platforms, all eager for content and comment, have led to a blurring of the traditional boundaries between news and sport. The lack of clear editorial boundaries in journalism is a central characteristic of the contemporary journalistic landscape.

Sports journalism on the web

There is no shortage of sports-related content available on the Internet. Journalists will use the web as a source for information, and in particular with official websites for sports teams attracting exclusive content, often this will be the first port of call for journalists looking for direct quotes from a player, manager or athlete. However, despite the explosion of material on the web, in terms of sports journalism, the wider institutional impact has been towards reinforcing already existing media brands.

In the UK official club football websites will carry material which they have gathered and sourced in-house and distribute it across the range of media platforms endorsed by the club. At the height of the dot com boom it was envisaged that the top clubs would have their own teams of in-house journalists generating content across a range of official digital media outlets for the club, with this exclusive content generating revenue through subscriptions and advertising (Boyle and Haynes, 2004). The reality was that the market and in some cases the technology was underdeveloped for such a fundamental restructuring of the sports news food chain. The key issue is the extent to which some element of trust and lack of complicity is required to give any sort of journalism legitimacy. Journalists working for club publications both on and offline are there to promote the club and work to a different agenda than those sports journalists working for other media organizations.

However the web has impacted on the already fraught issue of journalistic access to sports stars. As the stars of sport have developed a greater awareness of the importance and commercial value of image rights in the digital environment, this has been accompanied by a rise in personal websites attempting to offer exclusive comment.

The web also sees a lot of sports-related material and fans, websites generating considerable amounts of content, comment and information. Often this material is reacting against some comment or opinion that has appeared in the sports print media. Yet even in this unregulated market of sports journalism, some element of authority remains important and as a result, rather than any one simple source, fans use the web to access journalism from a range of sources, including official club websites, but also through established media brands such as the BBC and Sky.

The changing pace of news gathering

One key element that characterizes the digital sports news environment is the pace at which sports news stories are circulated in and across a range of media platforms. At the BBC journalists input copy that is then carried across the range of media platforms providing sports news for the Corporation. This pace of news is important as it both challenges the authority of the traditional print media sector that simply cannot keep up with delivering breaking news to their readers, but also offers an opportunity for that paper to extend its brand through an online presence. As noted earlier, newspapers during the 2008 Olympic Games used their websites to carry an initial story, with a view to driving readers to the more in-depth print version which would appear the following day.

However, the pace at which stories get picked up and carried across media outlets also presents a challenge for traditional notions of journalistic integrity. As the race to be first with a story has increased in an age of 24/7 rolling news, the accuracy and indeed the fundamental role of a journalist in the circuit of communication begins to change.

In sports news, the task of checking, filtering and making sense of stories for readers, listeners and viewers becomes more difficult as a lack of time become an increasing constraint for journalists. This is further complicated with the increasing use of the Internet as a news source for sports journalists. While this allows them access to the newswire services, many also use it for trawling for information and stories, often posted on fans, websites and often less than 100 per cent reliable. There is also the issue of the instant nature of the posting of information on the web, such as quotes from news conferences, which previously would have been eagerly retained and used exclusively by the print media.

The pressure of time has always been an aspect of print journalism culture, but in an age where news agencies can be posting quotes and comments from players on their websites almost as soon as a press conference (which may have been carried live on television and or radio) has concluded, the opportunities for a sports journalist to step back from a story and dig deeper have become less frequent. When this process is allied to the increasingly complex business-related stories that are part of the sports media landscape it can become a confusing and potentially difficult terrain for sportswriters.

Reputation management and sports journalism

The issue of the impact of the pressure of time, as previously rigid deadlines have tended to collapse and sports news is carried 24/7 across more media outlets, can be an issue for sportswriters, as is the growing awareness of the damage that (mis)information or opinion can have on someone's reputation in the age of almost instant dissemination via the Internet (Boyle and Haynes, 2006).

In an increasingly image-conscious media age where stories are picked up and reproduced across the digital landscape at great pace, sports people are willing to sue over issues raised in the sports pages. When this had occurred in the past, these stories tended to have been broken by news journalists and carried at the front end of newspapers. This tendency to extend litigation to the sports pages also gives some insight into the problems faced by sports journalists in covering sports-related stories that involve complex financial issues. In this instance, a growing willingness to sue can act as a deterrent to journalists wishing to probe parts of the sports industry that are already not particularly extensively covered. In an age where large amounts of sports journalism is devoted to comment and opinion (rather than factual information) and where the pace at which stories gets circulated around the public domain increases, cases of litigation involving either sports writers of even television sports 'pundits' who are able to have ghost columns carried in the print and online media are likely to grow as the commercial value of protecting reputation continues to escalate.

There is also a growing tendency for one part of a media institution to be affected by stories that have been generated in other parts of the organization or in other areas of journalism. For example, Manchester United manager Sir Alex Ferguson is in 2008 still refusing to give interviews to the BBC television football programme *Match of the Day* because of another BBC current affairs programme *Panorama* that made allegations about Ferguson's son, then a football agent. When a Chelsea football player was splashed over the front page of *the Sun* newspaper in early 2008 with allegations relating to his private life, the football club promptly banned a football reporter from that newspaper from attending their weekly press conference.

The growth of more sophisticated public relations (PR) and media management culture around elite sports and stars also means that access is increasingly controlled and the formalizing of media conferences for journalists mean that informal contact with sources in the sport has become more difficult (Sugden and Tomlinson, 2007). In one respect this has been positive in making information more openly available; in other ways, however, it has limited the ability of the journalist to 'get inside the story' and reveal inside information to the reader or viewer. For some sports journalists this is an era where they are simply handed more and more (controlled) information from which they build their copy without having to get out and chase a story.

As in other areas of journalism, the growth of PR has made being a journalist both easier (you are sent loads of information) and also more difficult as independent lines of enquiry are increasingly off limits and access to key players in the sports industry is carefully controlled. One of the most marked changes over the last decade has been the migration of PR practice associated with the entertainment industry of film and television into the world of sports, and football in particular. Elite stars can now demand copy, headline and photograph approval in a manner designed to control their media image. This is not simply agents seeking control for their sporting client, but increasingly sponsors such as Nike and Adidas controlling access and shaping the journalism associated with their brands. Simon Caney, editor of *Sport* magazine in the UK, argues:

> My view is that copy approval is something we have to live with, particularly where footballers are concerned. [It used to be as a sports journalist] all about who you had in your contacts book. Now you need about six phone numbers. You need Charlie Brookes at Nike and John Deacon at Adidas. . . . Sports journalism in the last 20 years has changed dramatically. (*Press Gazette*, 11 January 2008)

As the distance between the elite stars of sport and those journalists who report on them grows, so the nature of the journalism changes and the growth of promotional PR grows. Journalist Nick Davies (2008) argues that the volume of news stories that are generated by PR agencies and passed as news stories across the British media is growing and extensive, indicating that this is a challenge faced not simply by those working in the sports journalism arena.

The 'always on' sports journalist

If the media landscape within which sports journalists ply their trade has altered, so too has the relationship they have with technology and established patterns of working. The mobile phone means the journalist can be in constant contact with the office and potentially being directed by the sports desk while laptops and e-mail facilitate the sending of copy back to the desk and with wireless technology there now exists an ability to 'write on the road' and to file copy across a range of media platforms. Sports journalists working in 2008 are asked to produce considerably more copy than their counterparts of twenty years ago as the space to be filled, either on or offline, continues to expand.

What characterizes the digital sporting landscape is both the 'always on' nature of communication and the expansion in the range of media outlets that require to be serviced with sports content. A feature of the digital age in the UK has been the growth and reliance on freelance sports journalists. The growth in freelance journalists covering sport has been marked over the last decade or so as the range of print outlets from magazines to non-sporting publications which may carry sports material through to an expanded wire service has developed. In addition, newspaper sports sections will of course often use freelance journalists as regular contributors, particularly during the football season. The wire services such as the Press Association in the UK has expanded the numbers of journalists it has who work in the area of sports and service a range of media outlets across the print, broadcast and online sectors.

In the case of the financial funding of print sports journalism, the situation is often uneven across the sector. While a number of sports editors at UK national newspapers will argue that compared to their rivals they are under-resourced to compete, other news desks see the sports desk as being relatively well resourced. Indeed at a time when print journalism as a whole has seen resources (and editorial staff) cut, the increase in the profile of sports journalism has resulted in it being one of the better resourced areas of journalism, and while at the popular end of the print media market this has been the case for a number of years, the level of resource has increased at the broadsheet/compact end of the spectrum.

The sporting field: publish and be damned?

Finally we want to say something briefly about the explosion in writing about sports that has taken place beyond the newspaper and magazine arena. The original notion of the reflexive sportswriter who uses sports as a backdrop through which to write about life and broader themes has been an American tradition.

Of course, there have been journalists in Britain writing about sport in an intelligent manner (many influenced by the great US sports journalists such as Budd Schulberg and Damon Runyon), and there are non-football books which appeared during the 1980s which drew heavily on the US model of sportswriting epitomized by Norman Mailer's poetic commentary on the boxing industry. Perhaps the most interesting was by novelist Gordon Burn. His book *Pocket Money: Bad-Boys, Business-Heads and Boom-Time Snooker*, was published in 1986 at the height of the popularity of the sport in Britain.

Burn took the reader on a behind the scenes tour of the global snooker circuit, dominated by television, sponsors and money. However, in keeping with the US tradition, this is a book which tells us as much about Britain during the mid-1980s as about the sport of snooker. Here is a sport dominated by working-class players being transformed by television and sponsorship and being driven by the entrepreneurial Thatcherite skills of Barry Hearn. Burn returned to a sporting theme with his book *Best and Edwards: Football, Fame and Oblivion* (2006) in which he used these two iconic footballing stars from differing eras to examine their impact on popular culture and to reflect on the changing role and function of celebrity in modern media culture.

The growth in sports publishing is also reflected in the William Hill Sports Book of the Year award first instigated in 1989. Over the last decade or so trends have emerged so while there are a few books that deal with the challenges of, say, being a sports journalist – the best of which include Tom Humphries (2003) and Simon Hughes (2005) – the growth has been in fans writing about the role of sport in their lives, a genre kick-started in Britain back in 1992 with Nick Hornby's *Fever Pitch: A Fan's Life.* While US novelists have long used sport as an integral part of their narratives, more recently British writers such as David Peace in *The Damned Utd* (2006) and Joseph O'Neill in *Netherlands* (2008) have used, in very different ways, football and cricket and the literary fiction genre to explore particular moments in contemporary British and American social and cultural life.

Other books place sport in a broader social and cultural context, such as Butcher's (2004) account of the rivalry between Seb Coe and Steve Ovett that defined British athletics in the 1980s or Humphries' (2007) majesterial examination of one of the great rivalries in Irish sport between the gaelic football teams of Dublin and Kerry which dominated domestic sport in that country for a large part of the 1970s and early 1980s. Some offer genuine insider accounts of sport's often distasteful culture including a number of books around the sport of cycling such as Paul Kimmage's *Rough Ride* (2007) and accounts from David Walsh (2007) and Whittle (2008). Kimmage, a former rider who has reinvented himself as a journalist, adds the intriguing element of the 'poacher turned gamekeeper' to his account of the sport and its relationship with both drugs and the media. However, the bulk of sports-related books in what has become a major industry are ghosted by journalists and are biographies of sports stars past and present.

In turn the growing trend to publish high-profile and contro-versial accounts of sporting events while often still actively playing in the sport or being directly involved has prompted some debate around ethics and the role of journalism in this process. As journalists have found their social bond broken with the sports stars they cover because of (1) the extreme wealth that know insulates elite athletes from the rest of society, (2) the breakdown of trust between sports and journalism and (3) the rise in the panoply of people who protect and manage the media image of their clients, so getting 'up close and personal' with sports stars has become almost impossible. One way this can happen is by taking a ghosting job for a player and writing their autobiography.

Even this aspect of the sports media culture has changed. Most books make their money, not through direct sales but through selling the serialization rights to a newspaper. To do this, headline stories around scandal or controversy are given prominence by the newspaper. Given the levels of wealth among elite footballers, the need to engage in this activity is financially minimal. Not surprisingly, with a few exceptions – such as Eamon Dunphy's ghosted account of Roy Keane (Keane and Dunphy, 2003) – most footballer's book are anodyne and dull (Boyle and Haynes, 2006). Given that cricketers and rugby players are in sports that reward their stars less well than football it is unsurprising to see players and managers from these sports getting involved in the most controversial sports books.

England rugby world cup stars Lawrence Dallaglio (2008) and Mike Catt (2008) both attracted criticism for their breaking of dressing room confidences in their autobiographies which also lambasted the qualities of the then England coach. The governing body of the sport, the RFU, reacted by trying to introduce contractual bans on autobiographies among existing players. While former England head cricket coach Duncan Fletcher (2007) provided the sporting public with what one sportswriter, Kevin Mitchell, called the 'most wickedly entertaining read of the winter' (*The Observer*, 4 November 2007) as he told tales which included one involving a heavily drunk England star player turning up for net practice. Fletcher was again heavily criticized for breaking the 'sporting code of silence' by revealing what some felt should always be kept within the dressing room or on the training pitch.

In a digital age where all sports – and publishers – are competing for media and public attention, and there is money to made by selling controversy within a celebrity obsessed, expanding 24/7 media network, then one can expect the age of revelation to continue. Equally, in an era of sports image and media management consultants we would also expect to see the battle to control the stories emanating from behind the closed doors of sport also intensify, with sports journalists complicit in this complex process.

Conclusion: what is sports journalism for?

One of the challenges for newspapers is to adapt to the ongoing migration of readers online in search of news. It is also clear that sports news and journalism will continue to be an important aspect of this new online news ecology. One issue the decline of 'traditional journalism' and the rise of bloggers (and user-generated content) have raised is the challenge this process has for the legitimacy of journalistic authority. Much of this discussion has focused on the reporting of politics and the impact that the web and the rise of bloggers are having on political journalism.

However, in the arena of sports journalism there is a long tradition of dissent from 'mainstream' sports journalism through media platforms such as the print fanzine movement of the 1980s/1990s. Evolving out of this movement, sports fans were among the earliest groups on the web to establish communities and networks either to circulate information and organize themselves or to lampoon 'traditional media' coverage of their sport or team.

While this tradition continues, the breaking of sports news across the web and digital 24-hour news and sports television and radio channels has not eroded the appetite, particularly at the broadsheet/compact end of the market, for more in-depth and reflective sports journalism. Thus while the development of online sports journalism is certainly a key part of any news strategy in the digital age for an organization such as the BBC, the market for print sports journalism has also remained strong at a time when other areas of journalism, such as political coverage, appear to be suffering. Indeed it is striking the extent to which online web coverage of sport appears not to have significantly impacted on the appetite of readers for the traditional newspaper variety.

The expansion of journalism on the web has offered increased opportunities for journalists writing about sport and helped encourage the development of freelance sports journalism. Organizational change in these institutions over the last five years or so has seen a merger of editorial and strategic thinking with sports content and sports journalism being used to generate content across media platforms in organizations large enough to enjoy economies of scale.

Sports journalism in the digital age is of course characterized by continuity and change. It remains the case that sports fans require differing types of information, and will use different media at the appropriate times to access this. In sports fan culture, speed of information is of the essence, and in this traditional broadcasting, the web and mobile communications are ideal vehicles for results and breaking news stories. The web is particularly important for fans who live abroad allowing them to keep connected to their team or sport in a manner that was unimaginable a decade or so ago.

In the UK, the growing PR practice around the sports industry as its economic and political importance grows presents a challenge to journalists working in this field. But the challenges they face are similar to journalists in other areas. There remains a need to get out of the office and look beyond the neatly crafted media release and to question on behalf of readers and viewers. Sport, with its mixture of entertainment, drama and news values, offers a particular challenge for journalists in their need to both inform and entertain in an increasingly fast-paced news environment while addressing in many cases an increasingly knowledgeable audience.

Sport continues to offer a range of compelling narratives for the twenty-first century, and despite the rise of television sport, sports journalists remain one of the key cultural narrators of that ongoing story. In short, sports journalism should be about reporting, enquiring, explaining and at times holding to account sports on behalf of the fans. As sport becomes an increasingly central aspect of contemporary popular culture, the commercial value of sports journalism and selected sports journalists will continue to escalate. The challenge for sports journalists working, for example, in the UK is to offer uncomplicit, informative and entertaining journalism against the backdrop of an increasingly commercial and privatized media system. In such an environment the need for some parts of sports journalism to question, investigate and call to account the powerful within sports and its attendant political and commercial culture will become even more acute. And while sports journalism has correctly been criticized for its lack of investigative edge over the years, it should be noted that this area remains a small but growing aspect of the wider culture of sports journalism. Again, the decline in investigative journalism is not unique to sports coverage and is a concern across the spectrum of news journalism more generally (Davies, 2008).

Chapter 10

Consuming Sport:
Fans, Fandom and the Audience

The [Manchester] City takeover reminds us of this truth: the game may have originated here, but, even as it grows richer, it has become a pursuit in which its inventors are increasingly marginalized. We don't own the clubs and we don't play for them. We are merely spectators. (White, 2008)

Introduction

Being a sports fan has become an expensive passion. Much of our attention in this book has focused on the history, political economy and textual analysis of media sport. However, central to both the media and sporting industries is, of course, the fan and/or reader/ viewer, the people who consume sport, either in its relatively raw form or in its increasingly mediated form. Part of what we want to do in this chapter is to examine the consumption of mediated sport and attempt to develop an empirically grounded theory of audiences for televised sport. In the latter part of the book we have also been interested in the relationship between sport, media and identity formation. To this end it is also worth saying something about how fandom relates to this process and to re-emphasize the extent to which the media are not the sole agents shaping the process of identity formation among fans and other collectivities.

The masculine ritual of sport

The problems of developing an epistemology of watching televised sport become immediately apparent as soon as any attempt is made to conceptualize its audience who are characteristically referred to as 'armchair supporters'. This oft-quoted stereotype conjures up images of that other fictional social outcast the 'couch potato': sat in front of the screen with a 'four-pack' of beer and munching away at copious amounts of 'fast food'. One consequence of this characterization is the creation of a social and psychological pathology of televised sports audiences which conflates the individual viewer with an elitist perception of fandom as a deviant cultural phenomenon. As Jenson (1992: 9) has suggested with regard to images of fandom in general, this behaviour can frequently be seen to be obsessive, where 'Fandom is seen as a psychological symptom of a presumed social dysfunction.' The perceived slothful nature of this mode of consuming sport – isolated, lonesome and narcissistic – works to stigmatize individuals and groups seeking relief from the anxieties of modern life.

Moreover, by defining fandom in this way, Jenson argues that it allows a form of self-aggrandizement for those demarcated outside the fanatical, supporting 'the rational over the emotional, the educated over the uneducated, the subdued over the passionate, the elite over the popular, the mainstream over the margin, the status quo over the alternative' (Jenson, 1992: 24). While these overtly conservative images of fandom would not appear to relate in any way to the four million or so regular viewers who watch a programme like BBC television's *Match of the Day* on a Saturday night, certain dichotomies are invoked by the phrase 'armchair supporter'. Perhaps the most ubiquitous dichotomy would be between the passive experience of watching televised sport and the active experience of being among the supporters in the sports arena. This separation of the spectating experience has been at the heart of administrators' fears about the effect broadcasting would have on attendances at sport. For its part, television has gone out of its way to lure the 'armchair supporter' to the screen, and it is to the process by which the coverage of sport invokes a masculine mode of spectatorship that the analysis now turns.

Male spectatorship and televised sport

Influenced by feminist psychoanalytical film theory, recent critiques on male spectatorship have emerged to study the processes by which masculine subjectivities are constructed through visual pleasure and narrative structures (Nixon, 1996). Here, the spectator is constituted as a gendered subject, the dominant male gaze being characterized as voyeuristic, linear and contemplative. Drawing upon this theory of spectatorship which focuses on the 'interpellation' or mode of address of film discourses, Morse (1983) suggests that televised sports spectatorship elicits homoerotic desire as it involves a 'gaze at maleness'.

Moreover, as we have seen with the commentator's narrative (Chapter 4), the vernacular of televised sports invites the male spectator to participate in the 'world of sport' which confirms sport as a male preserve.

In a critique of this dominant position on classical male spectatorship, Rose and Friedman (1994) have argued that, while a degree of fetishization of the male body constitutes the 'hermeneutic process of reading and evaluating athletic performances', the 'analytic discourse' on the male spectator of televised sport should 'ultimately be qualified by the melodramatic'. In other words, as Morse herself realized but did not develop theoretically, televised sport can be viewed as a 'male soap opera' with multiple narratives which highlight 'personal struggle', 'social tension' and 'moral conflict'. Appropriating the theory of 'distraction' from the film theorist Kracauer (1926) and reinterpreting the notion of a 'rhythm of reception' from Modlenski (1983), Rose and Friedman state:

> What is ultimately at stake in our argument, then, is a reconceptualisation of masculine modes of consumption and production: we are suggesting that the distracted, decentred and other-oriented consumption of sport by television spectators reflects and reifies the patterns of perception and the skills required of the postindustrial male worker. (Rose and Friedman, 1994: 26)

As suggested in Chapters 2 and 3, television was integral to the standardization and commodification of sport, as new technologies were continually introduced to 'make sense' of the action for the viewers. The sports commentator places the spectator in relation to the melodrama of the event which, like a serial, is ongoing and continually fragmenting into new stories about players, managers, clubs and nations.

While the main commentator provides the narrative within the action – heightening the sense of actuality and 'liveness' – the co-commentator, or in-match summarizer, provides and draws upon wider narratives, which are far more speculative and function, according to Rose and Friedman (1994: 27), 'like the gossip of soap opera'. It is in the frame of this latter discourse, specifically, that the male spectator is interpellated to identify with sport as a masculine domain. Identification with the re-representation of the action is central to the popular pleasures produced by televised sport. The familiarity with the form and style of commentary and emotional identification with specific players and teams combine to dissolve the boundary of the television screen and invoke participation from the viewer. Again, we can recall early attempts to develop commentary techniques in radio and television which sought to address the listener as a friend. However, it could be argued that the 'friend' in question is distinctly male and, as O'Connor and Boyle (1993: 116) suggest in terms of football: 'If women are accommodated within the discourses of televised football . . . it is in a marginal and trivial manner'.

By engaging with this discourse, men view televised sport as an extension of their world and, as we will argue later in a case study of boxing, the metatexts of televised sport provide social tools with which men can operate in public domains, as part of a 'hegemonic masculinity' (Connell, 1987). Therefore, instead of analysing male spectatorship as distinct from a feminine mode of spectatorship, televised sport can be read as an 'open text' in which the 'dialogic activity' of spectating involves absorption into multiple identifications with characters, settings and narratives of the 'world of sport', in a 'rhythm of reception' which is distracted, partial and interrupted (a masculine counterpart to the standard reading of women's reception of soap opera). That fans should make paradigmatic readings of televised sport, focusing on the play of possibilities between stars, stories and action, should not, however, deflect from the actual, historically constructed power relations between men and women (and men and men) which are realized in televised sport and are characteristic of a dominant 'gender order' (Connell, 1987).

As we suggest in Chapter 7, televised sport practices and discourses continue to connote maleness. It is in this way that male images of sport, equating male sporting prowess with masculine superiority, contribute to the social reproduction of dominant cultural values. Sport remains a contradictory domain in which male emotions, culturally silenced in wider society (Rutherford, 1996), are legitimately expressed: the image of Paul Gascoigne's tears at Italia 90 being the most public 'show' of male grief in recent memory (later self-parodied by the England player in an advert for Walkers crisps in 1996).

The imaging of such personalized moments within televised football attempts to invoke an emotional attachment from the viewer and, in the case of Gascoigne, his tears were shed for his country. His actions, therefore, conflate masculinity, sporting pride and national identity – all familiar points of reference with which football fans can identify. The feminist study of 'women's genres' has placed gender at the centre of understanding television spectatorship in terms of wider relational connections and 'interpretive communities', which are characterized by a gravitation towards certain discursive modes of interpreting media content (Radway, 1984). In following this contextualizing of media reception, we can employ similar modes of analysis to research the reception of televised sport by men. The interrelationships between gender, genre and fandom become important dynamics to the study of men watching televised sport. As Livingstone (1996: 445) has argued, how these variables are negotiated by the viewer has 'consequences for their critical responses, their participation and involvement, and their motivations for viewing'. Having provided an overview of the discursive address of televised sport and the construction of the male spectator, the analysis now turns to the social and cultural consumption of the genre by men – this was conducted as part of the project Men Viewing Violence (Schlesinger et al., 1998) in which both authors were involved.

Men viewing boxing: Why study men? Why study violent sport?

Qualitative audience research has sought both to understand the ways that viewers use television in the belief that individuals have the power to engage actively with media to 'gratify' psychological needs and, on the other hand, to understand how a viewer's interpretation of television is informed by social group membership.

In the Broadcasting Standards Commission research project Men Viewing Violence, fifteen focus groups were conducted among men from various backgrounds to simulate broadly 'the ways in which people talk about what they see on the screen when presented with a common topic' (Schlesinger et al., 1998: 5). Participants viewed a range of violent programming so that how interpretations and reactions were influenced by social status, ethnicity, age, sexual preference and general life experiences could be studied. The study built on the research design of a previous project, Women Viewing Violence (Schlesinger et al., 1992), where programmes were chosen to stimulate group discussion on depictions of violence against women. In the men's study, we were acutely aware of the need to widen the range of programmes to include not only violence by men against women, but also men against men, including violence in sport. The introduction of sport, in particular boxing, to the screenings became important for several reasons.

Firstly, it allowed the investigation of men's identification with forms of aggressive masculinity. As we noted in Chapter 7, the connection between sport and masculinity is central to understanding the genre of media sport, and the researchers were eager to explore the various myths that connect gender with particular types of programming. Secondly, it enabled the exploration of men's reactions to various aspects of violence in sport: brutality, arrogance, drama and spectacle. To this end, men viewed two contrasting boxing events, one representing the competitive thrill and destructive violence of the sport (Nigel Benn against Gerald McLellan), the other representing the glitz and glamour of contemporary boxing on pay-television (Prince Naseem Hamed against Remigio Molina). A third reason for choosing sport as a stimulus was methodological. Audience studies of men remain a neglected field of media research, partly due to the problems associated with researching groups of men. In conducting focus groups with men, not only is the process of recruitment often difficult, but the moderating process can often be stifled by the intransigence of male participants to open up discussion and express their views and feelings.

However, sport offers one field of enquiry where men freely cooperate in a controlled group setting because, if managed properly, discussion can soon come to simulate the informal conversation familiarly associated with the social relations men experience in everyday life. Finally, and connected to this last point, the study was interested to explore men's general consumption of televised sport and examine how knowledge of sport carries currency in everyday social relations. Before conducting the focus groups respondents were also asked to complete a questionnaire that surveyed their media consumption and sporting interests. The overwhelming response, more than 80 per cent of the 88 men in the study, highlighted sport as the favourite type of television programme. However, fewer than 10 per cent had subscriptions to Sky Sports channels in the home, and only two respondents had paid for a pay-per-view sports event. The men's media consumption and preferences pointed to a stereotypical association between gender and genre, with evidence from the survey supporting the recognition of televised sport as a masculine domain. The notable exceptions to this dominant finding came from two groups of gay men from Glasgow and Manchester. These two groups showed a stark contrast to the other groups in the survey, in both the participation in and viewing of sport. Gay men in the study equated contact and team sports with dominant hegemonic masculinities that exemplified the macho, often violent, ideology displayed through sport by a large proportion of the male population. A general abhorrence of violence was crystallized through a specific dislike and avoidance of contact sports.

While the feeling of anti-sports violence was by no means exclusive to the gay men in the study, it did suggest that the way different masculine identities are constructed do have a significant bearing on the experiences and interpretative strategies of viewing violent sports on television.

The excitement of brutality

In the group discussions gay men continued to press home their dislike of boxing, with some participants equating violence in sport to other forms of violence in both public and private domains:

> I think in some people it will evoke thoughts of violence towards either their partner or somebody else who is watching at the time . . . because people who are immature may get some kick out of it and think, right, well, your missus is giving me some grief, or a partner . . . smack, I'll wallop you one. (Gay white man, 30–39, Manchester)

The sense that boxing could initiate violence among groups of men was not widely held, although one young working-class man did note that 'It always kicks off [trouble starts] in pubs when there's a boxing match on'. However, it was generally agreed across the groups that boxing could act as a cathartic outlet for male aggression:

> I've been to a couple of boxing matches and the crowd do generally get worked up, I think it does, I think that is one sport that does bring out a bit of aggressiveness in people. . . . and watching it on TV? I feel aggressiveness but I wouldn't necessarily say I would get aggressive, but you feel that aggressiveness there. (Middle-class white man, 30–39, Glasgow)

The notion that boxing represents a legitimate field of violent confrontation was widely understood, although not all men found the sport entertaining. For some men boxing presented something of a paradox – it could be engaging and challenge their moral outlook on violence in sport, at one and the same time:

> I see boxing as purely entertainment but even though I say that, after a fight, I can sit back and say, 'Oh shit, this is brutal!' You know? but when I am watching it, I see it as purely . . . I mean you feel the adrenaline you know . . . almost . . . sometimes you find you are moving about. (West African man, 18–29, Glasgow)

The dramatic intensity of the Benn/McLellan fight was viewed by men in the study to be central to the excitement of boxing.

As we have argued above and in previous chapters on the presentation of sporting narratives, a key aspect to people's enjoyment of media sport are the contingent aspects that rely on the unknown outcome of events and the importance of characterization in the unfolding story. Identification with winners and losers, favourites and underdogs, is, therefore, an important aspect of the viewer's experience of televised sport. Again, as one middle-class man from Manchester responded to viewing the Benn fight:

> I think it was the fact he was swinging from like . . . both sides . . . it looked like one guy was going to win, then it was the other guy. It kept swinging backwards and forwards so you were in limbo really. And it was action all the time. What I was thinking was, action, action, action, wasn't it? (Middle-class man, 30–39, Manchester)

The majority of the men in the study had a knowledge of the Benn/McLellan fight and were aware of the damage caused to the American boxer. This was viewed as an inevitable aspect of the sport, and it was widely held that boxers understood the dangers ahead of them in the ring. It was clear from the research that a significant number of men enjoy boxing because of the raw excitement it engenders. Moreover, while many of the men found the brutality of the sport abhorrent, they found no favour in wanting the coverage of the sport on television regulated or banned.

Boxing as spectacle and entertainment

We noted in Chapter 7 how the celebration of boxing by the media can serve to mask the brutality and violence associated with the sport. In the study, the discussion of how men engaged with television coverage of boxing led on to questions regarding the entertainment values of televised sport. In particular, the research focus turned to men's perceptions of BSkyB's coverage of boxing, which was discussed through a case study of the featherweight boxer Prince Naseem Hamed. Even for those men who disliked boxing, it was agreed that the entertainment values built into the coverage of the sport legitimized its appeal. Men above the age of thirty could remember the days when televised boxing was dominated by the BBC during the 1970s and 1980s. It was felt by some of the men that television coverage had dramatically changed over time. The intensive coverage given over to boxing on Sky Sports was considered to be overtly voyeuristic, in the sense that the camera dwelt on every punch and blow. For some, this had turned them away from viewing boxing. Again, particular examples were used to illustrate the point:

> Years and years ago, I would have enjoyed a big Muhammed Ali fight, and I would have been a typical sort of prime-time TV fan, wanting to watch it for the excitement. But as I got to know boxing and more about what goes on in boxing, in terms of moves and punches and that, I don't find it that entertaining. (Middle-class man, 30–39, Manchester)

> I think they've got to be very careful with Sky, in that now you've got the action replays, so close and so slow and so accurate, you can have different camera angles. It becomes very disturbing, to me personally. (Middle-class man, 30–39, Glasgow)

The hype that surrounds contemporary boxing and the spectacle garnered by television for stars like Prince Naseem Hamed was understood to be part and parcel of big-business sport.

Some men believed Hamed was deliberately 'mismatched' to ensure his longevity at the top, placing emphasis on 'showbiz' rather than sport, 'pulling in the punters . . . the audience who would not normally watch boxing' (Middle-class man, 40+, Leeds).

It was noted that Hamed's fights tended to be short, and some concern was raised regarding the cost of viewing boxing on subscription channels where there was no guarantee of value for money. The introduction of pay-per-view boxing also drew criticism from those who subscribed to Sky Sport, but were forced to pay extra to view major fights:

> I must admit, it goes against the grain with me, this pay per view thing. Because up until recently we did have Sky, more or less full packages, but I was determined not to pay an extra £10 for boxing matches, because I thought if you are paying for sports channels, why should you have to pay extra? (Middle-class man, 30–39, Glasgow)

Resistance to paying for televised sport was clearly a big issue for men in the study, even when they had subscribed to specialist sports channels.

As the study of men viewing boxing further illustrates, the extent to which new vistas of consuming televised sport are opened up heavily depends on social relations of age and gender. Younger men were far more likely to live in a household that subscribed to Sky Sport, and were also more likely to view sport in social settings like the pub. It was also apparent that discussion about boxing opened up men's imaginary connection to a wider popular culture, where sport was an important aspect of male cultural capital. Sport, then, provides a quintessential example of men's relationship to the public and private domains: where men's active engagement with televised sport, in this case boxing, connects with men's domination in public life.

Ten years on, we feel this study still reveals something about how sport is packaged for its audience. In the case of boxing its relative obscurity from free-to-air television led to the bizarre spectacle of British Heavyweight Champion Lennox Lewis picking up the BBC's Sports Personality of the Year Award in 1999 even though the vast majority of the BBC's viewers would not have seen him fight. This contrasts with a previous era of televised boxing when millions tuned in to watch Henry Cooper or Muhammad Ali. Indeed, it was ironic that in an attempt to gain wider public recognition for his achievements towards the end of his career Lewis fought Hasim Rahman in April 2001 in a one-off deal with the BBC. Lewis lost and in many ways the BBC lost faith in professional boxing. The BBC had one final dalliance with professional boxing in 2005 when it signed a multi-fight deal with Olympic gold medalist Audley Harrison who had just turned professional. But his fights were dull affairs and audiences switched off. The fan base for boxing remains firmly on niche pay-television and its demographic remains staunchly young and male.

Tribal instincts: fandom and the media

Euro 2008 posed something of a problem for television in Britain as there were no 'home' nations to support. In a tongue-in-cheek trailer for their coverage of the tournament the BBC used a range of vox-pop opinion's from factory workers to schoolboys, fishmongers to cab drivers to answer the question 'Euro 2008, who will you support?' Each answer depended on some spurious connection to one of the competing teams or simply fell back on familiar stereotypes. Although whimsical and inviting the audience to have a 'bit of fun' the trailer did reflect a more serious point that fandom is very much about identity. Euro 2008 may have prompted some British viewers to seek a different nation to support, but more generally sports fans do not as a rule change their allegiances.

The vibrancy of football fandom in the UK and, indeed globally, has remained as strong as ever. The configuration of football fandom arguably changed dramatically through the 1990s (King, 1998; Sandvoss, 2003) with the widening points of consumption of all things football – whether in all-seater stadiums, subscription sports channels, replica kits or the web – but there remain continuities in rituals, in communal identities and through participation in the sport that are long established in British football subcultures. We would argue that the passion play that draws people to the game still underscores any transformation fans may have experienced in their ritual trail to the match. Fears that all-seater stadiums would undermine the atmosphere at football grounds are overstated. Although the clustering of passionate, sometimes violent fans in football terraces across the country may have gone, there is still enough evidence to suggest imagined communal identities around football survive and prosper in contemporary football stadiums (Williams et al., 2001).

The 1990s saw a noticeable reappraisal of the role fans play in sporting cultures. As has been well documented in academic and popular fan writing on football supporters, for much of the 1970s and 1980s any association with the game immediately brought up issues of violence and hooliganism. While there is now a celebratory autobiographical genre of books (Redhead, 2004) and numerous television dramas and films that chart the exploits of hooligan crews both home and abroad, what Emma Poulton (2007) has termed 'Hooliporn', such narratives of football violence are seen for what they are and have become a niche form of voyeuristic male entertainment. The media perception of fans underwent a complex transformation after the events at Hillsborough in 1989, largely motivated by supporter activism through the Football Supporters Association, club-based independent supporters' organizations and football fanzines (Redhead, 1991; Haynes, 1995; Brown, 1998; King, 1998; Giulianotti, 1999; Boyle and Haynes, 2004; Williams, 2006). While the level of democratic control fans have at their disposal remains negligible where decisions really count (Brown and Walsh, 1999), since the 1990s football culture has by comparison with the previous decades enjoyed more favourable public relations thanks to its fans. Football as it is played, consumed, enjoyed and discussed has become a more public entity in everyday life.

There does, however, remain serious questions about how the increasing globalization of sport – especially in terms of ownership, media coverage and commodification – has impacted on how we understand the dynamics of sports spectatorship and issues of identity. The takeover of Manchester United by the Glazer family in 2005 prompted a strong reaction from a particular section of the clubs' local fan base. Annoyed and disturbed by the rampant commercialism and foreign ownership of the club which was viewed as undemocratic and burdening the club with outrageous debt, a group of supporters boycotted their long-held status as season ticket holders and established their own football club FC United of Manchester (FCUM). The idea, *pace* the formation of AFC Wimbledon following the move of Wimbledon FC from London to Milton Keynes, was to devise an alternative football experience to the one being offered by Manchester United. Adam Brown, both an academic researcher of football and activist in the formation of FCUM, has suggested the move to form a new club was born of a desire for a 'liminal match-going experience' as well as a reawakening of community pride and interest through football (Brown, 2007).

More broadly, the takeover of British clubs by foreign investors and the general privatization of football stadiums as places of entertainment has led to the social exclusion from football of certain groups in society who lack either the economic or cultural capital to participate in the sport at various levels (Crabbe and Brown, 2004).

The globalization of sporting cultures can also have other impacts and impressions on long-time football fans that enable local and global differences to emerge. For example, in a fascinating article on his summer love affair with the Toronto Blue Jays, the BBC radio presenter Colin Murray revealed how his upbringing in Northern Ireland and a chance trip to North America as a teenager transformed the monocultural role football had for many young boys like him in Britain. Contrasting the experience of British and North American sports spectatorship Murray recounts:

> Baseball fans could not be any more different from football supporters. Here, everyone drinks alcohol and mingles freely in the stadium, seldom reacting to a rival fan in the very next seat as they goad a nearby outfielder. When the game is over, they trundle home safely. The police presence is almost nonexistent and the only trouble I witness is two slightly drunken fans being ejected from the ground for informing Red Sox legend Manny Ramirez, in a deafening rasp, that he 'fucking sucked', which to be fair, he did. (Murray, 2008)

Of course, the spectator experience of some British sports (even lower levels of football) shares some of these traits.

But such observations reveal new forms of sports fandom that are no longer rooted in local identities but form part of an emergent fan tourism that is global and also influenced by exposure through television and other media outlets (Sandvoss, 2003). This process has led Giulianotti (2002) to suggest a taxonomy of contemporary fandom that is made up of 'supporters, followers, fans and flaneurs', the latter characterized by the postmodern playfulness with sporting cultures and identities engaged in by Murray above. Late-modern sports fans are of their very nature viewed as transnational global consumers in search of experience and participation through sport that now appears, at least to them, as missing or lacking in more local sports subcultures. Predominantly North American sports like baseball, ice hockey, basketball and American football therefore gain purchase among certain sections of British society for whom football, cricket and rugby hold little attraction for various reasons (Crawford, 2004; Falcous and Maguire, 2005).

Of course, these flows in sports spectatorship and consumption move in varied ways. We mentioned in Chapter 5 the importance of global sports stars as the marketers of key sports brands around the world. David Beckham's iconic status has opened up markets for the FA Premier League, Manchester United and Real Madrid across the world, and indeed his global celebrity has been drawn upon to build spectator interest in soccer in the USA and as part of the promotion for the countdown to the London Olympic Games in 2012.

The increasing dominance of an elite group of football clubs in Europe, previously given an economic and political voice through the European lobby group G14 but now ingrained in the structure of the Champions League, has also created some new dynamics in sports fandom and identity that pull away from the national to the supranational level. King's analysis of new regional superpowers in European sport suggests certain fan identities are more European in their focus than in previous generations. As a consequence some Manchester United fans eschew any identification with being English or even of supporting the English national side in favour of a new regional pride in their city's status in Europe as they compete symbolically and economically with their European rivals in Milan, Madrid, Barcelona and Munich (King, 2003).

Identities rooted around football, then, can be seen to transform themselves depending on the power and success of particular clubs. New identities around football are also contingent on the availability of certain clubs on television, the Internet or computer games and their promotion of star players and associated consumer goods and services. In a report on the 'consuming passions' of football fans Tim Crabbe and his colleagues suggest that young people in particular use 'computer gaming technology' as their connection 'to contemporary patterns of football support, consumption and understandings of the game' (Crabbe et al., 2006).

Such developments may frequently be held up as an erosion of tradition, particularly by older male generations. However, we would concur with the analysis of John Williams (2007) when he argues that to equate these developments with the dissolution of more localized fan cultures and the corrosion of some of British (and European) sporting values would be an overstatement and contra to empirical evidence of rising attendances at many football grounds across Britain. This is not to suggest that fandom is stuck in some locally grounded traditional paralysis. Rather, as Williams makes clear, there is a need to understand that there remain certain continuities in sports fandom that endure and inform fan identities at the same time as new, often challenging forms of consumption and experiences are emerging in sport.

Richard Giulianotti's (2005b) research on Scottish supporters, in particular the 'Tartan Army', reveals some of the complexities and contradictions in contemporary football fandom. The 'Tartan Army' are paraded on our television screens at every available opportunity during major tournaments involving Scotland and receive a far more sanguine press than their English counterparts. Reporters and journalists are even allocated the role of following the fans in order to report 'home' the latest views and opinions from the unofficial 'Scottish camp' (see Chapter 8). The 'Tartan Army' as it is perceived by the media – and possibly by those who consider themselves as members – is qualitatively different to that of the traditional associations with England fans. Where Scots are a contingent body that show bonhomie and good humour, the English are considered menacing, chauvinistic and potentially violent.

As Finn and Giulianotti (1998) have observed, the gregarious fan style of Scotland supporters not only trades off the negative stereotypes of England fans, but also benefits from the self-congratulatory tone of the Scottish media who praise the ambassadorial role performed by the fans. Recent research by Poulton (2003) suggests that some of these distinctions may be dissolving as evidence from the press coverage of the World Cup in 2002 revealed that initial media and police fears of England fan violence in South Korea and Japan simply failed to materialize. Nevertheless, such stereotypes die hard and will probably remain as imagery of conflict and war around the England national side continues.

At times the carnivalesque attitude spills through into club football, especially on jaunts around Europe. In 2003, an estimated 80,000 Celtic supporters made their way to Seville for the UEFA Cup final, many just to 'be there' and join in the celebratory atmosphere of reaching a major European final. But the mythology of Scottish fans, bonhomie with their hosts was significantly undermined by the violence of Rangers fans after the same final in Manchester in 2006 (see Chapter 6). Such episodes remind us that in order to understand sports fandom we need to contextualize the specific social relations of different fan groups and have a more nuanced approach to interpreting the dynamics and cultural politics of fandom in society and how they are rerepresented in the media. Our consumption of sport therefore can vary in time, space and cultural context.

To summarize this review of theoretical approaches to sports fandom our own view on the impact of highly mediated sporting experiences is similar to the following quote from Garry Whannel when he says:

> [T]he cultural experiences involved in consuming sport may be commercialized and commodified but they always also involve other forms of experience and exchange – to do with shared experience, with popular memory, with a sense of place and space, a sense of cultural tradition, and an awareness of and openness to the unpredictability of sports events. (Whannel, 2007: 150)

It is to the cultural importance of how traditions are constructed through sport and their mediation that we now turn, in particular the specific traditions and history of the 'Old Firm' in Scotland and of football culture in the city of Liverpool.

Tradition and history among football fans

Much of the recent debate regarding the future of football in Britain (and Europe) has centred around the perceived tension between the 'traditionalists' and the 'modernizers'. The first group is usually portrayed as supporters who invest the club with a symbolic significance, while the latter encompass the business and commercial community who view football as part of a wider media/leisure economy in which supporters are viewed as consumers (see Boyle and Haynes, 2004). In Simon Kuper's examination of football culture in over twenty different countries, he noted that in his experience it was only in British fan culture that history and tradition were deemed to be so important:

> British fans are historians. When two British sides play each other, their histories play each other too. This is especially true in Glasgow. (Kuper, 1994: 216)

He argues that, while this fixation with tradition is mirrored in British political culture, with continual debates about the dangers to British life of losing specific traditions (usually threatened by Europe), in Glasgow this concern is driven by specific ethnic and religious concerns unique to that city. Research carried out among fans by one of the authors in both Glasgow and Liverpool identified the role of the clubs and their positioning within ethnic and city identities as different and reflected by the supporters' concerns with their club and what they understand to be that club's tradition. Even in a media-saturated culture, football's emphasis on competition and rivalry at local, regional and national levels, allied with its close association with urban working-class culture and its attendant concern with the demarcation of territory, make it a potent cultural form for the expression of individual and collective identities.

Embedded in this cultural form is the centrality of tradition in informing how supporters come to think about their team, themselves and other supporters. As in the 'imagined community' of the nation, football culture celebrates its heroes and triumphs by weaving them into a powerful narrative which connects the past with the present. This not only draws on myths that exist within club histories, but also connects with deeper myths that circulate beyond the parameters of football and are embedded in wider society. This process is mediated through a number of institutions, including the media, family, school, supporters' clubs and so forth. Many official club histories (and indeed much history writing in general) attempt to map out and impose a narrative structure on past events. In so doing they also help to make sense of (or legitimize) aspects of the present. John Thompson has commented on how 'narrativization' is an important element in this process of legitimization:

> Claims are embedded in stories which recount the past and treat the present as part of a timeless and cherished tradition. Indeed traditions are sometimes invented in order to create a sense of belonging to a

community and to a history which transcends the experience of conflict, difference and division. (Thompson, 1990: 61–2)

History is a process of forgetting, as well as remembering, of legitimizing the present through one particular version of the past.

This process helps sustain the collective group identity among supporters and their allegiance to a particular club. The linkage between tradition and the selective interpretation of history is important, as it sustains particular discourses and allows them an ahistorical position: they become 'given' and 'natural'. Many of the discourses relating to national or cultural characteristics are represented through various forms of narrative as 'given' or 'fixed'. For example, many of the discourses relating to Irish immigration in nineteenth-century Liverpool and Glasgow are very similar to those which exist in certain social and political circles with regard to the position of the immigrant population in Britain in the early part of the twenty-first Century. It is 'our' traditions, 'our' jobs, 'our' heritage that is threatened by the 'wave' of immigrants. In this instance, aspects of 'tradition' are mobilized to legitimize current thinking and political actions.

In addition, traditional aspects of culture are perceived to belong to an earlier more innocent time. They become symbolic events that connect us with the past and hark back to a more secure, less complex society. In part this stems from a dissatisfaction with the modern world, allowing particularly comforting views of the past to function as nostalgia: a sense of longing for a more secure 'golden' era, which of course in reality may never have existed. As Chase and Shaw note with regard to modern human life experience:

> The only certainty is uncertainty, so that in this view nostalgia is the attempt to cling to the alleged certainties of the past, ignoring the fact that, like it or not, the only constant in our lives is change. (Chase and Shaw, 1989: 8)

Popular culture, and football – even mediated football, for to some extent all the fans' experience of the game comes through various channels of communication – in particular in the cities examined, becomes a site for this social process. It is not simply a case of one version of history versus another, but of how the clubs come to symbolize a sense of history, place and belonging to supporters who often view themselves as an integral part of the club and its historical narrative.

A sense of belonging in an era of change

For many fans, versions of tradition and history associated with football clubs and their cities provide a tangible link between the past and present. Football teams are always changing (players, managers and the like all come and go), yet the club exists in a space that is in part untouched by these changes (it is often remarked at Liverpool and Celtic that no one player is bigger than the club). To supporters the club offers a projection of a community which signifies, among other things, stability and continuity. If in Glasgow the centrality of the importance of religious and ethnic identities has been evident in the continuing rivalry that surrounds the position of Celtic and Rangers in the culture of the west of Scotland, by contrast in Liverpool it appears that football occupies a less divisive position in the cultural life of that city, and instead it provides a specific city identity which is placed in opposition to other regional and English national identities. In both cities there is another element of symbolic significance in the attachment and devotion of the supporters to their clubs.

The crisis in British football in one respect personifies a deeper concern about the future relationship of the individual to the wider collective in society. Among many supporters there exists a sense that yet another area of popular culture is being subjected to commercial pressures and interests which misunderstand the symbolic importance which football carries for many people. This is particularly true for those groups to whom football is interwoven with a range of other identities and experiences, and is not viewed as some optional extra which can be purchased as another part of the leisure economy. Stan Hey, talking about the seating of the Kop at Liverpool FC, encompasses this clash of tradition and change, and how this process is bound up with a sense of a specific place, identity and moment in history coming to an end. While aware of the dangers of lapsing into an uncritical account of contemporary society fuelled by nostalgia, it is worth quoting at length, touching as it does on a number of issues keenly felt among the supporters interviewed:

> As the factories die and their docks become shopping malls or art galleries, and the sea-faring, music-making past becomes part of the heritage industry, Liverpudlians, like most of the country, are bemused and wounded by the feeling of having lost a sense of community. The paradox of progress losing us more than we gain, of advancement for some, but not for all, may not be restricted to the streets if the Kop does indeed go.

'People have had some of the biggest moments of their lives there,' says Rogan Taylor. 'Moments they'll put in the big box, the one you take down to your death. The Kop has been the site of all this.' (Hey, 1993)

Despite television and sport increasingly addressing their fan base as consumers, for many people sport – even in its highly mediated forms – still carries with it a more rooted symbolism which connects with other areas of social life such as class and community. Understanding fandom means always attempting to locate it within that broader social context.

Conclusion

As we examined in Chapter 5, another impact of the increasingly close links between the media and sport, and how it is funded, is the growing financial gap between those who watch and those who play. This is particularly acute in the football industry, where the traditional supporters of the game, while still important, are no longer the major financial backers of the sport. While this differs from club to club and fans still matter when they are asked to consume vast quantities of officially endorsed club products, it is television and the money which flows from it into the game that has fuelled a massive increase in players' wages and media-related endorsement earnings.

In a sport such as football, which historically has been a working-class sport, a new generation of footballers, still drawn from this section of the community, are in a very short time moving in very different financial, social and often media-related circles. This gap, which has characterized sport in the US, is very much becoming the norm in the new age of satellite-backed and media-hyped football in Britain. Despite the globalization of major sporting events, the distinctive locale in which viewers engage with these events remains vital. The Lyons and Ticher (1998) collection of essays from twenty-five countries which examined how the world watched the 1998 football World Cup demonstrated that, while we may watch the same games, the context in which they are understood is more often than not determined by a country's wider political and cultural context. There is also an argument which suggests that the difference between watching sport live and watching live sport on television is breaking down, creating a 'hybridized viewer' (Siegel, 2002).

This suggests that all-seater stadiums, with giant video screens and a constant supply of food and drink provided for the spectators, has turned these venues into extensions of your front room. As Trevor Fishlock discovered on his tour of America back in the 1980s, it brings a very literal meaning to the marketing principle that fans should be viewed as consumers. At a baseball match in New York he commented on:

> The relentless mass chewing of junk food, an anorexic's nightmare of bulging squirrelly cheeks . . . . Soon our shoes were hidden in a litter of expended sachets, paper beer cups, ice cream cartons, peanut shells and ketchup-stained napkins. That evening the stadium had a crowd of 55,000 people and I calculated that the median fan was consuming three [hot] dogs . . . The reeking stadium sent up a thermal of sausage vapour. (Fishlock, 1986: 138)

While there have been major developments in football stadiums in Britain, replicating many of the characteristics found in America, the actual stadiums experience remains quite different.

Even in all-seater stadiums, fans in Britain do not go to football or rugby simply to spectate, they go to participate in the event, believing, with some degree of justification, that they may be able to influence the result of the game by supporting their team or creating an intimidating atmosphere for the opposition. Sometimes this hostile atmosphere is not even aimed at the opposition. In September 2008, Newcastle United supporters provoked an amazing reaction from the club's owner Mike Ashley as their outright hostility to Ashley forced him to publically admit he was selling the club as soon as could find a buyer.

Thus, while similarities exist, patterns and levels of fan intensity differ between sports and between countries. In many ways the notion of the global sports fan remains something of a media and marketing myth. In addition, of course, sport increasingly appears to be an adjunct of the entertainment media industry and, as we argue in the final chapter, this appears to involve the sports fan being asked to pay extra for the privilege of viewing the mediated event.

Chapter 11

Conclusion: Sport in the Digital Age

Even though we've left behind the stunning spectacle of Beijing, we know for certain that the Olympics will be one of the biggest themes in British life for the next four years and beyond. (Roger Mosey, Director of BBC Sport, BBC Sports Editors Blog, 25 August 2008)

There is a delight in seeing something well done – and Britain in Beijing was well done. So where next? The lessons for London in 2012 are awesome, and mostly terrifying. The worst lesson is that those seeking money from this government should wrap their demands in the flag, not in reason but in chauvinist shriek, abetted by that grotesque cheerleader, the BBC. (Simon Jenkins, *Guardian*, 27 August 2008)

Introduction: football is king?

Sport in the twenty-first century is never dull, it cannot afford to be. Sport is but one offering among the global mediated entertainment industries. Press, radio and television are but three possible outlets of sports information and entertainment. Websites, blogs, podcasts, video streams and various forms of mobile content summon the sports fan in an ever increasing array of services. The kind of information and news around sport is also more varied than ever before. In one particular week in September 2008 the news from English football and the extent of its coverage almost beggared belief. First there was the takeover of football club Manchester City by the oversees investment arm of the Abu Dhabi Royal Family. The new owners promptly showed their intent to rival neighbours Manchester United by signing Brazilian star Robinho from Real Madrid for a then British record signing of £32.5 million. This prompted comment by a happy celebrity City fan Noel Gallagher of the band Oasis whose bemusement at events was only trumped by Pele who thought Robinho would need counselling for choosing the Blues of Manchester over the Blues of Chelsea.

Later, 24-hour television channel Sky Sports News announced and updated news of the apparent sacking of Newcastle United manager Kevin Keegan. The rolling sports news channel strained every ounce of its news-gathering forces to cover the breaking story, only to discover by teatime that he hadn't in fact been sacked. The first departure of the 2008/09 season after only three games actually befell West Ham United manager Alan Curbishley who resigned over a dispute over the control of transfer dealings. Keegan now resurfaced, but promptly resigned twenty-four hours later over the same issue. To cap a calamitous week for the north-east club, its player Joey Barton was banned for six matches for violent play by an Football Association tribunal. All of these stories were major headlines through the week, generating massive amounts of news output and comment across all major media platforms. All of them in some shape or form were about the economics or politics of sport and only the success of Scottish tennis star Andy Murray in reaching the final of the US Open provided an actual sports story to divert attention away from the comings and goings of the Premier League and English football.

As we have suggested earlier in this book, football is the sine qua non of the media sports world. Without it newspapers would lose at least 25 per cent of their daily content and BSkyB would not be the pre-eminent pay-TV platform it has become. Even Lord Sebastion Coe, Chairman of the London 2012 Games, had to admit that football takes centre stage in the world of sport and insisted that Team GB enter a football team in the Games. It should be noted at the time that he was also a season ticket holder at Chelsea.

As the supply of communication grows in the digital age, so football appears to suck in exponentially high amounts of attention. In a sense, success breeds success. But the hegemony of football in the media coverage of sport and increasingly beyond is born of its constant reinscription in our consciousness and popular culture (Whannel, 2002). It carries the biggest stories that capture the largest audiences. In doing so this process also excludes other sports from any depth in coverage – most notably women's sports, including women's football – and also excludes wider audiences from sports news coverage who have no interest in football. In the 24-hour age of news production, football news is relentlessly researched, written and edited for delivery via the web or dedicated sports news channels that now also include club-specific sites and channels (Boyle and Haynes, 2004).

However, as we noted in Chapter 9, access to players and even managers (as the Keegan example above exemplified) means that journalists increasingly turn to other sources of information, such as the web, and tend towards gossip and hearsay rather than first-hand accounts. The claim that much of sports output, specifically on football, is predominantly 'churnalism' (Davies, 2008), the manufactured processing of information by journalists who rarely leave the enclaves of the newsroom and are dependent on news briefings and press releases, is symptomatic of this process of media proliferation. The speed of distribution of information in the digital economy of sports news means that journalists rarely get time to investigate stories in any depth and are constantly reacting to the manufacture of sports information in a complex, networked global media environment.

Whither BBC Sport?

In the same week as the furore at Newcastle United another dispute raged between free-to-air broadcasters the BBC and ITV who failed to reach a secondary rights agreement with pay-TV broadcaster Setanta to provide highlights of England's opening World Cup qualifying matches starting in September 2008. Setanta claimed neither broadcaster had offered enough money for the secondary rights and in doing so ignited a debate about the exclusion of viewers from premium sports coverage of national importance. The rapid transformations that have impacted on the 'sporting triangle' we reviewed in Chapter 3 have left the pioneers of sports broadcasting in the UK, and public service broadcasters of other nations, with growing pressures to adapt to the paradigmatic shift in the market for television sport. Cut-throat competition for sports rights and the corollary costs, have stretched the purse strings of many traditional broadcasters of sport. In 2002 inflated sports rights for coverage of the Football League had contributed to the implosion of the brash new digital terrestrial platform ITV Digital (Boyle and Haynes, 2004). The collapse of the service sent shockwaves through the sports rights market.

In 2002 the European Commission competition directorate DG4 opened proceedings against the English Premier League regarding the restrictive nature of the live television agreements it had with BSkyB. The spotlight turned to the collective sale of rights, exclusive agreements and its negative implications for broadcast markets and consumers. The EC argued that collective agreements restrict the number of games available to subscribers and were keen to explore the possibility of all games being opened up to the multi-channel broadcasting environment, including the Internet. As we have previously noted, the eventual ruling in 2004 opened the door for new pay-TV broadcaster Setanta to gain a small proportion of the live rights packages. The economic and regulatory pressures on sports rights in the new media age seemed to be deflating the spiral of rights fees across various sports. However, football, cricket, tennis, rugby union and Formula 1 have all enjoyed enhanced deals in the early twenty-first century. How can this be? The main reason remains the fierce competition for premium sports coverage that has increased since the arrival of digital television and the move by governing bodies of sport to 'unbundle' their 'basket of rights' to sport to sell the same event numerous times across different media platforms and modes of delivery (Haynes, 2005; Gratton and Solberg, 2007).

The extent to which public service broadcasters can juggle their responsibilities to all their viewers to include mass and minority audiences has placed further pressures on their ability to meet the needs of exposure-hungry sport. In the 1960s the introduction of BBC2 gave the BBC coverage of sport an important advantage over their rival ITV. In the multi-channel age, with dedicated niche programming, the BBC operates in an environment that affords expansive scheduling for sport and in-depth coverage but is up against competitors with more capacity and financial resources. As we noted in Chapter 4, the quantity of dedicated television coverage can often mean overkill and is not necessarily a marker of quality.

Broadcasters with long traditions in sport, like the BBC, often fall back on the belief they cover sport better than anyone else because of their impressive track record. However, such rhetoric can often pale in significance when sports bodies are seeking new arrangements with television. European television executives and sports administrators had observed with jealous eyes the revolution that struck the US sports broadcasting market in the early 1980s with the rise of ABC's dedicated sports channel ESPN. Ted Turner's Home Box Office had also pioneered the pay-per-view market through its promotion of heavyweight boxing, particularly Mike Tyson, bringing new riches to the world's top fighters and their promoters. Broader shifts in broadcasting regulation had given early signs that British television would be following the US example. Following the Thatcher government's free-market ideology, the 1990 Broadcasting Act did much to enable the foothold of BSkyB in the UK broadcasting market (Horsman, 1997).

As we mentioned in Chapter 4, new free-to-air channels like Channel 5 have also widened the market for televised sport. The cosy duopoly between the BBC and ITV companies was given initial competition from Channel 4 in the 1980s, particularly with the introduction of non-indigenous sports like American Football and later with the introduction of Football Italia in 1992. The introduction of Channel 5 in 1997 augured further competition for football, with the channel gaining its first coup when it screened England's World Cup qualifier against Poland during the first month of its launch. In 2008, the channel had the only free-to-air coverage of cricket, albeit highlights of England's home Test Matches, with live rights owned by BSkyB. Nevertheless, market intervention in sports rights endures in the form of the listed events based on economic welfare grounds (Gratton and Solberg, 2007). Such intervention seriously delimits the competition for rights in any one territory and in the era of interactive digital television and associated Internet presence, broadcasters that hold the rights to such events are increasingly using them to expand and bolster the sports coverage they provide.

BBC – the Olympic broadcaster

The BBC, whose budget for sport has struggled to match the inflated prices being negotiated for live sport (in particular football), has found its sports portfolio shrinking year on year. However, since the announcement in July 2005 that the Olympic Games would go to London in 2012 the economic, political and cultural position of sport in the UK has been transformed. Big sporting events are important for media organizations to prove their worth, whether it be to advertisers, subscribers or, in the BBC's case, their credentials as a public service broadcaster. When the Games were last held in London in 1948 the 'age of austerity' did not prevent the BBC from spending £250,000 on hosting the world's broadcasters, showcasing the new technology of television and wholeheartedly immersing itself in the ideology that hosting the Olympics was important for British prestige. Fast forward to 2008, and the BBC's role in championing Olympianism was as strong as ever and its technological innovation in the delivery of the Games was an undoubted opportunity to showcase its position in the digital media landscape. The Games in 2008 were available in HDTV for the first time, the BBC's iPlayer launched in 2007 was used to enable multiple live and on demand video streams, and its coverage encouraged interactive participation by its audience at every turn.

Given the huge investment of resources in the coverage of major sporting events like the Olympics, broadcasters are always eager to release positive figures reflecting high ratings and audience share. Roger Mosey, the BBCs Director of Sport, was in an ebullient mood as the 2008 Games came to a close:

> In the same way that Team GB has massively exceeded expectations, so have the audience figures. We predicted 30 million and privately hoped for about 35 million, so to get to 40 million even before the closing ceremony is terrific. (Conlan, 2008)

In an age of diminishing audiences for individual channels the figures were truly remarkable.

But the significance of equating the performance of the broadcaster to the athletes themselves makes all too apparent the pressure felt by the BBC to maintain its prestige in the coverage of the Games. The remarks hint at some of the wider pressures connected with the performance of the BBC in its coverage of sport. As a public service broadcaster it must transmit a range of programming to suit various audiences, as well as showcase those events like the Olympics that have broad national appeal. The problem for the BBC, noted above, is that budgets for sport are limited so when it covers sport the pressure is on to both draw a 'national' audience and maintain its historic position as 'the home of sport'. Arguably the former is increasingly difficult in a diverse multi-channel environment and the latter mantle of a leader in sports coverage has been significantly undermined by the growth and power of Sky Sports.

The BBC's television coverage of the Games had peaked at 7 million viewers on the second Thursday, and on the final Saturday took a very respectable 42 per cent share of the UK audience. When equated with audiences for sport in the 1970s and 1980s the Beijing Games does not compare favourably. But in the new media age the mainstream television coverage is only the partial story of its overall coverage. The BBC has attempted to respond to the challenges of multi-channel competition and dominant niche sports channels through its development of new web-based, interactive, high definition (HD) and on-demand services that provide far more depth to the coverage of individual events than ever before. The BBC introduced six live feeds via its website and a range of 'catch up' opportunities via its iPlayer with 400,000 users downloading the 100 metres final in one day alone (Mosey, 2008). The different modes of delivery do have some interesting consequences for the viewing experience.

The standard television format of linking to events from an anchor and panelists in the studio gets short-circuited when coverage is delivered online and on demand. In the online viewing experience the events stand alone and editorializing is by design of the web developer not the television producer. Although certain events are prioritized – invariably around British achievements and medalists – there is no framing of the event by the studio. It is almost a pure outside broadcast, in an old fashioned sense of television being there to capture the moment.

The BBCs HD coverage was mesmerizing in its depth and colour, but remained experimental in 2008. While the BBC broadcast more than 300 hours of the Olympics on its dedicated HD channel the number of households watching the service remained relatively small. Although more than forty per cent of British households had HD-ready television sets in 2008, only an approximate ten per cent could actually watch HDTV services (Beaumont, 2008). This was largely because of cost, as HD channels via the various television platforms in most cases came with an additional charge. This fracturing and bifurcation of audiences is an increasingly familiar pattern of sports viewing in the twenty-first Century. Even where viewers are watching the same sporting event their experiences of how they watch, where they watch and the technologies used may be incredibly varied.

The ideological battle the BBC faces in continuing to innovate in its television coverage of sport is a reflection of its wider institutional problems of justifying its existence and public funding in a highly liberalized, market-driven media environment. Many of the BBC's competitors, in television but especially in the online world, point to the relatively low level of commercial risk the BBC takes in innovating its coverage. Such subsidy is viewed as anti-competitive and drowning out new enterprise. The BBC's brand ensures it commands a prominent place in the minds of audiences and web users in the UK and increasingly globally. But, we would argue, without such a commitment to innovation in sports coverage the availability of quality sports programming, news and myriad services would be diminished, leaving certain social groups excluded from premium televised sport. Sport as a national shared experience would also suffer. This is not an argument that suggests things should stay the same and not innovate, a sentiment that comes through strongly in the following statement from Mosey:

Given this richness of our history – and we're enormously proud of it – there's an easy trap of thinking that the BBC is what the marketeers call a 'heritage brand'. A fantastic past – and plenty of glories in which it can luxuriate. But that is a fundamental misreading in my view of what the BBC is about – both in its past and in the future. The point about the people who launched all these wonderful new services is that they were pioneers not traditionalists. (Mosey, 2007a)

The pioneering spirit of the BBC Sports department is perhaps one of its most enduring features.

Its coverage of the 2008 Olympic Games may at times have been full of jingoism, of the sort that does harm to the BBC's claims to represent a multicultural society and heavily criticized by the likes of journalist Simon Jenkins whose quote prefaces this chapter. Having said this, its new media coverage enabled multiple and novel ways in which the Games and its cast of characters could be communicated. Television coverage was supplemented by blogs from producers and BBC journalists. There was more exposure and time given over to the variety of sports on show enabling the varied stories of the Games to be revealed. There were behind-the-scenes views of the Games itself, including some of the more contentious moments of the event. For instance, the arrest of the ITN journalist John Ray who went to cover one of the several protests against Chinese rule in Tibet was captured by a BBC crew and promptly put online as evidence of the overbearing surveillance that surrounded the Games in Beijing. In these ways and more, the mediation of the Olympic Games by the BBC opened up new vistas from which to experience the Games and to identify with athletes and nations.

BBC radio sport

The competition for sports also extends to radio. One of the success stories for BBC Sport has been the rejuvenation of its radio sports output. Ironically, it almost marked a return to a time when BBC Sport actually meant radio as opposed to television coverage. Thanks in part to the UK-wide Radio 5 Live news and sport station, the BBC has been able to command a pre-eminent position in the coverage of sport on radio. Central to this has been the ability of BBC radio to offer live football commentary on English Premier League matches.

Since the start of the Premier League in 1992 the BBC have retained the rights for live running commentary of the Premier League. Since

2000 the BBC unified its sports rights acquisition policy for all platforms which has meant that where it has failed in the television market it usually picks up some coverage of an event on radio. The best example of this is Premier League football which has never been shown live on BBC TV but has become a cornerstone of the increasingly popular BBC channel Radio 5 Live. The station's audience has gradually grown with a reach of more than 6 million listeners in 2007. The launch of Digital Audio Broadcasting (DAB) in 2006 also led to the development of its sister channel Radio 5 Live Sports Extra that enables additional live coverage of events when the main schedule is full. This spillover effect has also allowed more extensive coverage of cricket, where *Test Match Special* no longer has to leave listeners for the BBC Radio Four shipping forecast on long wave.

Radio 5 Live has not only offered more radio sport, supplemented by innumerable radio phone-ins, it has also extended certain areas of sports journalism. In particular its investigative programmes such as Garry Richardson's *Sportsweek* have become increasingly important in providing a range of sports journalism which goes beyond the mere reporting of sport and examines the broader range of social, economic and even political issues connected with sports. Its programming around sport has also been enriched by more interaction with the audience through SMS text messaging and e-mail's to presenters and discussion forums on the BBC website. Its highly successful 606 brand enables BBC listeners to create their own reports on sporting events including phone-in podcasts and creates an enormous hinterland of information beyond the radio channel itself. In a wider context of the BBC's public mission, 5 Live's approach epitomizes the BBC's Creative Future's vision launched in 2006 that 'the best content should be made available on every platform at the audience's convenience' (BBC, 2006).

However, as in television, radio has become an increasingly crowded and competitive marketplace in the UK. The commercial station TalkSport has extended its sporting portfolio to challenge the BBC's pre-eminence in its radio coverage of sport. Its approach is brasher, its perceived demographic audience is firmly male and arguably 'laddish', and its style of presentation is centred on ex-professional sporting celebrities delivering sports gossip and entertainment rather than any deep analysis. As its controller Moz Dee explained to one of its new presenters Martin Kelner, 'We're not here to provide a service particularly – the BBC does that – we are about entertainment and opinions, something the audience can react to' (Kelner, 2008). It has occasionally upset the BBC by snatching exclusive rights to key events, like overseas Test cricket tours, or where it has not successfully bid for rights has deployed its commentators to deliver commentary 'off-tube' where access rights to the event are not relevant. Even in radio, the old certainties no longer hold and the complexities of the bundling and unbundling of sports rights looks set to continue as new delivery systems all attempt to secure certain sports as core programming.

In 2006 TalkSport received a major boost in successfully bidding for one of seven rights bundles to cover the Premier League, thereby ending the BBC's monopoly of nationwide coverage of top-flight domestic football. The unbundling of audio-broadcasting rights packages to sport, including radio, and online streaming rights and podcasts has opened up new opportunities for sport to gain additional revenue streams as well as providing sports fans with different modes of engaging with sport.

Power play: digital and pay-per-view sport

The digital revolution that is impacting on sport has once more transformed the power play of media sport. Metaphors of democracy and open access have greeted the so-called information age since the 1960s, but it would appear that, as the pace of technological development reaches a state of hyper-intensity, issues around the liberalization of communication are paramount.

The regulation of new communications technologies has proved problematic as the pace of change has occurred too fast for state and supra-state policies to keep up with the often divergent needs of global corporate interests and end users or citizens (Kofler, 1998). Sport, as a global enthusiasm that can unite disparate communities as well as consolidate cultural distinctions, is once more at the cutting edge of these developments.

As we have seen with the BBC's coverage of sport, the production and consumption of sport cultures are set to change as these wider shifts in the media and communications industries take hold both among the traditional broadcasters and the more recent arrivals in the marketplace.

Free-to-air channels have invested heavily in digital television as a means of supporting their tight schedules for screening sport. As well as its 360 degree approach to the Olympic Games the BBC has used its digital television interactive services to enhance its coverage of Wimbledon, the Australian and the French Open tennis championships, the Open golf championship, the World Cup and is set to do the same with coverage of Formula 1. Where events have action that takes place in multiple locations at the same time this approach has proved revolutionary in terms of the range and depth of coverage offered to the viewer. BSkyB has done similar things with its coverage of the UEFA Champions League where subscribers to Sky Sports can choose from a multitude of matches on Wednesday evenings or watch games on demand online. The restrictions of multi-genre channels with tight schedules and competing programming have, to all intents and purposes, evaporated in the multi-platform digital age.

The arrival in the UK sports market of pay-per-view television sport was widely hoped to make inroads into the consumption patterns of sports fans whom, it was envisaged, would make micro-payments to watch individual sporting events. It was the unlikely setting of Oxford United's Manor Ground that saw the first pay-per-view football match in Britain in February 1999. But the uptake of pay-per-view in football has been patchy and not the financial windfall many in the sport and commercial broadcasters expected. Instead, pay-per-view has largely been the terrain of boxing that can build the hype around particular fighters and fights to encourage viewers to part with their money. Arguably Britain's first successful star of the pay-per-view model has been Ricky Hatton. But the approach is fraught with risk for the promoters who have to estimate the income from pay-per-view in order to provide the lucrative prize money craved by boxing stars to get the fights on in the first place. The problem with this model was exposed in September 2008 when Britain's new celebrity boxer Amir Khan fought his first pay-per-view bout against the Colombian Breidis Prescott and was unceremoniously knocked out after a mere thirty seconds of the first round. Sky Box Office had charged disgruntled viewers £14.99 for the fight and, according to some commentators, the emphatic defeat severely knocked the confidence of the boxing public in the belief that promoter Frank Warren could deliver a World Champion in Khan.

Despite the various figures which are often given for the potential growth in this market, the amount of money which pay-per-view will generate for both broadcasters and sport remains uncertain. However, even given the level of opposition and the cultural arguments made for the centrality of sport in national life – in Spain the showing of Barcelona v. Real Madrid on pay-per-view raised concerns about such a 'national game' not being available free to air – the growth looks set to continue, albeit incrementally, and most likely in micro-packaged events delivered online as well as through subscription television.

Longer term, of course, sport relies on competition to flourish and the danger of creating a wealthy minority in any sport is that in the long run competition dies. This has been recognized to some extent in the US, where the NFL has resisted the temptation to sell exclusive rights contracts to pay-TV benefiting the leagues and individual franchises. As Tom Lappin comments:

> The sport itself stays competitive by ensuring that the best young players join the weaker teams, maintaining a system of checks and balances. Strange that in America, the bastion of financial libertarianism, they should impose such restrictions to keep their sport alive. (*The Scotsman,* 25 February 1999)

There were cries of 'sellout' in 2006 when ESPN gained the rights to the traditional Monday Night Football game in a deal worth $1.1 billion up to 2013. Having been an institution of American network television for thirty-six years the movement to ESPN generated huge criticism from football fans. However, other rights deals for other matches means that the sport remains free-to-air on CBS and NBC and ensures national coverage and a wide audience at least up to 2011.

In the UK this longer-term vision appears to be largely absent, particularly in cricket where there is no live coverage of international matches on free-to-air television. Such developments raise awareness of the importance of televised sport to the wider sporting cultures. Removal of free-to-air televising of sport reduces exposure, diminishes the opportunities for young viewers and non-enthusiasts of sport to be exposed to particular events and damages the cultural importance certain nations place on particular sporting occasions. As this process increases, so the question of regulation will undoubtedly increase.

Nevertheless, the economic rewards of packaging channels and sports rights across other distribution platforms means that television organizations get more 'bang for their buck', effectively selling their product more than once, particularly where advertisers are concerned. The movement into this type of competition also raises questions about the funding of the BBC, and its use of the licence fee to open new markets. It is a problematic that broadcasting impresario Michael Grade picked up on shortly after the Corporation's initial partnership with BSkyB occurred in 1992:

> The BBC may hope that partnership with the Murdoch empire will soften the edges of the leaders and comment in the News International

papers during its argument with government for the renewal of the BBC charter and licence. That is a short-term gain to be measured against long-term suicide. (Quoted in Haynes, 1998: 104)

Further developments in the distribution of television services have forced the BBC to position itself strategically as one of the leading producers of quality broadcasting content, not just in the UK but globally.

Power play: the Internet – a new sporting superhighway

The globalization process that has transformed the organization of sport is also affecting the traditional ways in which media sport can be produced, delivered and consumed. Information and communication technologies (ICTs) have opened up new possibilities for sport to convey its message and create new markets. The rhetoric that accompanies the interactive era of digital telecommunication suggests a new 'computer age' in a rich equality-laden 'information society'.

Sport, as well as other facets of our daily lives, is set to be dramatically affected by the growing importance of the Internet, video gaming and other multimedia applications, placing more control in the hands of the consumer who may choose from a vast array of services through many-to-many communication. However, the rampant optimism that drives the promotional strategies of large computer-based corporations, is only heard and acted upon by a small technological elite (Loader, 1998).

In analysing the rapidly expanding 'online' services for the sports fan, we must guard critically against any oversimplified linear approach to technological change in media sport and its promise to empower its audience. While the interactive possibilities of the World Wide Web of sport are exciting, as we have argued throughout the book, any deeper understanding of media technologies of sport requires a concern for social, economic, political and cultural processes in order to appreciate the complex ways in which power is structured and manipulated.

In previous research done by the authors on the impact of the web and other digital technologies on the coverage of football in the UK it is clear that the ways in which the digital communication of sport becomes embedded in our lives is not always straightforward and clear (Boyle and Haynes, 2004). No one could have foreseen the mass use of SMS texting when mobile phone technology took off in the late 1990s, nor could they envisage that text messaging would, sometimes controversially, begin to structure certain elements in the production of televised sport from audience comment and interaction to competitions and the downloading of results, images and video.

These considerations now shape the planning and production of media sport like never before. It is no longer about serving the family viewers at home in their living rooms, but optimizing access through any means possible, in multiple locations and times that are convenient to the audience. On an experiential level the relationship people have with mediated sport is therefore changing dramatically although the social and cultural meanings around sport may endure and show stronger continuities.

Take, for example, the BBC's radio cricket programme *Test Match Special* which celebrated its fiftieth anniversary in 2007 (Baxter, 2007). The programme has a unique broadcasting style that has arguably become cult radio listening, having been shaped over the years by great names of British radio commentary from John Arlott to Brian Johnston. The programme has long encouraged participation by its listeners in the form of letters or, since the 1980s, the delivery of freshly baked cakes. In the new media age the programme now encourages e-mails and text messages to commentators while on air. Commentators will respond to messages as they deliver their running commentaries and analysis thereby broadening the flow of information the programme can draw upon and making its audience feel integral to the programme itself in a quite direct yet intimate way.

There are also more radical innovations in the coverage of sport that compete with the main players in the economic and political success of sport on the Internet. Fan websites are the corollary of a previous fan subculture, fanzines (Haynes, 1995). These developments have evolved with the nature and character of the web itself. Fans are now the authors of their own websites, blogs, discussion forums, online commentaries, social networking sites, podcasts and digital video productions distributed via YouTube. All these developments serve to reveal the passions that surround sport in new and creative ways (Sandvoss, 2003).

In Scotland, for example, there has been a long tradition of fan participation in sports broadcasting, and fan discourse on sport on the web, principally football, mimics many of these longer traditions. Dominant themes in Scottish football fan forums tend to be focused on issues of player performance, club management and ownership, the national team, transfer speculation, critiques of mainstream media narratives, ticket pricing and policies and the governance of the sport more broadly. All these are familiar and long-established discourses in Scottish sporting subculture but they are given additional impetus and communicative effect by new media which turns cultural consumption into forms of production. The key difference with mainstream online outlets like the BBC is that they are niche fan productions for niche audiences and therefore carry minimal influence on wider audiences and public understanding of football in Scotland. However, as we have noted in Chapter 9 and elsewhere, fan activity on the web can influence the circulation and flow of information in mainstream media as new insider information and rumour is released on fan sites only to be picked up and popularized by mainstream sports journalists (Boyle, 2005; Haynes and Boyle, 2008).

Another aspect of the blossoming fan cultures online is the disintermediation of sports media (Haynes and Boyle, 2008: 263). This process means that there is wider coverage of different sports from increasingly different perspectives. Where football dominates mainstream media, particularly press coverage of sport, online media sport provides a communicative space for sports that struggle to get exposure on television or by sports journalists. One particular dimension of this explosion is the use of YouTube by either governing bodies of sport, sports clubs and sports fans to distribute audio-visual coverage of sporting events. In 2006 the National Hockey League in the US was one of the first governing bodies of sport to launch its own YouTube channel. The channel enabled the NHL to bypass traditional television outlets, giving more direct editorial control of how the sport is produced and analysed as well as opening up other revenue streams through advertising and subscription. In 2007 Chelsea football club followed the same model launching their own YouTube channel to showcase news and interviews with players and the manager.

One problem of these 'official' channels is the lack of critical comment or investigative journalism. When editorial control goes in-house this is always likely to be the outcome. However, YouTube offers an antidote to the official views from sport. The proliferation of digital cameras and mobile phones with video capturing has led to a new phenomenon of 'home-made' videos being posted on the web. The ease of use, malleability and global distribution of material means that biographical accounts of 'going to the match' populate the web via YouTube. The view from the stadium may not offer any real insight into the action on the field of play, but they do reveal the social experience of many who watch live sport.

Governing bodies of sport are conscious of these developments and in some cases have banned the use of mobile phones and cameras at sporting venues in attempts to control the images that emerge from sport. Again, digital rights management of sports media and the policing of official, licensed coverage of sport has become big business. Company's like Net Result or Soccer Dataco, who are contracted by governing bodies of sport and sports broadcasters like BSkyB, lay vigil on the web to trace any copyright infringement of televised sports images on the web. Unsuspecting fans who copy copyrighted material – such as fixture lists – and distribute the images or information via the web receive curt and rapid legal writs if they do not desist. However, as the music industry has discovered, keeping a lid on the mass disobedience of copyright is no easy undertaking. Live feeds of BSkyB's coverage of the Premier League frequently appear on the Internet.

In a similar vein, some pub landlords across the UK have taken alternative satellite services from other parts of Europe to screen live Premier League football on Saturday afternoons in an attempt to evade what they see as prohibitive subscription fees for the public screening of Sky Sports which is distributed at different rates to domestic subscribers. Sky had introduced a discriminatory market as a response to a dispute with advertisers over their viewing figures. Pub viewing had grown exponentially since its first contract with the Premier League in 1992 so separating the market to extract more money from public places seemed a sensible marketing opportunity. Football has historically embargoed the screening of games on television between 3 and 5 p.m. on Saturdays; however, one particular pub landlady in Southsea challenged both the ban on showing Saturday afternoon football and Sky's right to discriminate against pubs in their pricing and ultimately took her case to the European court in 2008. Such manoeuvres are only possible in a global media environment and take advantage of the 'grey economy' and loopholes in the law.

The power play over the ownership of sports rights on the web has also led to more formal industrial disputes between sports rights holders and mainstream media. In what amounts to an economic and legal enclosure of sports information and images, sports governing bodies have exploited their production of fixture lists, rights of access for photographers and any secondary uses of audio-visual material. The cost of licences for these informational goods has at times led to deadlocked negotiations and all-out boycotts. In 2007 prior to the Rugby World Cup, the *Guardian*, *The Times*, the *Sun* and the French sports daily *L'Equipe* joined international news agency Reuters in limiting coverage over a rights dispute with the International Rugby Board. The dispute centred on licensing rules that limited the number of images newspapers could place on their websites.

The press, led by News International titles, threatened a boycott claiming the licence was restricting freedom of the press. The boycott of images was an attempt to upset the tournament sponsors who were paying high prices to gain high exposure of their brands across various media. As the tournament in France dawned the IRB eventually brokered a fairer deal, but the episode confirmed the complexities of rights associated with sport and how the arrival of the web makes distinctions between traditional media harder to decipher.

Endgame

Sport has become intertwined with the media to a greater extent than at any other time during the long relationship that has always existed between these two cultural forms. Football in particular remains the bridgehead which will allow new digital delivery systems to establish the patterns of market domination required to make them profitable.

Anybody who wishes to understand sport, whether an academic, a fan or a journalist, needs to understand the economic and political forces which are shaping and reshaping the contemporary sporting experience. For the media industries, sport offers a 'product' which can be transformed into a valuable commercial entity delivering readers, viewers, advertisers, customers and subscribers. Sport, it appears, is often only too happy to oblige as a willing victim in this process.

However, media sport is too important to be left solely to the political economists. It also remains a rich arena of myth, image, narrative and a compulsive world of storytelling. At a cultural and textual level the images that a community project onto the sporting field and the manner in which that image gets refracted through various media tell us much about our individual and collective identities. They also expose in a very public manner our values, priorities, hopes, dreams and aspirations like few other cultural forms. It is a publicly mediated arena which can be exciting, exhilarating, yet also inconsequential, but all the time saturated with the social forces and ideological energies which run through society.

Any analysis of the sport–media nexus needs to be alert to the importance of both approaches to the subject. Studies of the cultural dimension of sport often require sporting development to be placed within the context of a changing and increasingly complex media infrastructure. At the same time, the sensitivities people often bring to sporting identities more often than not originate in social spaces outside the media and can be rooted in deeper structures of class, gender, ethnicity and nationality. It remains important to locate media sport within the wider political, economic and cultural context within which it is both produced and consumed.

A study of media sport involves locating it firmly within the evolving cultural industries. Specific patterns of media development both in the UK and elsewhere in Europe have seen the extension of market forces and increased competition within this and other public-service sectors of the economy. The market lies at the centre of the new economic orthodoxy. In addition, the rise and increasing integration of the service and cultural industries both within and across economies has helped to propel professional sport into a closer relationship with the media.

Having helped create the political and economic climate in which global entrepreneurs and conglomerates could harness developing information technologies to make inroads into the previously closeted world of broadcast media, governments are only now becoming aware of some of the cultural implications of such a process. The result has been that arguments about the need to regulate or intervene in media markets has become more central to political debate in both the UK and Europe.

National governments and, to an extent, the EU are aware of the cultural and, by association, political importance of sport. However, they also see the digital industries as key drivers in the economy and as a source of employment and wealth creation. It is that balancing act between commerce and culture that sports have to confront as they become ever more closely identified with the media. As the television rights to top sports are sold to the highest bidder Will Hutton has noted that:

> For viewers the entry ticket to this world is the money to afford the subscriptions that are three times higher than the BBC licence fee . . . Great national sporting events . . . cease to be shared by us all . . . Both the sport and national life are therefore diminished. (Hutton, 1995: 222)

The longer-term danger is of course that what makes sport culturally different and commercially viable in the first place may be eroded over a period of time if short-term financial interests are prioritized.

Into tomorrow

Almost ten years on from the first edition of *Power Play* much has changed in the sports–media relationship, but there is also a strong element of continuity in the themes and issues we identified almost a decade ago. Continuity and change still characterize media sport development. Despite various trials and tribulations, sport's historical relationship with the media has largely been one of mutual benefit. The broadcast media in particular have helped create truly national and international sporting events, and in the process given democratic access to millions of people, consumers and citizens. In the digital age, however, the paradox is that we have entered an era based on media exclusivity rather than universal access. We now have a media landscape which, while dominated by the rhetoric of extending viewer choice, none the less addresses us not as citizens, but rather by our ability to pay for the consumption of new – and not so new – services.

The national and international governing bodies of sport, governments and media regulators need to be aware that, without a change in political will and a commitment to look further ahead than simply the next season, this process of fragmentation will continue apace.

It has proven to be notoriously difficult to predict future developments in both the media and sporting industries. As we demonstrated at the beginning of the book, few people could have foreseen the transformation of sport which has occurred in the last decade. As we look towards the next decade we can perhaps say with some degree of certainty that for fans, media executives and even academics, sport – in the fields of politics, economics and culture – will continue to matter.

Bibliography

Aamidor, A. (ed.) (2003) *Real Sports Reporting*. Bloomington: Indiana University Press.

Abel, S. and Long, A. (1996) 'Event sponsorship: does it work?', *Admap*, December.

Alabarces, P., Tomlinson, A. and Young, C. (2001) 'Argentina versus England at the France 98 World Cup: narratives of nation and the mythologizing of the popular', *Media, Culture and Society*, 23 (5), 547–66.

Aldgate, A. (1979) *Cinema and History: British Newsreels and the Spanish Civil War*. London: Scolar Press.

Allan, S. (ed.) (2005) *Journalism: Critical Issues*. Maidenhead: Open University Press.

Anderson, B. (1991) *Imagined Communities: Reflections on the Origin and the Spread of Nationalism* (2nd edn). London: Verso.

Andrews, D. L. and Grainger, A. D. (2007) 'Sport and globalisation', in G. Ritzer (ed.), *The Blackwell Companion to Globalisation*. Oxford: Blackwell.

Andrews, D. L. and Ritzer, G. (2007) 'The grobal in the sporting glocal', *Global Networks*, 7 (2), 113–53.

Andrews, M. (ed.) (2001) *Michael Jordan Inc.: Corporate Sport, Media Culture and Late Modern America*. New York: SUNY Press.

Andrews, P. (2005) *Sports Journalism: A Practical Introduction*. London: Sage.

Aris, S. (1990) *Sportsbiz: Inside the Sports Business*. London: Hutchinson.

Arlott, J. (1968) 'Over now to . . . The story of cricket on the air', in B. Johnstone (ed.), *Armchair Cricket*. London: BBC.

Arundel, J. and Roche, M. (1998) 'Media sport and local identity: British Rugby League and Sky TV', in M. Roche (ed.), *Sport, Popular Culture and Identity*. Aachen: Meyer & Meyer.

Badenhausen, K. (2007) 'Racing world puts four on Forbes.com's Top 25 earners list'. Online at: http://sports.espn.go.com/rpm/news/story?id=3085058 (accessed 2 August 2008).

Baillie, R. (ed.) (1994) *100 Years of Scottish Sport*. Edinburgh: Mainstream.

Bairner, A. (1994) 'Football and the idea of Scotland', in G. Jarvie and G. Walker (eds), *Sport in the Making of the Scottish Nation: Ninety-Minute Patriots?* Leicester: Leicester University Press.

Bairner, A. (1999) *Sport, Politics and the Press in Northern Ireland*. Paper presented at Sport, Media and National Identity Conference, Stirling Media Research Institute/ Sports Studies Department, University of Stirling, Scotland, 5 February.

Baker, A. (1997) 'A left/right combination: populism and Depression-era boxing films', in A. Baker and T. Boyd (eds), *Out of Bounds: Sports Media and the Politics of Identity*. Bloomington and Indianapolis: Indiana University Press.

Baker, A. (2008) 'Fans play their part in Twenty20 Cup's costume drama', *Daily Telegraph*, 28 July. Online at: www.telegraph.co.uk/sport/cricket/counties/2463762/Fans-play-their-part-in-Twenty20-Cups-costume-drama.html.

Barnett, S. (1990) *Games and Sets: The Changing Face of Sport on Television*. London: BFI.

Baxter, P. (2007) *Test Match Special – 50 Not Out*. London: BBC Books.

BBC (2006) *BBC Reorganises for an On-demand Creative Future*, BBC Press Release, 19 July. Online at: www.bbc.co.uk/pressoffice/pressreleases/stories/2006/07_july/19/future.shtml.

BBC Trust (2008) *The BBC Trust Impartiality Report: BBC Network News and Current Affairs Coverage of the Four UK Nations*. London: BBC.

BBCi (2004) 'Atkinson quits over racist slur'. Oneline at: http://news.bbc.co.uk/1/hi/entertainment/tv_and_radio/3648051.stm (accessed 22 April 2004).

Beattie, G. (1997) *On the Ropes: Boxing as a Way of Life*. London: Indigo.

Beaumont, C. (2008) 'The first high-definition Olympics', *Daily Telegraph*, 1 August.

Beech, J. (2006) *The Marketing of Sport*. London: Prentice Hall.

Bellamy, R. V. Jnr (1998) 'The evolving television sports marketplace', in L. A. Wenner (ed.), *MediaSport*. London: Routledge.

Benaud, R. (2005) *My Spin on Cricket*. London: Hodder.

Bernstein, A. (2002) 'Is it time for a victory lap? Changes in the media coverage of women in sport', *International Review for the Sociology of Sport*, 37 (3–4), 415–28.

Bernstein, A. and Blain, N. (2002) *Sport, Media and Culture: Global and Local Dimensions*. London: Routledge.

Bernstein, A. and Galily, Y. (2008) 'Games and sets: women, media and sport in Israel', *Journal of Jewish Women's Studies and Gender Issues*, Nashim, 15, 175–96.

Billig, M. (1995) *Banal Nationalism*. London: Sage.

Biscomb, K., Flatten, K. and Matheson, H. (1998) 'Read the paper, play the sport: a decade of gender change', in U. Merkel, G. Lines and I. McDonald (eds), *The Production and Consumption of Sports Culture*. Brighton: LSA.

Blain, N. and Boyle, R. (1994) 'Battling along the boundaries: Scottish identity-marking in sports journalism', in G. Jarvie and G. Walker (eds), *Sport in the Making of the Scottish Nation: Ninety-Minute Patriots?* Leicester: Leicester University Press.

Blain, N. and Boyle, R. (1998) 'Sport as real life: media, sport and culture', in A. Briggs and P. Cobley (eds), *The Media: An Introduction*. London: Longman.

Blain, N. and Boyle, R. (2009) 'Sport', in P. Cobley and D. Albertazzi (eds), *The Media: An Introduction* (3rd edn). London: Pearson.

Blain, N. and O'Donnell, H. (1998) 'European sports journalism and its readers during Euro 96', in M. Roche (ed.), *Sport, Popular Culture and Identity*. Aachen: Meyer & Meyer.

Blain, N., Boyle, R. and O'Donnell, H. (1993) *Sport and National Identity in the European Media*. Leicester: Leicester University Press.

Booth, D. (2008) *Talking of Sport: The Story of Radio Commentary*. London: Sports Books.

Bough, F. (1980) *Cue Frank!* London: MacDonald Futura.

Bourdieu, P. (1988) *Distinction: A Social Critique of the Judgement of Taste*. London: Routledge.

Boyle, J. (2003) 'The second enclosure movement and the construction of the public domain', *Law and Contemporary Problems*, 1 (2), 33–75.

Boyle, R. (1992) 'From our Gaelic fields: radio, sport and nation in postpartition Ireland', *Media, Culture and Society*, 14 (4), 623–36.

Boyle, R. (1995) *Football and Cultural Identity in Glasgow and Liverpool*. PhD thesis, University of Stirling, Scotland.

Boyle, R. (2006) *Sports Journalism: Context and Issues*. London: Sage.

Boyle, R. and Haynes, R. (1996) '"The grand old game": football, media and identity in Scotland', *Media, Culture and Society*, 18 (4), 549–64.

Boyle, R. and Haynes, R. (1998) 'Modernising tradition? The changing face of British football', in G. Lines and I. McDonald (eds), *The Production and Consumption of Sports Cultures*. Brighton: LSA.

Boyle, R. and Haynes, R. (2000) *Power Play: Sport, the Media and Popular Culture* (1st edn). London: Longman.

Boyle, R. and Haynes, R. (2004) *Football in the New Media Age*. London: Routledge.

Boyle, R. and Haynes, R. (2007) 'The football industry and public relations', in J. L'Etang and M. Pieckza (eds), *Critical Perspectives in Public Relations*. London: Lawrence Erlbaum.

Boyle, R. and Monteiro, C. (2005) '"A small country with big ambition": representations of Portugal and England in Euro 2004 British and Portuguese newspaper coverage', *European Journal of Communication*, 20 (2), 223–4.

Boyle, R., Morrow, S. and Dinan, W. (2002) '"Doing the business?" The newspaper reporting of the business of football', *Journalism: Theory, Practice and Criticism*, 3 (2), 161–81.

Brewer, J. D. (1992) 'Sectarianism and racism, and their parallels and differences', *Ethnic and Racial Studies*, 15 (3), 352–64.

Briggs, A. (1961) *The History of Broadcasting in the UK*. Vol. 1: *The Birth of Broadcasting*. Oxford: Oxford University Press.

Brookes, R. (2002) *Representing Sport*. London: Arnold.

Brown, A. (2007) 'Not for sale? The destruction and reformation of football communities in the Glazer takeover of Manchester United', *Soccer and Society*, 8 (4), 614–35.

Brown, A. (ed.) (1998) *Fanatics: Power, Identity and Fandom in Football*. London: Routledge.

Brown, C. (2004) 'Sexism in sport', *FitPro Network*. Online at: www.fitnessvenues. com/uk/sexism-in-sport.

Brown, C. G. (1993) *The People in the Pews: Religion and Society in Scotland since 1780*. Dundee: Economic and Social History of Scotland.

Bryant, J., Zillmann, D. and Raney, A. A. (1998) 'Violence and the enjoyment of media sports', in L. A. Wenner (ed.), *MediaSport*. London: Routledge.

BSkyB (1998) *Annual Report 1998*. London: BSkyB.

Buford, B. (1991) *Among the Thugs*. London: Secker & Warburg.

Burdsey, D. (2004) '"One of the lads"? Dual ethnicity and assimilated ethnicities in the careers of British Asian professional footballers', *Ethnic and Racial Studies*, 27 (5), 757–79.

Burdsey, D. (2007) 'Role with the punches: the construction and representation of Amir Khan as a role model for multiethnic Britain', *Sociological Review*, 55 (3), 611–31.

Burn, G. (1986) *Pocket Money: Bad-Boys, Business-Heads and Boom-Time Snooker*. London: Heinemann.

Burn, G. (2006) *Best and Edwards: Football, Fame and Oblivion*. London: Faber & Faber.

Buscombe, E. (ed.) (1975) *Football on Television*. London: BFI.

Butcher, M. (1999) 'Football in chaos over "New Bosman" ruling', *Observer*, 10 January.

Butcher, P. (2004) *The Perfect Distance – Ovett and Coe: The Record Breaking Rivalry*. London: Weidenfeld & Nicolson.

Butler, B. (1997) '1948: the way it was', in A. Adams (ed.), *50 Years of Sports Report*. London: CollinsWillow.

Campbell, A. (2008) *The 2008 Cudlipp Lecture: Journalism, a Growth in Scale, Alas, not in Stature*. London College of Communications, 28 January.

Campbell, V. (2004) *Information Age Journalism*. London: Arnold.

Cashmore, E. (1982) *Black Sportsmen*. London: Routledge & Kegan Paul.

Cashmore, E. (1996) *Making Sense of Sports* (2nd edn). London: Routledge.

Cashmore, E. (2004) *Beckham*. Cambridge: Polity.

Cashmore, E. (2005) *Making Sense of Sports* (4th edn). London: Routledge.

Catt, M. (2008) *Landing on My Feet*. London: Hodder & Stoughton.

Chadwick, S. (2007) 'Is sponsorship still sponsorship?', *International Journal of Sports Marketing and Sponsorship*, July, p. 287.

Chase, M. and Shaw, C. (1989) 'The dimensions of nostalgia', in C. Shaw and M. Chase (eds), *The Imagined Past: History and Nostalgia*. Manchester: Manchester University Press.

Clapson, M. (1992) *A Bit of a Flutter: Popular Gambling and English Society, c.1823–1961*. Manchester: Manchester University Press.

Clarke, A. and Clarke, J. (1982) 'Highlights and action replays', in J. Hargreaves (ed.), *Sport, Culture and Society*. London: Routledge & Kegan Paul.

Clarke, J. and Critcher, C. (1985) *The Devil Makes Work: Leisure in Capitalist Britain*. Basingstoke: Macmillan.

CNN/Sports Illustrated (1999) 'Up in the Air'. Online at: http://cnnsi.com/basket-ball/nba/news/1999/01/07/nba_comebac/index.html.

Coakley, J. (2003) *Sports in Society* (8th edn). Maidenhead: McGraw-Hill Higher Education.

Cohen, P. (1988) 'Tarzan and the jungle bunnie: class, race and sex in popular culture', *New Formations*, 5, 25–30.

Collantine, K. (2008) 'ITV F1 ratings grow slowly', 2 July. Online at: www.f1fanatic.co.uk/2008/07/02/itv-f1-tv-ratings-grow-slowly/.

Conlan, T. (2008) 'Olympics: BBC's Games audience hits 40 million', *Guardian*, 22 August.

Conn, D. (1997) *The Football Business: Fair Game in the '90s?* Edinburgh: Mainstream.

Conn, D. (2005) *The Beautiful Game? Searching for the Soul of Football*. London: Yellow Jersey Press.

Connell, R. (1987) *Gender and Power: Society, the Person and Sexual Politics*. Cambridge: Polity Press.

Connell, R. (1997) *Masculinities*. Cambridge: Polity Press.

Corner, J. (1995) *Television Form and Public Address*. London: Edward Arnold.

Cosgrove, S. (1998) 'The Tartan Army, France 98', *Observer Guide to the World Cup*, 7 June.

Cowgill, B. (2006) *Mr Action Replay*. Stratford-upon-Avon: Sports Masters International.

Crabbe, T. and Brown, A. (2004) '"You're not welcome anymore": the football crowd, class and social exclusion', in S. Wagg (ed.), *British Football and Social Exclusion*. London: Routledge.

Crabbe, T., Brown, A., Mellor, G. and O'Connor, K. (2006) 'Football: an all consuming passion?', EA Sports Research, Substance. Online at: www.substance.coop/files/ea_sports_footballconsuming_passion_report.pdf.

Cramer, J. A. (1994) 'Conversations with women sports journalists', in P. Creedon (ed.), *Women, Media and Sport: Challenging the Gender Order*. London: Sage.

Crawford, A. (2004) *Consuming Sport: Fans, Sport and Culture*. London: Routledge.

Craxton, A. (1958) 'Pressing the buttons', in B. Johnston and R. Webber (eds), *Armchair Cricket*. London: BBC.

Creedon, P. (1994) *Women, Media and Sport: Challenging the Order*. London: Sage.

Critcher, C. (1992) 'Is there anything on the box? Leisure studies and media studies', *Leisure Studies*, 11 (2), 97–122.

Cronin, M. (1997) 'Which nation, which flag: boxing and national identities in Ireland', *International Review for the Sociology of Sport*, 32 (2), 131–46.

Curran, J. (1978) 'Capitalism and control of the press, 1800–1975', in J. Curran, M. Gurevitch and J. Woollacott (eds), *Mass Communication and Society*. London: Edward Arnold, pp. 195–230.

Dallaglio, L. (2008) *It's in the Blood: My Life*. London: Headline.

Davies, B. (2008) *Interesting, Very Interesting: The Autobiography*. London: Headline.

Davies, H. (1990) *The Glory Game* (2nd edn). Edinburgh: Mainstream Publishers (orig. published 1972).

Davies, N. (2008) *Flat Earth News*. London: Chatto & Windus.

Davies, P. (1990) *All Played Out: The Full Story of Italia 90*. London: Heinemann.

Davies, R. O. (2006) *Sports in American Life: A History*. London: Wiley-Blackwell.

Davis, R. D. and Harris, O. (1998) 'Race and ethnicity in the US sports media', in L. A. Wenner (ed.), *MediaSport*. London: Routledge.

Deford, F. (1999) 'A man for his time', *Sports Illustrated: Michael Jordan – A Tribute*, 20 January.

Delgado, F. (2005) 'Golden but not brown: Osca De La Hoya and the complications of culture, manhood and boxing', *International Journal of the History of Sport*, 22 (2), 196–211.

Deloitte (2008) *Deloitte Annual Review of Football Finance*. London: Deloitte.

Denney, R. (1989) *The Astonished Muse*. New Brunswick, NJ: Transaction.

Desbordes, M. (ed.) (2006) *Marketing and Football: An International Perspective*. London: Butterworth-Heinemann.

Dobson, S. and Goddard, J. (2007) *The Economics of Football*. Cambridge: Cambridge University Press.

Donegan, L. (1997) *Four-Iron in the Soul*. London: Penguin.

Dowell, B. (2007) 'ITV a winner from rugby final', 22 October. Online at: www.guardian.co.uk/media/2007/oct/22/tvratings.bendowell.

Duke, V. and Crolley, L. (1996) *Football, Nationality and the State*. Manchester: Manchester University Press.

Dunning, E. (1989) 'The figurational approach to sport and leisure', in C. Rojek (ed.), *Leisure for Leisure: Critical Essays*. London: Routledge.

Dunning, E. and Rojek, C. (eds) (1992) *Sport and Leisure in the Civilising Process*. London: Macmillan.

Dunning, E. and Sheard, K. (1979) *Gentlemen, Barbarians and Players: A Sociological Study of the Development of Rugby*. Oxford: Oxford University Press.

Dunning, E., Murphy, P. and Williams, J. (1988) *The Roots of Football Hooliganism: An Historical and Sociological Study*. London: Routledge.

Dyson, M. E. (1993) 'Be like Mike? Michael Jordan and the pedagogy of desire', *Cultural Studies*, 7 (1), 64–72.

Easton, S. and Mackie, P. (1998) 'When football came home: a case history of the sponsorship activity at Euro '96', *International Journal of Advertising*, 17, 99–114.

Eco, U. (1986) 'Sports chatter', *Travels in Hyper-Reality*. London: Picador.

Edelman, R., Andrews, A. and Wagg, S. (2006) *East Plays West: Sport and the Cold War*. London: Routledge.

Falcous, M. and Maguire, J. (2005) 'Globetrotters and local heroes? Labour migration, basketball and identities', *Sociology of Sport Journal*, 22, 137–57.

Fielding, R. (1972) *The American Newsreel, 1911–1967*. Norman: University of Oklahoma Press.

Finn, G. and Giulianotti, R. (1998) 'Scottish fans, not English football hooligans! Scots, Scottishness and Scottish football', in A. Brown (ed.), *Fanatics! Power, Identity and Fandom in Football*. London: Routledge.

Fishlock, T. (1986) *The State of America*. London: Faber & Faber.

Fletcher, D. (2007) *Behind the Shades: The Autobiography*. London: Simon & Schuster.

Forgacs, D. (ed.) (1988) *A Gramsci Reader*. London: Lawrence & Wishart.

Fraser, D. (2008) *Nation Speaking Unto Nation: Does the Media Create Cultural Distance between England and Scotland?* London: IPPR.

Frei, M. (1997) *Italy: The Unfinished Revolution*. London: Mandarin.

Frindall, B. (2005) *Bearders: My Life in Cricket*. London: Orion.

Fynn, A. and Guest, L. (1994) *Out of Time*. London: Simon & Schuster.

Gardiner, S. (1998) 'The law and hate speech: "Ooh Aah Cantona" and the demonisation of "the other"', in A. Brown (ed.), *Fanatics! Power, Identity and Fandom in Football*. London: Routledge.

Garland, J. (2004) 'The same old story? Englishness, the tabloid press and the 2002 Football World Cup', *Leisure Studies*, 23 (1), 79–92.

Germain, J. (1994) *In Soccer Wonderland*. London: Booth-Clibborn Editions.

Gilroy, P. (1993) *Small Acts: Thoughts on the Politics of Black Cultures*. London: Serpent's Tail.

Giulianotti, R. (1991) 'The Tartan Army in Italy: the case for the carnivalesque', *Sociological Review*, 39 (3), 503–27.

Giulianotti, R. (1994) 'The Patriots' tour of duty', *The Herald*, 22 January.

Giulianotti, R. (1999) *Football: A Sociology of the Global Game*. Cambridge: Polity.

Giulianotti, R. (2002) '"Supporters, followers, fans and flaneurs": a taxonomy of spectator identities', *Journal of Sport and Social Issues*, 26 (1), 25–46.

Giulianotti, R. (2005a) 'The sociability of sport: Scotland football supporters as interpreted through the sociology of Georg Simmel', *International Review for the Sociology of Sport*, 40 (3), 289–306.

Giulianotti, R. (2005b) *Sport: A Critical Sociology*. Cambridge: Polity Press.

Giulianotti, R. and Williams, J. (eds) (1994) *Games Across Frontiers: Football, Identity and Modernity*. Aldershot: Arena.

Glanville, B. (1999) *Football Memories*. London: Virgin.

Glendinning, M. (2007) 'VISA evaluates RWC sponsorship', *Sport Business International*, December.

Goldblatt, D. (2007) 'Taking sport seriously', *Prospect*, No. 141, December.

Goldlust, J. (1987) *Playing for Keeps: Sport, the Media and Society*. Melbourne: Longman.

Goodwin, P. (1998) *Television under the Tories: Broadcasting Policy 1979–1997*. London: BFI.

Gratton, C. and Solberg, A. (2007) *The Economics of Sports Broadcasting*. London: Routledge.

Groot, L. (2008) *Economics, Uncertainty and European Football: Trends in Competitive Balance*. London: Edward Elgar.

Guinness Sports Yearbook (1994) London: Guinness.

Guoqi, X. (2008) *Olympic Dreams: China and Sports, 1985–2008*. Cambridge, MA: Harvard University Press.

Guttmann, A. (1994) *Games and Empires: Modern Sports and Cultural Imperialism*. New York: Columbia University Press.

Hagerty, B. (2005) 'It's cricket, but is it journalism?', *British Journalism Review*, 16 (3), 79–84.

Hall, A. E. (1985) 'How should we theorize sport in a capitalist patriarchy?', *International Review for the Sociology of Sport*, 20 (1), 109–16.

Hall, W. and Parkinson, M. (1973) *Football Report: An Anthology of Soccer*. London: Sportsmans Bookclub.

Hamilton, I. (1994) 'A victory of sorts', *Weekend Guardian*, 4 June.

Hand, D. and Crolley, L. (2006) *Football and European Identity*. London: Routledge.

Harcup, T. (2004) *Journalism: Principles and Practice*. London: Sage.

Hargreaves, I. (2003) *Journalism: Truth or Dare?* Oxford: Oxford University Press.

Hargreaves, Jen (1994) *Sporting Females*. London: Routledge.

Hargreaves, Jen (1997) 'Women's boxing and related activities: introducing images and meanings', *Body and Society*, 4 (1), 77–98.

Hargreaves, John (1986) *Sport, Power and Culture*. London: Polity.

Hattenstone, S. (2008) 'When the blacksmith is worth a dozen Tendulkars', *Guardian. co.uk*, 30 July. Online at: http://blogs.guardian.co.uk/sport/2008/07/30/when_the_blacksmith_is_worth_a_1.html.

Haynes, R. (1995) *The Football Imagination: The Rise of Football Fanzine Culture*. Aldershot: Arena.

Haynes, R. (1998) 'A pageant of sound and vision: football's relationship with television, 1936–60', *International Journal of the History of Sport*, 15 (1), 211–26.

Haynes, R. (1999) '"There's many a slip twixt the eye and the lip": an exploratory history of football broadcasts and running commentaries 1927–39', *International Review of the Sociology of Sport*, 34 (2), 143–56.

Haynes, R. (2004) 'The fame game: the peculiarities of sports image rights in the UK', *Trends in Communication*, 12 (2 & 3), 101–16.

Haynes, R. (2005) *Media Rights and Intellectual Property*. Edinburgh: Edinburgh University Press.

Haynes, R. (2007) 'Footballers image rights in the new media age', *European Sports Management Quarterly*, 7 (4), 361–74.

Haynes, R. and Boyle, R. (2008) 'Media sport', in N. Blain and D. Hutchison (eds), *The Media in Scotland*. Edinburgh: Edinburgh University Press.

Hearn, J. (1994) 'Research in men and masculinities: some sociological issues and possibilities', *Australian and New Zealand Journal of Sociology*, 30 (1), 47–70.

Helland, K. (2007) 'Changing sports, changing media', *Nordicom Review*, Jubilee Issue, 105–19.

Hey, S. (1993) 'The Kop's last stand', *Observer*, 2 May.

Hill, D. (1989) *'Out of his Skin': The John Barnes Phenomenon*. London: Faber & Faber.

Hoberman, J. (1984) *Sport and Political Ideology*. London: Heinemann.

Hoberman, J. (1997) *Darwin's Athletes: How Sport Has Damaged Black America and Preserved the Myth of Race*. New York: Mariner Books.

Holland, B. L. (1997) 'Surviving leisure time racism: the burden of racial harassment on Britain's black footballers', *Leisure Studies*, 16, 261–77.

Holmwood, L. (2008) 'Olympics win US ratings gold for NBC', *Guardian.co.uk*, 20 August. Online at: www.guardian.co.uk/media/2008/aug/20/television.usa.

Holt, M. (2007) 'Global success in sport: the effective marketing and branding of the UEFA Champions League', *International Journal of Sports Marketing and Sponsorship*, October, 51–61.

Holt, R. (1989) *Sport and the British*. Oxford: Oxford University Press.

Hopcraft, A. (1988) *The Football Man* (2nd edn; orig. published 1968). London: Sportspages.

Hornby, N. (1992) *Fever Pitch: A Fan's Life*. London: Victor Gollancz.

Hornby, N. (ed.) (1993) *My Favourite Year*. London: Witherby.

Horne, J. (2006) *Sport in Consumer Culture*. Basingstoke: Palgrave Macmillan.

Horne, J., Jary, D. and Tomlinson, A. (eds) (1987) *Sport, Leisure and Social Relations*. London: Routledge & Kegan Paul.

Horsman, M. (1997) *Sky High: The Inside Story of BSkyB*. London: Orion.

Hoskins, C., McFadyen, S. and Finn, A. (1997) *Global Television and Film*. Oxford: Oxford University Press.

Houlihan, B. (1994) *Sport and International Politics*. Hemel Hempstead: Harvester Wheatsheaf.

Houlihan, B. (1997) 'Sport, national identity and public policy', *Nations and Nationalism*, 3 (1), 113–37.

Houlihan, B. (ed.) (2007) *Sport and Society: A Student Introduction*. London: Sage.

Hudson, R. (1968) 'The commentary: radio', in B. Johnston (ed.), *Armchair Cricket 1968*. London: BBC Publications.

Huggins, M. (2007) 'Projecting the visual: British newsreels, soccer and popular culture 1918–39', *International Journal of the History of Sport*, 41 (1), 80–102.

Hughes, S. (2005) *Morning Everyone: A Sportswriter's Life*. London: Orion Books.

Humphries, T. (1996) *Green Fields: Gaelic Sport in Ireland*. London: Weidenfeld & Nicolson.

Humphries, T. (2003) *Lap Dancing and the Nanny Goat Mambo: A Sports Writer's Year*. London: Pocket Books.

Humphries, T. (2007) *Dublin v Kerry: The Story of the Epic Rivalry that Changed Irish Sport*. London: Penguin Books.

Hutton, W. (1995) *The State We're In*. London: Jonathan Cape.

Inglis, S. (1987) *Soccer in the Dock: A History of British Football Scandals 1900 to 1965*. London: Willow Books.

James, C. L. R. (1963/1983) *Beyond a Boundary*. London: Hutchinson.

Jarvie, G. (2006) *Sport, Culture and Society*. London: Routledge.

Jarvie, G. and Maguire, J. (1994) *Sport and Leisure in Social Thought*. London: Routledge.

Jarvie, G. and Reid, I. (1997) 'Race relations, sociology of sport and the new politics of race and racism', *Leisure Studies*, 16, 211–19.

Jarvie, G. and Walker, G. (eds) (1994) *Sport in the Making of the Scottish Nation: Ninety-Minute Patriots?* Leicester: Leicester University Press.

Jarvie, J. (1991) 'Sport, racism and ethnicity', in G. Jarvie (ed.), *Sport, Race and Ethnicity*. London: Falmer.

Jeanrenaud, C. and Kesenne, S. (2006) *The Economics of Sport and the Media*. Cheltenham: Edward Elgar.

Jefferson, T. (1998) '"Muscle", "hard men" and "Iron" Mike Tyson: reflections on desire, anxiety and the embodiment of masculinity', *Body and Society*, 4 (1), 77–98.

Jenson, J. (1992) 'Fandom as pathology: the consequences of characterization', in L. A. Lewis (ed.), *The Adoring Audience: Fan Culture and Popular Media*. London: Routledge.

Johnston, B. (ed.) (1968) *Armchair Cricket 1968*. London: BBC Publications.

Jones, K. (2000) 'Decline and fall of popular sportwriting', *British Journalism Review*, 11 (1), 39–43.

Jones, S. G. (1992) *Sport, Politics and the Working Class*. Manchester: Manchester University Press.

Jordan, M. (1994) *Rare Air: Michael on Michael*. San Francisco: Collins.

Katz, D. (1994) *Just Do It: The Nike Spirit in the Corporate World*. Holbrook, MA: Adams Media Corporation.

Keane, R. and Dunphy, E. (2003) *Keane: The Autoboigraphy*. London: Penguin.

Kelly, S. F. (ed.) (1993) *A Game of Two Halves*. London: Mandarin.

Kelner, M. (2008) 'Without the Olympics what does a sports station do?', *Guardian*, 18 August.

Kimmage, P. (2007) *Rough Ride* (new edn). London: Yellow Jersey Press.

King, A. (1998) *End of the Terraces: The Transformation of English Football in the 1990s*. Leicester: Leicester University Press.

King, A. (2003) *The European Ritual*. Aldershot: Ashgate.

King, C. (2007) 'Media portrayals of male and female athletes: a text and picture analysis of British national newspaper coverage of the Olympic Games since 1948', *International Review for the Sociology of Sport*, 42 (2), 187–99.

Kofler, A. (1998) 'Digital Europe 1998: policies, technological development and implementation of the emerging information society', *Innovations*, 11 (1), 53–71.

Kolah, A. (1999) *Maximising the Value of Sports Sponsorship*. London: Financial Times Media.

Koppett, L. (1994) *Sports Illusion, Sports Reality: A Reporter's View of Sports, Journalism and Society*. Urbana and Chicago: University of Illinois Press.

Koppett, L. (2003) *The Rise and Fall of the Press Box*. Toronto: Sport Media Publishing.

Kraucauer, A. (1926) 'The cult of distraction', reprinted in *New German Critique* (1987), 40, 91–6.

Kuper, S. (1994) *Football Against the Enemy*. London: Orion.

Kuper, S. (ed.) (1998) *Perfect Pitch: Foreign Field*. London: Headline.

Laine, T. (2006) 'Shame on us: shame, national identity and the Finnish doping scandal', *International Journal of the History of Sport*, 23 (1), 67–81.

Larson, J. L. and Park, H. S. (1993) *Global Television and the Politics of the Seoul Olympics*. Boulder, CO: Westview Press.

Leigh, D. and Vulliamy, E. (1997) *Sleaze: The Corruption of Parliament*. London: Fourth Estate.

Lewis, J. (2008) *Cultural Studies: The Basics* (2nd edn). London: Sage.

Lines, G. (2001) 'Villains, fools or heroes? Sports stars as role models for young people', *Leisure Studies*, 20 (4), 285–303.

Livingstone, S. (1996) 'On the continuing problems of media effects research', in J. Curran and M. Gurevitch (eds), *Mass Media and Society* (2nd edn). London: Edward Arnold.

Loader, B. D. (ed.) (1998) *Cyberspace Divide: Equality, Agency and Policy in the Information Society*. London: Routledge.

Lowerson, J. (1989) 'Golf', in T. Mason (ed.), *Sport in Britain: A Social History*. Cambridge: Cambridge University Press, pp. 187–214.

Lowerson, J. (1993) *Sport and the English Middle Class, 1870–1914*. Manchester: Manchester University Press.

Lowes, M. D. (1997) 'Sports page: a case study in the manufacture of sports news for the daily press', *Sociology of Sport Journal*, 14, 145–59.

Lyons, A. and Ticher, M. (1998) *When Saturday Comes: The First Eleven*. London: WSC.

McChesney, R. W. (1998) 'Media convergence and globalisation', in D. K. Thussu (ed.), *Electronic Empires: Global Media and Local Resistance*. London: Arnold.

MacClancy, J. (ed.) (1996) *Sport, Identity and Ethnicity*. Oxford: Berg.

McCormack, M. (1967) *Arnold Palmer: The Man and the Legend*. London: Cassell.

McIlvanney, H. (1995) *McIlvanney on Football*. Edinburgh: Mainstream.

MacKay, A. (1997) 'How it all began', in A. Adams (ed.), *50 years of Sports Report*. London: CollinsWillow.

MacNeill, M. (1998) 'Sports journalism, ethics and Olympic athletes' rights', in L. A. Wenner (ed.), *MediaSport*. London: Sage.

MacPherson, A. (1991) *Action Replays*. London: Chapman.

MacRae, D. (1997) *Dark Trade: Lost in Boxing*. Edinburgh: Mainstream Publishers.

Maguire, J. and Tuck, J. (1997) 'Global sports and patriot games: rugby union and national identity in a United Sporting Kingdom', in M. Cronin and D. Mayall (eds), *Sporting Nationalisms: Identity, Ethnicity, Immigration and Assimilation*. London: Frank Cass.

Malac, M. A. (1995) *The Social Roles of Sport in Caribbean Societies*. Luxembourg: Gordon & Breach.

Malik, S. (1998) 'Race and ethnicity', in A. Briggs and P. Cobley (eds), *The Media: An Introduction*. London: Longman.

Mangan, J. A. (1981) *Athleticism in the Victorian and Edwardian Public School*.

London: Cambridge University Press.

Mangan, J. A. (ed.) (1996) *Tribal Identities: Nationalism, Sport, Europe*. London: Frank Cass.

Mangan, J. A. and Park, R. J. (1986) *From 'Fair Sex' to Feminism*. London: Frank Cass.

Mann, M. (1992) 'The emergence of modern European nationalism', in J. A. Hall and I. C. Jarvie (eds), *Transition to Modernity*. Cambridge: Cambridge University Press.

Mantle, J. (1999) 'Luciano's magical drive', *EuroBusiness*, April.

Marqusee, M. (2001) 'In search of the Unequivocal Englishman: the conundrum of race and nation in English Cricket', in B. Carrington and I. McDonald (eds), *'Race', Sport and British Society*. London: Routledge.

Martineau, G. D. (1957) *They Made Cricket*. London: Sportsman's Bookclub.

Martin-Jenkins, C. (1990) *Ball By Ball: The story of Cricket Broadcasting*. London: Grafton Books.

Maskell, D. (1988) *Oh I Say!* London: Collins.

Mason, T. (1988) *Sport in Britain*. London: Faber & Faber.

Melechi, A. and Hearn, J. (1992) 'The transatlantic gaze: youth, masculinities and the American imaginary', in S. Craig (ed.), *Men, Masculinities and Social Theory*. London: Unwin Hyman.

Mellor, A. (1991) 'Enterprise and heritage in the Dock', in J. Corner and S. Harvey (eds), *Enterprise and Heritage: Crosscurrents of National Culture*. London: Routledge.

Messner, M. A. (1990) 'When bodies are weapons: masculinity and violence in sport', *International Review for the Sociology of Sport*, 25 (3), 203–20.

Messner, M. A. (1992) *Power at Play: Sports and the Problem of Masculinity*. Boston: Beacon Press.

Messner, M. A. (2007) *Out of Play: Critical Essays on Gender and Sport*. Albany, NY: State University of New York Press.

Messner, M. A. and Sabo, D. (eds) (1990) *Sport, Men and the Gender Order: Critical Feminist Perspectives*. Champaign, IL: Human Kinetics Publishers.

Miller, T., Lawrence, G., McKay, J. and Rowe, D. (2001) *Globalization and Sport: Playing the World*. London: Sage.

Mitchell, K. (2001a) 'Fighting for life', *Observer Sports Magazine*, 4 November.

Mitchell, K. (2001b) *War, Baby: The Glamour of Violence*. London: Yellow Jersey Press.

Modlenski, T. (1983) *Loving with a Vengeance: Mass-Produced Fantasies for Women*. Hamden, CT: Shoe String Press.

Modood, T. (1992) *Not Easy Being British: Colour, Culture and Citizenship*. London: Trentham Books.

Moorhouse, H. F. (1991) 'On the periphery: Scotland, Scottish football and the new Europe', in J. Williams and S. Wagg (eds), *British Football and Social Change: Getting into Europe*. Leicester: Leicester University Press.

Moorhouse, H. F. (1994) 'From zines like these? Fanzines, tradition and identity in Scottish football', in G. Jarvie and G. Walker (eds), *Scottish Sport in the Making of the Nation: Ninety-Minute Patriots?* Leicester: Leicester University Press.

Morse, M. (1983) 'Sport on television: replay and display', in E. A. Kaplan (ed.), *Regarding Television*. Los Angeles: AFI.

Morse, M. (1992) *Power at Play: Sports and the Problem of Masculinity*. Boston: Beacon Books.

Mosey, R. (2007a) Speech given to Broadcast Sports Forum, Hilton Waldorf Hotel, London, 29 November. Online at: www.bbc.co.uk/pressoffice/speeches/stories/mosey_broadcast.shtml.

Mosey, R. (2007b) 'Our challenge to cricket in a digital age', 3 May. Online at: www.bbc.co.uk/blogs/sporteditors/2007/05/roger_mosey_may_2.html.

Mosey, R. (2008) 'Olympic figures continue to impress', BBC Sport Editors Blog, 18 August. Online at: http://www.bbc.co.uk/blogs/sporteditors/2008/08/i_said_in_my_last.html.

Murray, C. (2008) 'The DJ and the Blue Jays', *Observer Sports Magazine*, 31 August.

Newman, P. (2007) '"Back the bid": the 2012 Summer Olympics and the governance of London', *Journal of Urban Affairs*, 29(3), 255–67.

Nicolson, M. (2007) *Sport and the Media: Managing the Nexus*. London: Butterworth-Heinemann.

Nixon, S. (1996) *Hard Looks: Masculinity, Spectatorship and Contemporary Consumption*. London: UCL Press.

Noble, R. (1955) *Shoot First! Assignments of a Newsreel Cameraman*. London: Pan Books.

O'Conner, B. and Boyle, R. (1993) 'Dallas with balls? Televised sport, soap opera and male and female pleasures', *Leisure Studies*, 12, 107–19.

O'Donnell, H. (1994) 'Mapping the mythical: a geopolitics of national sporting stereotypes', *Discourse and Society*, 5 (3), 345–80.

O'Donnell, H. (1999) 'France '98: Discourses of Identity'. Unpublished paper for the Sport, Media and National Identity: One Day Seminar, University of Stirling.

O'Neill, J. (2008) *Netherlands*. London: Fourth Estate.

Oates, J. C. (1994) *On Boxing*. London: Doubleday.

Panagiotopoulou, R. (2007) *The Image of Athens and Greece in the International and Greek Press during the Preparation and Staging of the Olympic Games Athens 2004*, International Olympic Academy, 11th International Seminar for Sports Journalists, Greece.

Paxman, J. (1998) *The English: A Portrait of a People*. London: Penguin.

Peace, D. (2006) *The Damned Utd*. London: Faber & Faber

Phelops, W. L. (2008) 'Understanding the impact of new technologies on sports sponsorship contracts', *Journal of Sponsorship*, 1 (1), 15–19.

Polley, M. (1998) *Moving the Goalposts: A History of Sport and Society since 1945*. London: Routledge.

Polley, M. (2006) *Sports History: A Practical Guide*. Basingstoke: Macmillan.

Poulton, E. (2003) 'New fans, new flag, new England? Changing news values in the English press coverage of World Cup 2002', *Football Studies*, 6 (1), 19–36.

Poulton, E. (2007) '"Fantasy football hooliganism" in popular media', *Media, Culture and Society*, 29 (1), 151–64.

Puijk, R. (ed.) (1997) *Global Spotlights on Lillehammer: How the World Viewed Norway during the 1994 Winter Olympics*. Luton: John Libbey.

Puttnam, D. (1997) *The Undeclared War: The Struggle for Control of the World's Film Industry*. London: HarperCollins.

Rader, B. (1984) *In Its Own Image: How TV has Transformed Sports*. New York: Free Press.

Radway, J. (1984) *Women Read the Romance*. Chapel Hill: University of North Carolina Press.

Real, R. M. (1998) 'MediaSport: technology and the commodification of postmodern sport', in L. A. Wenner (ed.), *MediaSport*. London: Routledge.

Redhead, R. (2004) 'Hit and tell: a review essay on the soccer hooligan memoir', *Soccer and Society*, 5 (3), 392–403.

Redhead, S. (1987) *Sing When You're Winning: The Last Football Book*. London: Pluto.

Redhead, S. (1991) *Football with Attitude*. Manchester: Wordsmith.

Redhead, S. (1997) *Post-Fandom and the Millenial Blues: The Transformation of Soccer Culture*. London: Routledge.

Regester, C. (2003) 'From gridiron and the boxing-ring to cinema screen: the African American athlete in pre-1950s cinema', *Sport in Society*, 6 (2–3), 269–92.

Rines, S. (2007) *Driving Business Through Sport* (2nd edn). London: International Marketing Reports.

Riordan, J. and Kruger, A. (1999) *International Politics of Sport in the 20th Century*, London: Spon Press.

Robinson, J. S. R. (2008) 'Tackling the anxieties of the English: searching for the nation through football', *Soccer and Society*, 9 (2), 215–30.

Roche, M. (2006) 'Mega-events and modernity revisited: globalization and the case of the Olympics', *Sociological Review*, 54 (2), 25–40.

Rojek, C. (1985) *Capitalism and Leisure Theory*. London: Routledge.

Rojek, C. (1992) 'The field of play in sport and leisure studies', in E. Dunning and C. Rojek (eds), *Sport and Leisure in the Civilizing Process*. London: Macmillan.

Rose, A. and Friedman, J. (1994) 'Television sport as a mas(s)culine cult of distraction', *Screen*, 35 (1), 22–35.

Rose, D. and Wood, N. (eds) (1996) 'Introduction. Sport, globalization and the media', Special Edition of *Media, Culture and Society*, 18, 4.

Rose, T. (1994) *Black Noise: Rap Music and Black Culture in Contemporary America*. Hanover, NH: Wesleyan University Press.

Rosie, M., MacInnes, J., Petersoo, P., Condor, S. and Kennedy, J. (2004) 'Nation speaking unto nation? Newspapers and national identity in the devolved UK', *Sociological Review*, 437–58.

Rowe, D. (1992) 'Modes of sports writing', in P. Dahlgren and C. Sparks (eds), *Journalism and Popular Culture*. London: Sage.

Rowe, D. (1995) *Popular Cultures: Rock Music, Sport and the Politics of Pleasure*. London: Sage.

Rowe, D. (1996) 'The global love match: sport and television', *Media Culture and Society*, 18 (4), 565–82.

Rowe, D. (1997) 'Apollo undone: the sports scandal', in J. Lull and S. Hinerman (eds), *Media Scandals: Morality and Desire in the Popular Culture Marketplace*. Cambridge: Polity Press.

Rowe, D. (2003a) 'Sport and the repudiation of the global', *International Review for the Sociology of Sport*, 38 (3), 281–94.

Rowe, D. (2003b) *Sport, Culture and the Media: The Unruly Trinity* (2nd edn). Maidenhead: Open University Press.

Rowe, D. (ed.) (2004) *Critical Readings: Sport, Culture and the Media*. Maidenhead: Open University Press.

Rowe, D. (2005) 'Fourth estate or fan club? Sports journalism engages the popular', in S. Allan (ed.), *Journalism: Critical Issues*. Maidenhead: Open University Press.

Rowe, D., McKay, J. and Miller, T. (1998) 'Come together: sport, national-ism and the media image', in L. A. Wenner (ed.), *MediaSport*. London: Routledge.

Rowe, D., Lawrence, G., Miller, T. and McKay, J. (1994) 'Global sport? Core concern and peripheral vision', *Media, Culture and Society*, 16, 661–75.

Russell, A. (2007) 'Time for a new game?', *New Statesman*, 29 October, p. 16.

Rutherford, J. (1996) 'Who's that man?', in R. Chapman and R. Rutherford (eds), *Male Order: Unwrapping Masculinity*. London: Lawrence & Wishart.

Sabo, D. and Curry Jansen, S. (1998) 'Prometheus unbound: constructions of masculinity in sports media', in L. A. Wenner (ed.), *MediaSport*. London: Routledge.

Samuel, M. (2007) 'Le Saux: Beckham called me a poof', *The Times*, 8 September.

Sandvoss, C. (2003) *A Game of Two Halves: Football, Television and Globalisation*. London: Routledge.

Scannell, P. and Cardiff, D. (1991) *A Social History of British Broadcasting*. Oxford: Basil Blackwell.

Schlesinger, P. (1991) *Media, State and Nation*. London: Sage.

Schlesinger, P., Dobash, R. E., Dobash, R. and Weaver, K. (1992) *Women Viewing Violence*. London: BFI.

Schlesinger, P., Haynes, R., Boyle, R., McNair, B., Dobash, R. E. and Dobash, R. (1998) *Men Viewing Violence*. London: Broadcasting Standards Commission.

Scott, M. (2008) 'Olympics: TV holds key to midnight 100m in London', *Guardian*, 19 August.

Scully, G. W. (1995) *The Market Structure of Sports*. Chicago: University of Chicago Press.

Siegel, G. (2002) 'Double vision large-screen video display and live sports spectacle', *Television and New Media*, 3 (1), 49–73.

Silverstone, R. (1994) *Television and Everyday Life*. London: Routledge.

Simmons, K. (2007) *Women's Football: Tapping the Potential of the Fastest Growing Sport*. Paper presented at Raising the Game: The Future for Women's Sport, 15 November, London.

Singer, J. (2008) 'Playing regulatory games', *SportBusiness International*, No. 131, January.

Sloop, J. M. (1997) 'Mike Tyson and the perils of discursive constraints: boxing, race and the assumption of guilt', in T. Boyd and A. Baker (eds), *Out of Bounds: Sports, Media and the Politics of Identity*. Bloomington: Indiana University Press, pp. 102–22.

Smit, B. (2007) *Pitch Invasion: 'Adidas', 'Puma' and the Making of Modern Sport*. London: Penguin Books.

Smith, A. and Porter, D. (eds) (2004) *Sport and National Identity in the Post-war World*. London: Routledge.

Smith, S. J. (1995) 'Women, Sport and the British Press: The Under-representation of Sporting Females'. Unpublished BA (Hons) Film and Media Studies dissertation, Stirling, University of Stirling.

Steen, R. (2008) *Sports Journalism: A Multimedia Primer*. London: Routledge.

Steenveld, L. and Strelitz, L. (1998) 'The 1995 Rugby World Cup and the politics of nation building in South Africa', *Media, Culture and Society*, 20 (4), 609–29.

Strutt, J. (1841) *The Sports and Pastimes of the People of England* (orig. published 1801). London: Thomas Tegg.

Sugden, J. (1996) *Boxing and Society*. Leicester: Leicester University Press.

Sugden, J. and Bairner, A. (1993) *Sport, Sectarianism and Society in a Divided Ireland*. Leicester: Leicester University Press.

Sugden, J. and Tomlinson, A. (eds) (1994) *Hosts and Champions: Soccer Cultures, National Identities and the USA World Cup*. Aldershot: Arena.

Sugden, J. and Tomlinson, A. (1998) *FIFA and the Contest for World Football*. Cambridge: Polity Press.

Sugden, J. and Tomlinson, A. (2007) 'Stories from Planet Football and Sportsworld: source relations and collusion in sport journalism', *Journalism Practice*, 1 (1), 44–61.

Taylor, R. (1992) *Football and Its Fans*. Leicester: Leicester University Press.

Thompson, J. B. (1990) *Ideology and Modern Culture*. Cambridge: Polity Press.

Tomlinson, A. (1986) 'Going global: the FIFA story', in A. Tomlinson and G. Whannel (eds), *Off the Ball: The Football World Cup*. London: Pluto.

Tomlinson, A. (1994) 'FIFA and the World Cup: the expanding football family', in J. Sugden and A. Tomlinson (eds), *Hosts and Champions: Soccer Cultures, National Identities and the USA World Cup*. Aldershot: Arena.

Tomlinson, A. (ed.) (2006) *The Sports Studies Reader*. London: Routledge.

Tomlinson, A. and Young, C. (eds) (2005) *National Identity and Global Sports Events*. New York: State University of New York Press.

Toulmin, V. (2006) '"Vivid and realistic": Edwardian sport on film', *Sport in History*, 26 (1), 124–49.

Tuck, J. (2003) 'The men in white: reflections on rugby union, the media and Englishness', *International Review or the Sociology of Sport*, 38 (2), 177–99.

Tuggle, C. A., Huffman, S. and Rosengrad, D. (2007) 'A descriptive analysis of NBC's coverage of the 2004 Summer Olympics', *Journal of Sports Media*, 2 (1), 54–75.

Tunstall, J. (1996) *Newspaper Power: The New National Press in Britain*. Oxford: Oxford University Press.

Turner, B. (2004) *The Pits: The Real World of Formula 1*. London: Atlantic Books.

Vamplew, W. (1988) *Pay-up and Play the Game: Professional Sport in Britain, 1875–1914*. Cambridge: Cambridge University Press.

Vamplew, W. (2007) 'Playing with the rules: influences on the development of regulation in sport', *International Journal on the History of Sport*, 24 (7), 843–71.

Vande-Berg, L. E. (1998) 'The sports hero meets mediated celebrityhood', in L. A. Wenner (ed.), *MediaSport*. London: Routledge.

Vialli, G. and Marcotti, G. (2007) *The Italian Job: A Journey to the Heart of Two Great Footballing Cultures*. London: Bantam.

Vincent, J., Pedersen, P. M., Whisenant, W. A. and Massey, D. (2007) 'Analysing the print media coverage of professional tennis players: British newspaper narratives about female competitors in the Wimbledon Championships', *International Journal of Sport Management and Marketing*, 2 (3), 281–300.

Wacquant, L. (1995) 'Pugs at work: bodily capital and bodily labour among professional boxers', *Body and Society*, 1 (1), 65–93.

Waddell, S. (1979) *The Book of World Darts*. London: BBC Publications.

Waddell, S. (2007) *Bellies and Bullseyes: The Outrageous True Story of Darts*. London: Ebury Press.

Wagg, S. (ed.) (1995) *Giving the Game Away: Football, Politics and Culture on Five Continents*. Leicester: Leicester University Press.

Wakelam, H. T. B. (1938) *Half Time 'The Mike and Me'*. London: Nelson.

Walsh, D. (2007) *From Lance to Landis: Inside the American Doping Controversy at the Tour de France*. London: Ballantine Books.

Watts, J. (2008) 'The pressure from 1.3 bn people hurt him', *Guardian*, 18 August.

Weaver, P. (2008) 'The Twenty20 revolution that turned innocent sideshow into hunt for millions', *Guardian*, 26 July.

Webb, T. (2008) 'How a European sport had changed in the way that it sells its sponsorship packages', *Journal of Sponsorship*, 1 (1), 20–7.

Weeks, A. (2004) *Under Auntie's Skirts: The Life and Times of a BBC Sports Producer*. Lewes: Book Guild.

Weight, R. (1999) 'Raise St George's standard high', *New Statesman*, 8 January.

Wenner, L. A. (1998) 'Playing the MediaSport game', in L. A. Wenner (ed.), *MediaSport*. London: Routledge.

Wensing, E. H. and Bruce, T. (2003) 'Bending the rules: media representations of gender during an international sporting event', *International Review for the Sociology of Sport*, 38 (4), 387–96.

Westerbeek, H. and Smith, A. (2003) *Sports Business in the Global Marketplace*. Basingstoke: Macmillan.

Whannel, G. (1991) 'Grandstand, the sports fan and the family audience', in J. Corner (ed.), *Popular Television*. London: BFI.

Whannel, G. (1992) *Fields in Vision: Television Sport and Cultural Transformation*. London: Routledge.

Whannel, G. (1998) 'Reading the sports media audience', in L. A. Wenner (ed.), *MediaSport*. London: Routledge.

Whannel, G. (2000) 'Stars in whose eyes?', *Index on Censorship*, 29 (4), 48–54.

Whannel, G. (2001) *Media Sports Stars: Masculinities and Moralities*. London: Routledge.

Whannel, G. (2007) *Culture, Politics and Sport: Blowing the Whistle Revisited*. London: Routledge.

Whannel, G. (2008) *Culture, Politics and Sport*. London: Routledge.

Wheatcroft, G. (2005) *Le Tour: A History of the Tour de France, 1903–2003*. London: Simon & Schuster.

White, J. (1994) 'They thought it was all over', *Radio Times*, 28 May – 3 June.

White, J. (1999) 'One for the ghetto', *Guardian Weekend*, 23 January.

White, J. (2008) 'We're just spectators in a global soap opera', *Daily Telegraph*, 3 September.

Whitson, D. (1998) 'Circuits of promotion: media, marketing and the globalization of sport', in L. A. Wenner (ed.), *MediaSport*. London: Routledge.

Whittle, J. (2008) *Bad Blood: The Secret Life of the Tour de France*. London: Yellow Jersey Press.

Wignall, T. (1936) 'Introduction', in Hodder T. Knowles (ed.), *Daily Express Book of Popular Sports*. London: Daily Express Publications.

Williams, C. L., Lawrence, G. and Rowe, D. (1985) 'Women and sport: a lost ideal', *Women's Studies International Forum*, 8 (6), 639–45.

Williams, J. (1991) 'Having an away day: English football supporters and the hooligan debate', in J. Williams and S. Wagg (eds), *British Football and Social Change*. Leicester: Leicester University Press.

Williams, J. (1994) 'The local and the global in English soccer and the rise of satellite television', *Sociology of Sport Journal*, 11 (4), 376–9.

Williams, J. (2006) 'Protect me from what I want: football fandom, celebrity cultures and "new" football in England', *Soccer and Society*, 7 (1), 96–114.

Williams, J. (2007) 'Rethinking sports fandom: the case of European soccer', *Leisure Studies*, 26 (2), 127–46.

Williams, J., Long, C. and Hopkins, S. (eds) (2001) *Passing Rhythms: Liverpool FC and the Transformations of Football*. London: Berg.

Williams, R. (1974) *Television, Technology and Cultural Form*. London: Collins.

Williams, R. (1998) *Racers*. London: Penguin.

Williams, R. (2008) 'Spanish fans' racist jibes require firm action, not mere lip service', *Guardian*, 5 February.

Willis, P. (1982) 'Women in sport in ideology', in Jen Hargreaves (ed.), *Sport, Culture and Ideology*. London: Routledge & Kegan Paul.

Wilson, B. (1997) '"Good blacks" and "bad blacks": media constructions of African-American athletes in Canadian basketball', *International Review for the Sociology of Sport*, 32 (2), 177–89.

Wilson, B. and Sparks, R. (1996) '"It's gotta be the shoes": youth, race and sneaker commercials', *Sociology of Sport Journal*, 13, 398–427.

Wolstenholme, K. (1956) *Sports Special*. London: Stanley Paul.

Women's Sport and Fitness Foundation (2008) *Women in Sport Audit: Backing a Winner: Unlocking the Potential in Women's Sport*. WSFF: London.

Woodward, K. (2004) 'Rumbles in the jungle: boxing, racialization and the performance of masculinity', *Leisure Studies*, 23 (1), 5–17.

Wooldridge, I. (2007) *Searching for Heroes: Fifty Years of Sporting Encounters*. London: Hodder & Stoughton.

Wynne-Jones, G. V. (1951) *Sports Commentary*. London: Hutchinson's Library of Sports and Pastimes.

Index

ABC, 53, 81, 207
Abramovich, Roman, 59
Abu Dhabi Royal Family, 44, 59, 107, 204
Ackerman, Val, 125
Adidas, 47, 48, 50, 55, 75, 87, 126, 178
Adlington, Rebecca, 2
advertising
  audience, 67–9
  image rights, 100
  Internet, 65
  revenue, 68
  Rugby World Cup, 56
  sponsorship, 44, 45, 169
  sports stars, 92
advertising rights, 49–50
AFC Wimbledon, 195
aggression, 138, 188–9, 190
Air China, 55
Air Jordan, 94, 95
Akhavan, Hamid, 60
alcohol problems, 156
Ali, Muhammad, 41, 78, 116, 193
All England Croquet Club, 23
All England Lawn Tennis Association, 132
Allison, George, 34, 79
Alliss, Peter, 82, 84, 93
Alonso, Fernando, 111
Alston, Rex, 34, 35
amateurism, 21, 46
American Football, 42, 51, 101, 208
Anderson, B., 20
Anderson, Rachel, 124
Andrews, D. L., 159
Andrews, Eamonn, 34–5
Andrews, M., 95
APCS (Association for the Protection of Copyright in Sport), 38
Arena, 164
Aris, S., 91–2
aristocracy/patronage, 20, 22, 45

Arlott, John, 34, 35, 217
Armstrong, Lance, 130
Arundel, J., 160
Ascot, 38
Ashes series, 19, 25–6, 70, 166
Ashley, Mike, 203
Asian Cup, 149
Asian sports people, 108, 109, 116, 120
Association for the Protection of Copyright in Sport (APCS), 38
Aston Villa, 59
Atherton, M., 132–3
Athletic News, 23
Atkinson, Ron, 109–10
attendance numbers, 36, 46; *see also* fans; spectatorship
audience
  advertising, 67–9
  cinema, 27, 28, 30
  consumption, 16–17
  e-mails, 212
  exclusive sports, 28
  family, 39
  gender, 26, 125
  hybridized, 202
  live events, 56–7
  replays, 76–7
  stereotypes, 184–5
  text messaging, 212
  see also spectatorship
audience research, 76, 188–9
Austin, Tracy, 133
Australia, 1, 19, 55
autobiographies, 137, 180–1
L'Auto-Velo, 25

Bain, Martin, 155
Bairner, A., 117, 120
Baker, Andrew, 75
Bardsley, Tom, 155
Barnes, Simon, 128

Barnett, S., 8, 9, 51
Barton, Joey, 205
baseball, 1, 63, 101, 195, 203
basketball, 93–4, 95, 98, 101
Bassett, Dave, 135
BBC
    Audience Research Unit, 76
    boxing, 193
    Creative Future, 212
    cricket, 74
    Formula 1, 58, 69–70, 214
    game shows, 71
    ideology, 210–11
    iPlayer, 208–10
    licence fee, 215, 221
    Light Programme, 34
    national coverage, 14
    public service, 32–3, 46, 69, 70
    radio sport, 31–2, 131, 211–13
    Scottish sports, 161
    sports programming, 11, 31, 37–8, 207
    sports rights, 212
BBC Handbook, 33
BBC Scotland, 160–1
BBCi, 110
beat reporters, 166, 169
Beckham, David, 88, 89–90, 99, 100, 137, 196
Beech, J., 10
Bell, Ian, 156
Bell's Life, 22
Benchmark Sport Holdings, 43
Benn, Nigel, 139, 140, 141, 189, 191
Benson & Hedges, 47
Bentley, J. J., 23
Berlusconi, Silvio, 59
Bernstein, A., 3–4, 143
betting, 22, 24
BFI (British Film Institute), 9
Biograph films, 27
biological determinism, 120, 122, 138
Bird, Larry, 94, 102
Birmingham University, CCCS, 10
Biscomb, K., 126
Bishop, Ian, 133
black sports people
    boxers, 115
    British sports, 108–9
    as media celebrities, 110–11, 120
    popular culture, 94
    US, 95, 108
    see also ethnicity; race
Blain, N., 3–4, 9, 72, 128, 145, 153, 162, 169
Blair, Tony, 173
Blatter, Sepp, 98
blogging, 182, 211
Boat Race, 32, 33

body images, 128, 129, 130; see also female body; male body
Bolt, Usain, 68
Boorstin, D., 89
Borg, Bjorn, 78
Bosman, Jean-Marc, 98
Bourdieu, P., 126
boxing
    aggression, 138, 190
    BBC, 193
    brutality, 139–41
    early, 22
    ethnicity, 115–16
    experience ring-side, 142–3
    on film, 27
    injuries, 139–40
    masculinity, 138–41
    pay-per-view, 192, 214
    racism, 112
    Rumble in the Jungle, 41
    as spectacle, 142–3, 191–3
    sports stars, 113–15
    televised, 37–8, 50, 78, 141–3
    violence, 115, 141, 190–1
Boyle, J., 100
Boyle, R., 100, 128, 134, 162, 171, 173, 187
Bradford disturbances, 116
branding
    elite sport, 43–4, 48
    global, 50–2, 89
    sponsorship, 178
    sports journalism, 172, 175
    sports stars, 100
Brazil, 56, 68
Brewer, J., 117, 118
bribery, 103–4, 170
Britain
    Broadcasting Act (1990), 57
    devolution, 150–2
    ethnicity/sport, 108–9
    football in crisis, 201–2
    national sports coverage, 161
    religion/sport, 114
    spectator experience, 195–6
    sports pages, 126
    see also separate countries
British Cultural Studies, 9–10
British Film Institute (BFI), 9
British Movietone News, 28–9
Britishness, 77, 112–13, 116, 157–8
Broadcasting Act, UK (1990), 57, 207–8
Broadcasting Standards Commission, 188
Brown, A., 195
Brown, Cathy, 129
Brown, Gordon, vii, 152
Bruce, T., 127–8
Bruno, Frank, 128
brutality, 139–41, 190–1

Bryant, J., 141
Bryant, Kobe, 95
BSkyB
    Beckham, 89
    boxing, 141
    Champions League, 214
    and Channel 4, 70
    cricket, 74–5, 208
    dominance of, 2, 11, 14, 56, 69
    Manchester United, 58–9
    Premier League, 206–7, 219
Budweiser, 53, 55
Burdsey, D., 109, 113
Burn, Gordon, 179–80
Burnham, Andy, 98
Burns, Tommy, 154, 155, 157
Buscombe, E., 9
business--sport linkages, 47–8
Butcher, M., 98, 180
Butler, Bryon, 30

Calvalcade of Sport, 40
Campbell, Alastair, 173
Canada, 108
Caney, Simon, 178
Cantona, Eric, 104–5
Cardiff, D., 32
Cardus, Neville, 25
Caribbean, 1
Carr, John, 75–6
Cashmore, E., 4, 44, 89–90, 145
Catt, Mike, 181
CBS, 215
celebrity culture, 87–91, 92, 100, 181–2
Celtic, 107–8, 117–19, 157, 162, 198, 201
Centre for Contemporary Cultural Studies,
    10
Chadwick, S., 43
Champions League (UEFA)
    BSkyB, 214
    ITV, 68, 109
    marketing, 52
    Moscow final, 65, 156
Channel 4, 41–2, 70
Channel 5, 70, 208
Chase, M., 200
Chelsea Football Club, 59, 65, 156, 218
Chicago Bulls, 93–4, 102
China, 2, 7, 54, 60; see also Olympic Games,
    Beijing (2008)
Christie, Linford, 91
cigarettes: see tobacco advertising
cinema, 27, 28, 30
Clapson, M., 22
Clarke, Giles, 71
class
    commentators, 80, 110
    Marxist analysis, 4
    masculinity, 136–7

newspapers, 23, 168
    race, 108
    sexuality, 136–7
    sport, 20, 23, 118, 136–7, 165, 202
    sports journalism, 23, 165
CNC, 55
Coca-Cola, 53, 54, 87, 92, 126
Cock, Gerald, 32–3, 36, 37
Coe, Sebastian, 180, 205
Cohen, P., 107
Coleman, David, 39, 81, 82
collective bargaining, 101–2
Collins, Steve, 140, 141
commentaries, 14, 33, 34–5, 67, 76, 78–9, 83–4
commentators, 79–84, 110, 217
commercialism, 12, 53, 61, 100, 195
commercialization, 159–60, 167
commodification, 62, 87, 96, 186
Commonwealth Games, Glasgow, 146
communication technology, 160, 178–9, 213,
    216
communications policy, 163
community
    imagined, 199
    interpretive, 187–8
    nostalgia, 201–2
    online, 182, 218
computer gaming technology, 197
Conlan, T., 209
Conn, D., 96–7
Connell, R., 136, 138, 187
Connery, Sean, vii–viii
consumption, 5
    fans, 184, 194
    spectator experience, 202–3
    style magazines, 137
Coonan, Clifford, vii
Cooper, Henry, 193
copyright issues, 38, 219
Corner, J., 77–8
corporate capitalism, 53, 63
corruption, ix, 61, 104
Cowes, 28
Coxon, J. W., 32
CPS Emitron cameras, 38
Crabbe, T., 197
Craxton, Anthony, 73, 74
Creative Future, 212
creative industries, x, 10
Creedon, P., 4, 125
cricket
    amateur, 21
    Ashes, 19, 25–6, 70, 166
    Australia, 1, 19
    BSkyB, 74–5, 208
    Caribbean, 1
    class, 165
    commentaries, 34, 35
    county matches, 72, 74

Englishness, 133, 144
global branding, 50–2
IPL, 75
one-day game, 50–1, 74
personalization of stars, 75
replica shirts, 75
televised version, 72–4
Test Matches, 29, 32, 50, 70–1, 74, 208
Twenty20 competition, 70, 72–3, 74, 75–6
West Indies, 146–7
cricket administration, 72–4
Cricket Reporting Agency, 25
Cricketers' Almanac, 25
Croatia, 112
Crolley, L., 146
Cronin, M., 118, 119
Cronje, Hansje, 104
Crooks, Garth, 105, 110
cultural capital, 126, 193
cultural studies approach, 4–5, 138, 146–7,
    213, 220–1
Curbishley, Alan, 205
Curry Jansen, S., 138
cycle racing, 24–5, 33, 45, 60, 180; see also
    Pendleton; Romero

DAB (Digital Audio Broadcasting), 212
Daily Express, 19, 24, 26
Daily Mail, 24, 98–9, 135
Daily Mirror, 24, 25–6
Daily Record, 105, 155
Daily Telegraph, 50, 75, 86, 156, 166
Dallaglio, Lawrence, 181
darts, 74
Davies, Barry, 81
Davies, Nick, 173, 178
Davies, R. O., 7
Davis, R. D., 108
De La Hoya, Oscar, 113–15, 116
De Lotbiniere, Seymour Joly, 34, 79, 83
Dee, Moz, 212
DeFreitas, Phillip, 133
Delgado, F., 113–14, 116
Deloitte, 99–100
Denney, Reuel, 64
Derby, 27, 32, 33
Desailly, Marcel, 109
Desbordes, M., 10
Deutsche Telekom, 60
devolution, 14, 148, 150–2, 158, 160–1, 162
Digital Audio Broadcasting (DAB), 212
digital broadcasting, xi
    and BBC, 69, 213–16
    commentaries, 84
    media consumption, 63–4
    media sport, 213–16
    news gathering, 175–6
    pay-per-view, 214–16

profitability, 220
sports journalism, 11, 170–1, 173–4,
    183
synergies, 100, 173–4
Dimmock, Peter, 39, 82
DLF Universal, 51
Dobson, S., 10
drug-taking, 60, 61–2, 145, 180
Duke, V., 146
Dunphy, Eamon, 181
Durex, 47
Dyke, Greg, 66
Dyson, M. E., 95

Easton, S., 54
EBU (European Broadcasting Union), 40
Ecclestone, Bernie, 62
Economist, 47, 63, 149
Edelman, R., 7
Edison, Thomas, 27
Edwards, Billy, 27
Elias, N., 5
elite sport
    audience access, 28
    branding, 43–4
    commercialism, 61
    media, 160, 178
    money matters, 18
    sponsorship, 50, 54–5, 99
    sports stars, 87–90, 178
e-mails, 212, 217
employment contracts, 96
endorsement earnings, 202; see also
    sponsorship
England
    fans, 152–3, 197–8
    football, 59, 70, 99–100, 144
    Premier League, 58, 59, 99–100, 206–7
    Rugby World Cup, 56
    see also Englishness
England and Wales Cricket Board, 70, 71,
    75–6
English, Tom, 155
Englishness, 113, 133, 144, 157–8
L'Équipe, 25, 45, 220
ESPN, 207, 215
essentialist discourse, 95, 105, 108, 120, 123
ethics of sport, 104
ethnicity, 108, 110, 113, 114, 115–16, 117; see
    also race
Eubank, Chris, 139
Euro 96, 151
Euro 2004, 146
Euro 2008, 193
Europe, Eastern, 98
European Broadcasting Union (EBU), 40
European Commission, 206–7
European Court of Justice, 98

European Football Championship, viii, 40, 51–2, 54
European Union, 43, 58, 98
Eurovision, 40–2
Evans, Gavin, 142
event television, 56, 65
excitement, 190–1

FA: *see* Football Association
al-Fahim, Sulaiman, 44
faking on film, 27
fandom, 138, 185, 196, 198, 202
fans
  consumption, 16–17, 115, 184, 194, 198
  copyrighted material, 219
  identity, 193
  nationality, 76, 77
  online communities, 182, 218
  popular culture, 200
  Rangers, 154–6, 198
  role in sporting culture, 194
  Scotland, 152–3, 197, 217–18
  spectator experience, 73, 202
  sports tourism, 196
  violence, 194
  websites, 217
  see also audience
fanzines, 84, 217
fashion, 152–3.137
FC United of Manchester (FCUM), 195
Fédération Internationale de Football Association: *see* FIFA
Fédération Internationale de l'Automobile: *see* FIA
Federer, Roger, 95
female athletes, 127, 128–9
female body, 128, 130, 143
feminist approaches, 4–5, 123, 138, 185
Ferguson, Alex, vii–viii, 177
FIA (Fédération Internationale de l'Automobile), 62–3, 111, 121
Field, 23
FIFA (Fédération Internationale de Football Association), 49, 98, 112, 124–5; *see also* World Cup
figurational sociology, 5
Finland, 145
Finn, G., 197
Fishlock, T., 203
Five Nations rugby, 32
Fletcher, Duncan, 181
football, 1, 71
  autobiographies, 137
  class, 136–7, 202
  commercialism, 195
  cultural significance, 137, 198, 199
  Cup Finals, 29, 32
  endorsement earnings, 202
  Italy, 16, 208

media coverage, ix, 205
  mediated experience, 200
  relationships with society, 153
  revenue, 96–7
  Scotland/England/Wales, 2, 59, 70, 80–1, 99–100, 144, 150–1
  season extending, 167
  sexual politics, 137–8
  Spain, 146, 153
  spectator experience, 202–3
  symbolic significance, 198–9, 201
  see also FIFA; television rights; UEFA; World Cup
Football Association (FA), 14, 32–3, 40, 69, 159–60
football clubs
  ownership, 48, 59, 195
  wealth, 17–18
  websites, 175
football coupons, 24, 31
Football Italia, 208
Football League, 23, 39, 40
Football Supporters Association, 194
Forbes list, 99
Forman, George, 41
Formula 1
  BBC, 58, 69–70, 214
  Brazil, 56
  FIA, 62–3, 111, 121
  Irvine, 100
  ITV, 57–8
  revenue, 68
  sexism, 124
  sponsorship, 48, 57
  website, 57
Fowler, Robbie, 136, 137
Fox TV, 69
fragmentation process, 222
France, Rugby World Cup, 55–6
freelance sports journalism, 182
Freeman, Cathy, 127–8
Friedman, J., 186

G14 lobby group, 196
Gaelic Athletic Association (GAA), 117–19
Gaelic games, 1, 12, 144, 161–2
Galily, Y., 143
Gallagher, Noel, 204–5
gambling, 22–4, 31, 58
game shows, 71
Gardiner, S., 105
Garland, J., 157–8
Gascoigne, Paul, 187
Gaumont, 28, 29
gay men study, 189–90
Gazzetta dello Sport, 24
gender
  audience, 26, 125
  commentators, 81–2, 83

essentialism, 123
genre, 189
leisure patterns, 4
media sport, 15–16, 167
national identity, 131
physical power, 138
sexuality, 136–7
spectatorship, 187–8
sports journalism, 133–4
stereotyping, 15, 123
gender relations in sport, 4–5, 89,
        122–4
genre/gender, 189
Germany, 146, 153
ghost-writing, 180–1
Gillett, George, 59
Gilroy, P., 110–11
Giro Ciclista, 24
Giulianotti, R., 152–3, 196, 197
Glanville, Brian, 168
Glasgow, 199, 200, 201; *see also* Celtic;
        Rangers
Glazer family, 59, 195
Glendenning, Raymond, 34
globalization, x, 222
        ICTs, 216
        identity, 158, 160
        spectatorship, 194–5
        sports journalism, 68–9, 170–2
Goddard, J., 10
Goldblatt, D., vi, ix
Goldlust, J., 9, 36, 72
golf, viii
        commentators, 82
        IMG, 49
        Open Championship, 32
        Senior Tours, 93
        televised, 92–3
        US Masters, 78
        women players, 124, 125–6
Good Friday Peace Agreement, 120
Gower, David, 76
Grade, Michael, 215–16
Grainger, A. D., 159
Gramsci, A., 1
Grand National, 29, 32, 78
Grand Prix, Brazil, 68
Grandstand, 39
Gratton, C., 10
Graydon, John, 39–40
Greer, G., ix
Greyhound Racing Association, 38
Grisewood, Fred, 79
Grobbelaar, Bruce, 103–4
Groot, L., 10
Guardian, ix, x, 66, 72, 110, 111, 126, 130,
        133, 140, 142, 148–9, 166, 204, 219
Guinness Sports Yearbook, 91
Gunnell, Sally, 91

Guoqi, X., 7
Gutteridge, Reg, 140

Haim, Tal Ben, 107
Hamed, Naseem, 115–16, 142, 189, 191,
        192
Hamilton, Lewis, x, 56, 68, 88, 111, 121
Hancock, Nick, 76
Hargreaves, Jen, 4, 123
Hargreaves, John, 81, 84
Harris, O., 108
Harrison, Audley, 193
Harvey, Len, 37–8
Hattenstone, S., 72
Hatton, Ricky, 214
Haynes, R., 100, 128, 171, 215–16
HDTV (high definition television), 69, 208–9,
        210
Hearn, Barry, 180
Helland, K., 6–7
Henderson, R., 133
Henley Regatta, 28
Henri, Thierry, 95
Herald, vii
Heskey, Emile, 112
Hey, Stan, 201–2
Hicks, Tom, 59
high definition television: *see* HDTV
Hillsborough, 10, 194
Hingis, Martina, 128
historical perspective, 12–13, 19–20
Hoberman, J., 94, 95, 120, 147
Holt, R., 20–1, 52, 99, 150–1
Home Box Office, 207
homoerotic desire, 185–6
homophobia, 136
Honda, 57
hooliganism, 194
Hornby, Nick, 180
Horne, J., 4–5, 60
Horse and Hound, 23
horse racing
        Ascot, 38
        betting, 24
        commentators, 82
        Derby, 27, 32, 33
        Grand National, 29, 32, 78
        Jockey Club, 22
        sporting press, 21–2
Hoskins, C., 71
Houlihan, B., 145–6, 159
Hoy, Chris, vii, 2
Hudson, Robert, 35
Huggins, M., 30
Hughes, Simon, 180
Hulton, Edward, 22, 23
Humphries, Tom, 180
hunting, 23
hurling, 144, 162

Hurst, Geoff, 76, 78
Hutton, W., 221

ICC World Cup, 74
ice hockey, 101
identification, 1, 186–7, 188–9, 191
identity
    collective, 148, 149, 199, 200
    cultural, 150–1
    fans, 193
    globalization, 158, 160
    ideology, 15
    Internet, 196–7
    localism, 151
    media sport, x, 10–11
    multiple, 111
    religious/ethnic, 114, 115, 116, 199, 201
    transformation, 196–7
    see also national identity
identity formation, 159, 162–3
ideology
    amateurism, 21
    BBC, 210–11
    identity, 15
    Media Studies sport, 7–8
    national identity, 14, 67
    national sporting events, 71
    race, 95
    sociology of sport and leisure, 6–7, 147
    symbolism, 144–5
image rights, 100
IMG (International Management Group),
    49, 91–2
Independent, vi, vii, 140
Independent on Sunday, 132, 133
Independent Television Authority, 39
India, viii, 51, 159–60
Indian Premier League (IPL), 50–1, 70, 75
industrial society, 20–1
IndyCar series, 63
information society, 216
informational goods, 100, 219
infotainment, 169
intellectual property, 171
International Management Group (IMG),
    49, 91–2
International Olympic Committee (IOC),
    53, 170
International Rugby Board (IRB), 55–6, 220
International Sport and Leisure (ISL), 49–50,
    54
Internet
    advertising, 65
    communication, 160
    European Commission, 207
    identities, 196–7
    instantaneity, 176–8
    interactivity, 63, 100

    and print media, 11
    racism, 117
    Rangers fans, 155
    see also IPTV
IOC (International Olympic Committee),
    53, 170
IPL (Indian Premier League), 50–1, 70, 75
iPlayer, 208–10
IPTV (Internet protocol television), 69
Iranian sports stars, 101
Iraq, 149
IRB (International Rugby Board), 55–6, 220
Ireland, Gaelic games, 1, 12, 144, 161–2, 180
Ireland, Northern
    devolution, 152
    Good Friday Peace Agreement, 120
    media/sport, 120
    sectarianism, 108, 117–19
Irvine, Eddie, 100
ISL (International Sport and Leisure), 49–50,
    54
Israeli studies, 143
Italy, 16, 144, 208
ITV, 2, 39–40
    Champions League, 68, 109
    motor racing, 57–8, 148
    Rugby World Cup, 56
ITV Digital, 206

Jackson, Colin, 110
Jacques, Martin, x
James, C. L. R., 19
Japan, 42
Jarvie, G., 3, 109
Jarvie, J., 108
Jeanrenaud, C., 10
Jenkins, Simon, 204, 211
Jenson, J., 185
Jewell, Jimmy, 80
Jockey Club, 22
Johns, Hugh, 82
Johnson, Ben, 103
Johnson, Magic, 94, 102, 103
Johnston, Brian, 35, 217
Jones, S. G., 6–7
Jordan, Michael, 94–5, 102
journalism
    British/US, 16–17
    hierarchies in, 165
    legitimacy, 175
    media institutions, 172–3
    objectivity, 28; see also newspapers; print
        media; sports journalism
jurisprudence in sports, 96

Keane, Roy, 181
Keegan, Kevin, 205, 206
Kelner, Martin, 212

Kesenne, S., 10
Ketchum Sport and Sponsorship, 49
Key, Robert, 72
Khan, Amir, 112–13, 115–16, 214
Kimmage, Paul, 130, 180
Kindalan, Mario, 115
King, A., 196
King, C., 127
King, Don, 141
Klammer, Franz, 78
Kodak, 53, 54
Koppett, L., 102
Kournikova, Anna, 129
Kracauer, A., 186
Kruger, A., 7
Kuper, S., 198–9

Labour Government, 152
Lady's Magazine, 21
Lappin, Tom, 215
Lawell, Peter, 157
Lawson, Mark, 66, 67–9
Le Saux, Graham, 136, 137
Leibovitz, Annie, 130
Lennon, Neil, 118–19
Lerner, Randy, 59
Levi-Strauss, 53
Lewis, Carl, 78
Lewis, J., 116
Lewis, Lennox, 193
Liddle, Rod, 107
Lineker, Gary, 76
Lines, Gill, 91
Listener, vi
litigation, 177
live events, 56–7, 66, 218
Liverpool, 198, 200, 201
Liverpool Football Club, 59, 201
Livingstone, S., 188
Lloyd, Chris Evert, 128
Lloyd, Peter, 82
localism, 151, 159
London bombings, 112–13, 116
Louis, Joe, 115
Lowerson, J., 23
Lubin, Sigmund, 27
Lumière brothers, 27
Lyons, A., 202

McAvoy, Jock, 37–8
McChesney, Robert, 68
McCoist, Ally, 157
McCormack, Mark, 48–50, 86, 91–2, 93
MacDonald, Ramsay, 28
McDonald's, 53
McIlvanney, Hugh, 164, 167
Mackay, Angus, 34
Mackie, P., 54

McLaren, Bill, 83–4, 191
McLellan, Gerald, 139, 189
MacPherson, Archie, 80–1
Macpherson, Stewart, 34
Mahmoud, Younis, 149
Mailer, Norman, 179
Major Leage Baseball, 101, 102
Malaja, Lilia, 98
Malcolm, Devon, 133
male body, 143, 186
male gaze, 185
Manchester, 22, 23, 198
Manchester City, 44, 59, 107, 184, 204
Manchester Guardian, 25; *see also* Guardian
Manchester United
    BSkyB, 58–9
    Cantona, 104–5
    Champions League final, 65, 156
    Glazer family, 59, 195
    and Manchester City, 204
    marketization of news, 172
    ownership of, 58, 59
Mandela, Nelson, 148–9
manliness, 26, 136; *see also* masculinity
Marca, 111
marginalization process, 91, 122–3, 143
Marshall, Howard, 34
Martineau, G. D., 21
Marxist analysis, 4, 123
masculinity
    boxing, 138–41
    class, 136–7
    diverse, 135–6, 189–90
    hegemonic, 88–9, 136, 187
    media institutions, 135–6
    power, 136, 138
    reconceptualized, 186
    violence, 115, 116, 123
Maskell, Dan, 82
mass communications, 12–13, 20
MasterCard, 126
Match of the Day, 39, 135, 177, 185
match-fixing, 104
Matthews, Stanley, 97
Mays, Harold, 80
media
    commercialization, 17, 159–60
    demand-led, 17
    elite sport, 160, 178
    exclusivity/universal access, 222
    gay men study, 189–90
    internationalization, 148–9
    regulatory change, 17
    sports coverage, ix, 14, 205, 222
    stereotyping, 108
media corporations, 48
media institutions, 61, 123, 135–6, 147, 171–3,
    177–8

media sport
  academic study, 3–4
  cultural significance, 220–1
  digital technology, 213–16
  gender, 15–16, 167
  as genre, 189
  identity, x
  nationality, 15–16
  political economy, 10, 11, 13
  race, 15–16
  sports stars, 95–6
  transformation process, 7–8, 13–14, 20, 147
Media Studies, x, 3–4, 7–8
mediated experience of sport, 10–11, 88, 107, 200
Mellor, Adrian, 150
Men Viewing Violence project, 188
merchandizing, 86, 102
Messner, M. A., 123, 136
Mickelson, Phil, 93
Microsoft, 54
El Mindo Deportivo, 25
Mitchell, Kevin, 139, 140–1, 144, 181
Mitchell & Kenyon films, 27
Mitford, Mary Russell, 21
mobile phone technology, 216–17
Modlenski, T., 186
Modood, T., 116
Molina, Remigio, 189
Montana, Joe, 78
Monte Carlo Rally, 40
Moore, Brian, 81, 82, 135
Morse, M., 185–6
Moseley, Max, 121
Mosey, Roger, 70, 209, 210–11
motor racing, 25, 47, 48, 82, 148; *see also* Formula 1
Motson, John, 81, 135
Mott, S., 86
Mullan, Harry, 140
Murdoch, Rupert, 56, 58–9, 68–9, 164, 167, 215–16
Murray, Andy, viii, 88, 131, 205
Murray, Colin, 195, 196
Muslim identity, 114, 115, 116

Nadal, Rafael, viii
Nally, Patrick, 49
narrativization, 66, 77–8, 183, 199–200
National Basketball Association: *see* NBA
national character, 16, 145, 156, 157
National Collegiate Athletic Association (NCAA), 102
National Football League: *see* NFL
National Hockey League (NHL), 101, 218
national identity
  devolution, 162
  fans, 76, 77

gender, 131
  ideology, 14, 67
  politics, 7
  race, 107–8, 114–17
  and religion, 114–15
  sports, vii, viii, ix, 14, 144–5, 151–3
national prestige, 145, 146
national sporting events, 71, 161
nationalism, 15–16, 98–9
nationhood, 32, 113, 151
Navratilova, Martina, 128
NBA (National Basketball Association), 93–4, 101, 102–3
NBC, 67–8, 102, 127, 215
NCAA (National Collegiate Athletic Association), 102
neo-marxist approach, 4–5
Net Result, 219
New York, 203
New Zealand, 1
Newbon, Gary, 140
Newcastle United, 203, 205, 206
news agencies, 176
News Corporation, 68–9
news coverage, ix, 175–6
News International, 215–16, 220
News of the World, 24, 131
Newspaper Proprietors' Association (NPA), 30, 32
newspapers
  circulation pressures, 24, 167
  class, 23, 168
  commercial development, 12
  devolution, 148
  Europe, 24–5
  racism, 148
  sports coverage, 23–4
  websites, 176
  see also print media
newsreels, 26, 27–8, 29, 30
NFL (National Football League), US, 42, 101, 215
NHL (National Hockey League), 101, 218
Nicholson, M., 10
Nicklaus, Jack, 49, 92
Nike, 48, 50, 56, 75, 87, 94–5, 105, 158, 178
Noble, Ronnie, 29
Nordic World Ski championships, 145
nostalgia, 200, 201–2
NPA (Newspaper Proprietors' Association), 30, 32

Oatley, Jacqui, 135
OBs: *see* outside broadcasts
Observer, viii, 25, 66, 130, 134, 139, 166, 181
Observer Sports Magazine, 130, 144
O'Connor, B., 187
O'Donnell, H., 145, 147, 153, 169

Old Firm rivalries, 119, 162, 198
Oldham disturbances, 116
Olympic Games
    Athens (1896), 24
    Athens (2004), 114, 127
    Atlanta (1996), 125
    Beijing (2008), vii–viii, 2, 17, 54–5, 68,
        86–7, 101, 146, 166, 208–9, 211
    London (1948), 38, 208
    London (2012), viii, 2, 54, 55, 70, 146, 196,
        204, 205, 208
    Los Angeles (1984), 52, 53, 54
    Montreal (1976), 53
    Rome (1960), 40
    Sydney (2000), 127–8
    Tokyo (1964), 41, 52–3
Olympic Games coverage
    BBC, 213
    Team GB, 205, 209
    televised, 40–2, 52–5, 67, 78
    timing of events, 50, 68
    transformed by media, 171
O'Neal, Shaquille, 95
O'Neill, Joseph, 180
online communities, 182, 218
online journalism, 164, 166, 182, 216
online viewing, 210
Open Golf Championship, 32
O'Sullivan, Peter, 82
outside broadcasts (OBs), 31, 32–3, 34–5,
    37, 83
Ovett, Steve, 180
ownership of football clubs, 48, 59, 195

Packer, Kerry, 75
Palmer, Arnold, 49, 86, 91–2, 96
Panorama, 177
paralympic athletics, 166
paternalism, 46
Pathé, Charles, 28
patriarchy, 122, 123, 143
patriotism, 26, 113; *see also* national identity
patronage, 20, 22, 45, 60
Pattinson, Darren, 132
Paul, Robert, 27
pay-per-view
    boxing, 141, 192, 214
    competition, 2
    elite Scottish sport, 161
    multi-channel, 69
    sports coverage, ix, 43, 70, 71, 161
    television rights, 99
Peace, David, 180
Pele, 41, 78, 205
Pendleton, Victoria, 122, 129–30, 131, 134
Pepsi, 51
PFA (Professional Footballers Association),
    97, 98, 124

PGA (Professional Golfers Association), 24
Phelops, W. L., 64
Phelps, Michael, 68
photojournalism, 28, 168–9
physical power, 136, 138, 143
Pierce, Mary, 128
Pilling, M. J., 41
Platini, Michel, 98
Player, Gary, 49, 92
Player, John, 47
political economy, 10, 11, 13
politics/sport, vii–viii, 7, 18, 26, 63, 221
Polley, M., 7, 12, 45, 108–9, 124
popular culture
    black, 94, 95
    class, 20
    fans, 200
    football, 137
    media/sport, 2, 30
Porter, D., 7
Poulton, E., 194, 197
power, physical, 136, 138, 143
power discourses, 4–6, 18
Premier League, England
    BBC radio, 211–12
    BSkyB, 206–7, 219
    club ownership, 58, 59
    foreign players, 98–9
    TalkSport, 213
Prescott, Breidis, 214
Press Association, 179
Press Gazette, 166, 172, 178
Preston, E., 133
print media, 11, 126–7, 164, 168, 169, 176; *see
    also* newspapers
Pro-Celebrity tours, 92–3
Professional Footballers Association: *see* PFA
Professional Golfers Association (PGA), 24
professionalism, 21, 83, 97–8, 165–7
Pro-Serv, 94–5
pub viewing, 219
public relations, 61, 171, 177–8, 183
public service broadcasting, 9, 32–3, 69, 70,
    207
Puskas, Ferenc, 40
Puttnam, D., 27

A Question of Sport, 71

race
    class, 108
    essentialism, 105
    ideology, 95
    media sport, 15–16
    national identity, 107–8
    politics of, 95
    stereotyping, 106
Racing Calendar, 22

racism
  boxing, 112
  casual, 109, 110
  FIFA on, 112
  Internet, 117
  newspapers, 148
  Polley, 108–9
  sectarianism, 117–19
Radcliffe, Paula, 67
Rader, B., 9
Radio 5 Live, 134, 211–12
radio sports coverage, 30–2, 34–5, 36,
    211–13
Radio Times, 31–2, 33, 37, 38, 41, 78, 79
Radway, J., 188
Rahman, Hasim, 193
Raikkonen, Haki, 99
Ramirez, Manny, 195
Randall, D., 132
Rangers, 108, 117, 118, 162
    fans, 154–6, 198
Ray, John, 211
Red Rum, 78
Red Sox, 195
Redgrave, Steve, 78
Redhead, S., 96
Reebok, 48
Regan, Mich, 155
Regester, C., 108
Reid, I., 109
Reid, John, 157
Reith, Lord, 31
religious labelling, 117–18, 119
reputation management, 176–8
Reuters, 220
Rezazadeh, Hossein, 101
RFU (Rugby Football Union), 181
Richardson, Gary, 114–15, 212
Rickman, John, 40
Riddell, Lord, 30
Riordan, J., 7
Robinho, 204, 205
Robinson, J. S. R., 158
Robson, Laura, 131–2, 133
Roche, M., 160
Rojek, C., 5
rolling news channels, 173, 176, 205
Rome, Treaty of, 98
Romero, Rebecca, 130–1, 134
Rose, A., 186
Rose, Justin, 88
Rosie, M., 148
Rowe, D., 9, 103, 159, 168, 169, 170
Ruddock, Alan, viii
rugby
  class, 165
  Englishness, 144, 158
  Five Nations, 32

national identity, 1
Twickenham, 37
Rugby Football Union (RFU), 181
Rugby World Cup
  advertising, 56
  Australia (2003), 55
  France (2007), 43, 44, 55–6, 68
  rights disputes, 219–20
  South Africa (1995), 148–9, 154
  Visa, 48
Runyon, Damon, 179
Rushdie, Salman, 116
Russell, A., 149

Sabo, D., 136, 138
Salmond, Alex, vii
Samsung, 54, 60
Samuel, M., 137
satellite television, 52–3, 56, 219
Saudi Arabia, 149
Scannell, P., 32
Schlesinger, P., 148, 151, 162–3, 188
Schulberg, Budd, 179
Scotland
  alcohol problems, 156
  Beijing Olympics coverage, 166
  devolution, 152, 160–1
  fans' participation, 217–18
  football, 2, 80–1, 144, 150–1
  global pressures, 160–1
  national characteristics, 156, 157
  national identity, vii, viii, 14, 152–3
  Old Firm rivalries, 119, 162, 198
  pay-per-view, 161
  sectarianism, 108
  Tartan Army, 152–3, 197
  see also Glasgow
Scotland on Sunday, 155
Scotsman, 215
Scottish National Party, 152, 161
Scottish Parliament, 152
Scottish Television, 161
sectarianism, 15, 108, 117–19, 199
'Senior' sport, 93
serialization rights, 181
Setanta Sports, 2, 14, 51, 206, 207
sexism, ix, 124, 127, 137–8
sexuality, 128–9, 136–7
Sharapova, Maria, 99
Shaw, C., 200
shinty, 161
Shooting Times, 23
Siegel, G., 202
Silverstone, R., 76
Simmons, K., 124–5
Simpson, O. J., 103
Singer, Jamie, 58
Singh, Vijay, 93

Sky Box Office, 141, 214
Sky Sports, 70, 75, 141, 189, 192, 193, 214, 219
Sky Sports 1, 125
Sky Sports News, 205
sleaze, 103
Slot, O., 134
Smith, A., 7, 10
Smith, Robin, 133
Smith, S. J., 126, 134
Snead, Sam, 91
Snickers, 55
snooker, 51–2, 66–7, 180
Soccer Dataco, 219
sociology of sport and leisure, 3–4, 6–7, 138, 147
Solberg, A., 10
Sony, 57
Sony Television, 51
South Africa, 148–9, 154
Soviet Union, 146
Spain
    football/politics, 146, 153
    pay-per-view, 214
    racist abuse, 111–12
    sponsorship market, 48
    sports successes, viii
spectatorship
    British sports, 195–6
    consumption, 202–3
    fans, 73, 202
    football, 202–3
    gender, 187–8
    globalization, 194–5
    live experience, 56, 142–3, 202, 218
    masculine, 185–6, 187
    violence, 138
    see also audience
sponsorship, 13, 42, 45–7
    advertising, 44, 45, 169
    branding, 50–2, 178
    commercial, 45, 47, 59–60
    elite, 50, 54–5, 99
    Formula 1, 48, 57
    newspapers, 24
    Olympic Games, 53
    online, 63–5
    and patronage, 60
    sports stars, 61, 99
    tobacco manufacturers, 47
    World Cup, 126
sport
    biological determinism, 120, 122, 138
    class, 20, 23, 118, 136–7, 165, 202
    cultural significance, ix, 7, 30, 147, 213
    gender, 4–5, 89, 122–4
    industrialization, 97
    as narrative, 66, 77–8, 183, 199–200

national identity, vii, viii, ix, 14, 144–5, 151
    origins, 20–1
    politics, vii–viii, 7, 18, 26, 63, 221
    social cohesion, 116–17
    stereotypes, 147
    values, 197
    violence, 190–1
    see also televised sport
Sport, 178
Sport on Friday, 105
SportBusinessInternational, 43, 47, 68, 102–3, 125
Sporting Chronicle, 22
sporting events, 36, 146, 166
Sporting Life, 22
sporting press, 21–2; see also print media
sports agent, 14, 87, 96
sports brokers, 48–50
sports coverage
    gender bias, 126, 167
    hierarchy, 166
    media, 14
    national dimension, 145
    newspapers, 23–4
    pay-TV, 43
    print media, 126–7, 164
    selectivity, 26
sports economy, 10, 17
Sports Formbook, 40
sports governing bodies, 46, 49–50, 70–1, 101–2, 219
sports industries, 10, 172, 183
sports journalism, 25–6, 50, 182
    access to players/managers, 168, 171–2, 175
    branding, 172, 175
    class, 23, 165
    communication technology, 178–9
    complicity, 172, 174, 175, 183
    copy approval, 178
    digital media, 11, 173–4, 183
    editorial decisions, 174
    European, 24–5
    by ex-sports stars, 170
    financial funding, 179
    freelance, 182
    gender, 133–4, 138
    ghost-writing, 180–1
    globalization, 68–9, 170–2
    hard news, 168, 169, 174
    Internet, 174–5
    litigation, 177
    local/global, 171
    media institutions, 171–2
    orthodox rhetoric, 168, 170
    political economy of, 170–9
    PR information, 177–8
    professionalism, 165–7
    reflexive analysis, 168, 170

sports journalism (*cont.*)
  reputation management, 176–8
  soft news, 168, 169
  and sports commentary, 81
  time pressures, 176, 178–9
  video technology, 166
sports labour markets, 96–7
sports presenters, 81–2
sports programming, 167
  BBC, 11, 31, 37–8, 207
  competition for, 46
  transformation, 38
sports publishing, 179–82
Sports Report, 34
sports reporters, 168
sports rights
  BBC, 212
  bidders for, 221
  bundling, 213
  collective sale of, 206–7
  competition, 38–40, 206
  digital, x, 219
  distributon platforms, 215
  holders of, 64
  live rights packages, 207
  secondary agreements, 206
  on web, 219
Sports Special, 39, 83
sports stars
  advertising, 92
  boxing, 113–15
  branding, 89, 100
  commodification, 96
  elite, 87–90, 178
  feel-good factor, 169
  games shows, 71
  gossip, 169
  heroes/villains, 90–1, 103–5
  Iran, 101
  media sport, 95–6
  mediated sport, 88
  power, 101–2
  press reporting, 104–5
  as role models, 91, 105–6
  sponsorship, 61, 99
  US, 101–3
Sports Studies, 4, 17
sports teams' websites, 174–5
sports writers, 16–17, 168; *see also* sports
  journalism
Sportstour, 40
Sportsview, 39
Sportsweek, 212
Springboks, 148–9
Steenveld, L., 149
stereotyping
  Asian sports people, 116
  audience, 184–5

English fans, 197–8
  ethnicity, 117
  gender, 15, 123
  international sports, 147
  media, 108, 120
  patriarchy, 123
  race, 106
  sport, 147
  women's boxing, 143
Strachan, Gordon, 157
Strelitz, L., 149
Strutt, J., 21
style magazines, 137
subscription sports channels, 69; *see also* pay-
  per-view
Sugden, J., 1, 117, 141, 177
sumo wrestling, 42
Sun, 103–4, 147, 177, 219
Sunday Herald, 156
Sunday Mirror, 132
The Sunday Times, 107, 122, 130, 132
Super Bowl, 78
Super-Middleweight Championship of the
  World, 139
Sykes Committee, 30
symbolic significance, 144–5, 148–9, 198–9,
  201
Syncom III satellite, 41

TalkSport, 100, 212–13
Tartan Army, 152–3, 197
Tattersall's Rings, 22
Taylor, Gordon, 97, 98
Taylor, Rogan, 202
team game values, 144
Team GB, 209
TEAM (The Event Agency and Marketing
  AG), 51–2
technological development, 13, 83
telegraph, 22
telephoto lens, 37
televised sport
  analysis of, 9–10
  audience, 184–5
  global, 40–2
  as male soap opera, 186
  naturalism/construction, 78
  origins of, 30, 35–6
  outside broadcasts, 37–8
  and radio, 36
  transformation, 66–7, 84–5, 94
  voyeuristic gaze, 138, 194
  see also pay-per-view
television, 9–10
  commodification, 62
  historical perspective, 19–20
  sponsorship, 13
  timing of sports events, 8, 68

tobacco advertising ban, 46
transformation, 79
see also sports programming
television rights, 45, 69–70, 99–100, 102; *see also* sports rights
Telstar satellite, 52
tennis
  BBC coverage, 213–14
  commentators, 82
  Nadal, viii
  Wimbledon, 32, 78, 131–2
  women players, 128
Test Match Special, 35, 212, 217
text messaging, 212, 216–17
The Event Agency and Marketing AG (TEAM), 51–2
They Think It's All Over, 76
Thompson, J. B., 7, 199–200
Thompson, Peter, 80–1
three foreigners rule, 98
Tibet, 60, 211
Ticher, M., 202
Tiger Aspect Productions, 49
The Times, 60, 128, 130, 132, 133, 134, 166, 219
The Times magazine, 131
timing of sports events, 8, 50, 51–2, 68, 166
tipping sheets, 24
T-Mobile, 60
tobacco manufacturers, 43, 46, 47, 58
Tomlinson, A., 1, 7, 177
Tomlinson, C., 135
topicals, on film, 26, 28
Toronto Blue Jays, 195
Toshiba, 56
Toulmin, V., 27
Tour de France, 45
Townsend, Phil, 172
trainers, 94–5
Trans World International (TWI), 49
transfer fees, 96, 98
transformation process
  commentaries, 67
  identity, 196–7
  media, 2, 7–8, 13–14, 20, 147
  sports programming, 38
  televised sport, 9, 66–7, 79, 84–5, 94
  Victorian, 21
  Whannel, 67, 72
Tsingtao, 55
Tuck, J., 158
Tuggle, C. A., 127
Turner, Beverly, 124
Turner, Ted, 207
Twentieth Century Fox, 28–9
Twenty20 competition, 70, 72–3, 74, 75–6
TWI (Trans World International), 49

Tyler, Martin, 81
Tyson, Mike, 105, 139, 207

UEFA (Union of European Football Association)
  foreign players, 98
  ISL, 54
  Manchester Cup Final, 154–5
  racist abuse, 111–12
  Seville Cup FInal, 198
  television rights, 52
  see also Champions League
United States of America
  baseball, 1
  credit crunch, viii
  ethnicity in sport, 114
  female sport, 125
  sports stars, 101–3
US Masters, 78
user-generated content, 164, 182

Vamplew, W., 22
Vande-Berg, L. E., 94
Vaughan-Thomas, Wynford, 34
video technology, 53, 166
Vincent, J., 128
violence
  boxing, 115, 141, 190–1
  dislike of, 189–90
  fandom, 138
  fans, 194
  masculinity, 115, 116, 123
  spectator experience, 138
Visa, 48, 53, 54, 56
Vitagraph, 27
voyeuristic gaze, 138, 194

Wacquant, L., 141
wage-capping, 101
Wakelam, Teddy, 34, 79
Wales, 1, 152
Walker, Murray, 82
Wall Street Journal, 164
Walsh, David, 180
Walton, Ken, 82
Ward, Bill, 39–40
Warren, Frank, 141, 214
Watt, Jim, 140
WBC (World Boxing Council), 139
Weaver, P., 72, 76
Webb, Tony, 63
Weight, R., 157
Wenner, L. A., 9
Wensing, E. H., 127–8
West, Peter, 74
West Ham United, 205
West Indies, 146–7
Westerbeek, H., 10

WestNally, 49
Whannel, G.
  BBC, 39
  celebrity culture, 87, 88
  consumption of sport, 9, 76, 198
  on Crooks, 110
  manliness, 136
  naturalism/construction, 78
  spectator experience, 73
  sponsorship, 44
  sports broadcasting, 83
  text/ideology, 8
  transformation of sport, 66, 67, 72
  vortextual effect, 89
When We Were Kings, 41
White, Jim, 156–7, 184
Whitson, D., 47–8
Whittle, J., 180
Who Do You Think You Are?, 110
Wignall, Trevor, 19, 26
William Hill Sports Book of the Year,
  180
Williams, C. L., 123
Williams, J., 197
Williams, Raymond, vi, 77
Williams, Richard, 62–3, 111, 120–1,
  130
Williams, Venus, 128
Wilson, B., 108
Wimbledon Championships, 23, 32, 78,
  131–2, 143
wire services, 179
Wisden, John, 25
Wisden Cricket Monthly, 133
WNBC (Women's National Basketball
  Association), 125
Wolstenholme, Kenneth, 39, 76, 77, 79, 80,
  82, 83
women
  boxers, 115, 143
  financial rewards, 126
  footballers, 124–5, 126, 205–6
  genres, 187
  golfers, 124, 125–6
  marginalization, 91, 122–3, 143
  media institutions, 123
  sports journalists, 15, 133–4
  sports pages, 126, 134, 143
  tennis players, 128

US, 125
  see also female body; gender
Women Viewing Violence, 188
Women's Hour, 131
Women's National Basketball Association
  (WNBC), 125
Women's Sport and Fitness Foundation, 125,
  126
Woods, Tiger, 78, 93, 95, 99, 100
Woodward, K., 115
World Boxing Council (WBC), 139
World Cup (FIFA)
  England's qualifying matches, 206
  English fans, 197–8
  Scotland's qualifying games, 161
  sponsorship, 126
  televised, 40–2, 78
  timing of games, 50
  transformed by media, 171
World Cup (FIFA) finals
  Argentina (1978), 145
  Chile (1962), 41
  England (1966), 46, 76, 82
  France (1998), 202
  Germany (1974), 9
  Germany (2006), 67–9
  Mexico (1970), 41
  Mexico (1986), 50
  South Africa (2010), 146, 161
  South Korea/Japan (2002), 197
  US (1994), 50
World Federation Wrestling, 141–2
World Heavyweight Boxing, 50
World Ski Championships, 145
World Sports Group, 51
Wright, Billy, 40, 97
Wright, Ian, 110
Wynne-Jones, G. V., 34

Xiang, Liu, 86–7

Yanjing, 55
Young, C., 7
youth sporting events, 60
YouTube, 155, 217, 218

Zee-TV, 51
Zenit St Petersburg, 154–5
zoom lenses, 38